Avatars of Vengeance

Frontispiece. Ichikawa Danjūrō VII as Soga Gorō sharpening arrows in *Ya no ne*, color woodblock print, by Utagawa Toyokuni III (Kunisada), 1852. Courtesy of Waseda University Tsubouchi Memorial Theater Museum.

Avatars of Vengeance
Japanese Drama and the Soga Literary Tradition

Laurence R. Kominz

Center for Japanese Studies
The University of Michigan

Ann Arbor, 1995

Address: Center for Japanese Studies, The University of Michigan, 108 Lane Hall, 204 S. State Street, Ann Arbor, MI 48109-1290

Michigan Monograph Series in Japanese Studies, Number 13

Library of Congress Cataloging-in-Publication Data

Kominz, Laurence Richard, 1952-
Avatars of vengeance : Japanese drama and the Soga literary tradition / Laurence R. Kominz.
xiii, 282p. 23.5cm. — (Michigan monograph series in Japanese studies ; 13)
Includes bibliographical references and index.
ISBN 0-939512-69-6 (cloth : alk. paper)
1. Soga monogatari. 2. Soga monogatari—Dramatic production—history. 3. Soga, Sukenari, 1172-1193—In literature. 4. Soga, Tokimune, 1174-1193—In literature. I. Title. II. Series.
PL7980.S63K6 1995
895.6'322—dc20 95-2897
CIP

Jacket design by Judy Stopke.
This book was set in Galliard.

The paper used in this publication meets the requirements of the ANSI Standard Z39.48-1984 (Permanence of Paper).

∞

Printed in the United States of America

Contents

Preface

Avatars of Vengeance would have been impossible without the guidance and support of many teachers and colleagues, and it is a pleasure to record my gratitude to them. My interest in theatrical versions of the Soga vendetta began during graduate school at Columbia University where Professors Paul Varley and Carol Gluck helped me with my preliminary work. And I could not have had a more patient and thorough thesis advisor than Donald Keene. His accomplishments and his love for Japanese literature and drama were an inspiration to me. In Japan Professor Kitagawa Hiroshi of Shiga University helped me to read and understand *The Tale of the Soga Brothers.* I am indebted to Michael Cooper and James Brandon for their encouragement and assistance in publishing introductions to Noh and Kabuki plays about the Soga brothers in *Monumenta Nipponica* and the *Asian Theatre Journal.* These short projects were important stepping stones on the path that led to the completion of *Avatars of Vengeance.*

As I struggled through medieval and Edo-period play texts in Kyoto in the early 1980s, my spirit was rejuvenated by taking lessons in and performing traditional Japanese drama. This activity kept me ever aware of how vibrant and alive traditional theater still is. I studied Noh under Udaka Michishige of the Kongō School and *kyōgen* under Shigeyama Sengorō (now Shigeyama Sensaku, a living national treasure). My lessons in *gidayū* chanting under the superb lady *shamisen* player Tsurusawa Jūteru brought Chikamatsu Monzaemon's long unperformed Soga texts alive in a way that would have been impossible had I not been singing Chikamatsu's puppet plays with her every week. Having begun to study Japanese performance, I found I could not give up my lessons, and I began to study *buyō* dance after coming to Portland, Oregon. After fifteen years of studying Soga drama, it was thrilling to make my debut in *buyō* as Soga Gorō. My *buyō* teacher, Fujima Kan'riye, has helped enrich the cultural life of the Oregon/Washington Japanese-American community since the early 1950s, but I doubt that she has ever had to teach as enthusiastic yet inept a pupil as me.

So many people have helped with the final stages of *Avatars of Vengeance* it is impossible to list them all. Most of all I am indebted to Bruce Willoughby, Managing Editor of the Center for Japanese Studies at the University of Michigan, who stuck with *Avatars* despite a long review process. I was fortunate in 1992–93 to be able to join a graduate seminar at Waseda University in which Visiting Professor Takei Kyōzō guided his students in reading the very difficult diary of the first Ichikawa Danjūrō, and that diary made it possible to add Danjūrō's personal convictions to the story of his transformation of Soga Gorō in Kabuki. Two leading scholars of Kabuki history, Gunji Masakatsu and Hattori Yukio, made time in their busy schedules to meet with me and discuss the roles of religion and art in Edo-period Kabuki. Ichikawa Danjūrō XII met with me twice to talk about his family heritage and his commitment in his own stage career to keeping alive the traditions that elevated the Soga brothers to the highest level of prominence in Kabuki.

Illustrations are an integral part of *Avatars of Vengeance*, and Morita Tōshirō, staff photographer at the Tokyo National Theater and one of the finest theater photographers in Japan, generously allowed me to use many of his photographs. Professor Torigoe Bunzō at the Waseda University Tsubouchi Memorial Theater Museum and Shimane Kiyoshi, the museum's administrative manager, had new reproductions made so we could create the book's cover illustration, and librarians and curators at Tokyo Geijutsu Daigaku, the Philadelphia Museum of Art, and Odawara City Kyōdō Bunkakan generously provided illustrations and reproduction rights.

Perhaps I should include a word of thanks to the spirits of the Soga brothers themselves. I had been working on the book off and on for over ten years when in May of 1993 I attended a funeral service at Kōzenji in the village of Shimo Soga, commemorating the 800th anniversary of the death of the brothers. In the presence of the Soga brother's spirit I wrote a prayer on a votive tablet (*ema*) and hung it beside their graves, a prayer that through my work their story might reach new readers across the seas. A month later I sat down to do another rewrite of the manuscript, and since then the road to publication has been straight and steady. None of this would have been possible without the support of the Japan Foundation. A Japan Foundation Dissertation Fellowship funded my first year of research on Soga drama in 1982–83, and I did my final revision in 1993 while on a Japan Foundation Professional Fellowship at Waseda University's Tsubouchi Memorial Theater Museum.

For the past twelve years I have taught Japanese language and literature at Portland State University, and my departmental colleagues and friends have always stood behind me in my academic endeavors. In this project, and in all of my work, I enjoy the support and understanding of my wife Toshimi and our children Leo and Maya, who believe me when I tell them that I have "important work to do" and must stay at the office late, working on academic projects. I hope my children will some day find careers they enjoy as much as I do researching, performing, teaching, and writing on traditional Japanese drama.

Illustrations

Chapter One: Introduction

In the summer of 1193 Japan's first shogun, Minamoto Yoritomo, held a great hunt at the base of Mount Fuji. At midnight on the last night of the hunt, the twenty-eighth day of the fifth month, two young samurai, Soga Jūrō Sukenari and Soga Gorō Tokimune, broke into the camp quarters of Kudō Suketsune, one of the shogun's chief advisors, and murdered him. Kudō's retainer had assassinated the father of the two brothers seventeen years before. The shogun's guards intervened after the vendetta, and the Soga brothers killed and injured several of them in the ensuing melee. Jūrō, the elder brother, was slain that night. Gorō was captured and the next day was brought before the shogun for interrogation. Gorō informed the shogun of the poverty and humiliation he and his brother had suffered during their youth, and of their unswerving devotion to the vows they had made as children to avenge their father. Now that their revenge was complete, Gorō declared that he had no further purpose in life and requested permission to kill himself. The shogun, although impressed by the brothers' perseverence, bravery, and filial devotion, ordered Gorō to be executed. Gorō had committed the crimes of engaging in a private vendetta on a public occasion and of killing retainers of the shogun.

The story of the Soga brothers' revenge was soon being recited to musical accompaniment in the Kantō region (eastern Honshū). The performers were itinerant monks and nuns who belonged to various religious sects, each of which imposed its own values and moral lessons on the basic frame of the Soga story. A century and a half after the original event, *Soga monogatari* (The Tale of the Soga Brothers) had become an important part of the oral literature of Japan. Minstrels carried the tale to the farthest reaches of the country, and for four hundred and fifty years the Soga tale was Japan's most popular revenge story. With the appearance in the following centuries of Japan's great traditional theaters (notably Noh, Kabuki, and the puppet theater), playwrights repeatedly turned to the story of the Soga brothers for source material. The Soga plays form a significant thematic category in every genre of serious traditional drama in Japan.

Between 1400 and 1900 the main characters from the Soga story were featured in a vast number of plays. Noh plays based on the Soga story figure importantly in the repertory of dramatic, "this world" (*genzai*) Noh plays. Chikamatsu Monzaemon (1653–1724), often called Japan's greatest playwright, wrote thirteen Soga plays for the puppet and the Kabuki theaters. Soga Kabuki plays became so popular that all the theaters in Edo (premodern Tokyo) put them on during the first few months of every year. Soga plays became a regular feature of the urban New Year celebration.[1] New Soga plays were presented for every New Year's show, and thus the total number of Soga Kabuki plays was prodigious—more than one thousand, including dance dramas.[2] Few other stories in Japan or in the world have stimulated so much dramatic activity as *The Tale of the Soga Brothers.*

Avatars of Vengeance illuminates changes in the Soga story and its characters as they appeared onstage over a four-hundred-year period. In analyzing how and why these changes took place, it becomes apparent that the story and the characters serve as an excellent indicator source, making possible new insights into the dynamics of continuity and creativity in traditional Japanese drama. My discussion of the Soga story onstage will take two perspectives: (1) the story and its characters as subjects of scrutiny—to ascertain the development of this archetypical revenge story over time; and (2) a study of changes in the Soga vendetta and its protagonists as keys to understanding the dynamics of change in theater. The two perspectives are related, because cultural archetypes strongly influence play writing and staging, and, oppositely, major changes in performance contexts can modify archetypes that seemed static and permanent for years or even centuries.

THE SOGA STORY ONSTAGE TODAY

Today the Soga tradition can still be seen in performance at Noh and Kabuki theaters. Gorō, who appears in three commonly performed plays—the Noh play *Youchi Soga* (Night Raid by the Soga Broth-

1. See chapter 7 for a discussion of Soga Kabuki plays performed for the New Year.
2. See Hattori Yukio, ed., *Kotobuki kongen Soga,* vol. 46 of *Kokuritsu gekijō jōen shiryō shū* (Kokuritsu Gekijō, 1970), 1–79 for all Soga Kabuki plays performed in the Edo period, not including short dance dramas.

ers), the Kabuki play *Ya no ne* (The Arrow Sharpener), and the Kabuki dance drama *Gorō*—varies so much from one play to the next that uninitiated Japanese viewers, and certainly non-Japanese audiences, would hardly suspect that the same character is being portrayed. The vastly different approaches to Gorō's character are not the work of innovative contemporary play directors, as one might suppose. On the contrary, each play is a classic, and Gorō is depicted in almost exactly the same way every time each of these pieces is performed. There are no directors involved in or needed for any of these plays.

In *Youchi Soga*, Gorō is a filial son and obedient younger brother totally dedicated to avenging his father. He is a strong warrior who defeats several enemy samurai in single combat (see fig. 1), but he is overcome by superior numbers while fighting in the shogun's camp. His costume is subdued for Noh and announces that he is a samurai of average rank. In *Ya no ne*, Gorō's huge arrows, oversized costume, and red stripes painted on his face identify him as a Kabuki superhero. The brothers' revenge is virtually irrelevant to the play. Instead we witness Gorō celebrating the New Year's holiday. The only martial combat in the play is an easily won fight with a lowly radish seller, and Gorō makes an undignified but humorous exit, riding the radish seller's market horse (see fig. 2). In *Gorō* (see fig. 3), Gorō is carrying an umbrella and looks like a young dandy off to see his lover in the pleasure district. Only two lines of lyrics refer to the Soga vendetta. Although the words accompanying the dance conclude with an advertisement for a festival celebrating Soga Gorō as a Shinto deity, most of the dance drama is in a lyrical and romantic vein, concerned with Gorō's love for his mistress, Shōshō, and with her feelings toward him. In this incarnation Gorō is strikingly handsome and dashing. The unappealing stripes on his face are replaced with bold strokes of makeup that accentuate the actor's eyes and nose, making him look virile and attractive. His kimono is back to human proportions, and instead of oversized weapons he carries one or two swords. A few visual signals, the butterfly crest on the actor's outer robe and the pattern on the back of his inner kimono, tell audiences in-the-know that this is indeed Gorō, who was, in former incarnations, a martial superhero.

The two other main characters of the Soga tale, Soga Jūrō and his mistress Tora, underwent similar transformations as, over the centuries, they took their place on center stage in innumerable ballads and plays. Tora's transformation is the most dramatic. In the medieval period she was a rustic prostitute who only found true purpose

Fig. 1. Gorō (Matsuura Shin'ichirō) advances in front of Gosho no Gorōmaru (Yamamoto Akihiro) in the Noh play *Youchi Soga*. Osaka, 1982. Photo by author.

Fig. 2. Gorō (Onoe Shōroku II) in the Kabuki play *Ya no ne.* Photo by Morita Tōshirō.

Fig. 3. Gorō (Bandō Mitsugorō IX) in the *buyō* dance drama *Gorō*. Photograph by Morita Tōshirō.

in life after becoming a pious and learned nun. As interest in her increased, she became the focus of a tale that traced her life from birth to enlightenment. In some variant versions of the Soga story she became a model samurai wife, and by 1700 she had become the most beautiful and accomplished courtesan in the pleasure district, a woman for whom a religious career was completely unnecessary.

These sorts of changes were imposed on all of the characters of the story—its heroes, villains, and bit players, not only across literary and dramatic genres, but within them as well. Discovering how and why these dramatic reinterpretations were carried out sheds new light on the relationships between the different theatrical genres and provides a new perspective on the conflicting pulls of tradition and change over a long period of literary and theatrical creation.

CHŪSHINGURA AND THE SOGA REVENGE

Because of its important role in New Years' holiday celebrations during the Edo period (1600–1868), the Soga story played a more dominant role in Kabuki than in any other theatrical genre, and it is not surprising that today Soga plays are most prominent on the Kabuki stage. When Japan entered the modern era in the 1860s, the Soga story was one of two archetypical, popular revenge stories—both were known primarily through Kabuki and Bunraku presentations.

In Japan today the best known traditional revenge story is *Chūshingura,* the revenge of the forty-seven loyal retainers, not the story of the Soga brothers. The vendetta of the forty-seven *rōnin* of Akō was first presented in the guise of a Soga play. The godlike status of the forty-seven samurai was made possible by generations of adulation for and worship of the Soga brothers,[3] and *Chūshingura* borrows important motifs from Edo-period Soga plays. The replacement of the Soga brothers by the loyal forty-seven as the focus of adulation for Edo-period townsmen resulted partly from the Akō samurai's proximity in time and closeness in culture to theater audiences, and partly from the excellent plays that were written embellishing the revenge.[4] By the end of the eighteenth century, *Chūshingura* and its variants had become the plays that were sure to salvage a theater season ravaged

3. Maruya Saiichi, *Chūshingura to wa nani ka* (Kōdansha, 1984), 41–56.
4. Henry Smith, "Rethinking the Story of the 47 Ronin," Modern Japan Seminar, Columbia University, 13 April 1990, p. 12.

by box office failures. A theater proverb said, "Soga plays are Kabuki's daily vitamins, and *Chūshingura* is its smelling salts."

In the modern period detailed, factual accounts of the Akō retainers are available, whereas similar historical material on the Soga brothers is not. This has made it possible over the years for playwrights to research, reinterpret, and update the *Chūshingura* story in ways that have not been possible for the Soga story. In the 1930s and 1940s Mayama Seika wrote for Kabuki a nine-play cycle called *Genroku Chūshingura* (The Genroku-Period Treasury of Loyal Retainers) that was supposedly more historically accurate and more true to the reality of Japan in 1700 than any previous Kabuki version of the Akō vendetta. Several of the plays are fine works and invariably well received, and thus they are performed quite often. New films and television shows depicting the *Chūshingura* story appear almost every year. Sometimes they reinterpret the story, but more often they follow Seika's version or the ever-popular *Kanadehon Chūshingura* (The Treasury of Loyal Retainers) version, while relying on popular actors and actresses to achieve commercial success.

More than any other factor, it is the different Edo-period performance contexts that have maintained the popularity of *Chūshingura* and driven the Soga story into relative obscurity in postwar Japan. In the Edo period, plays of the *Chūshingura* cycle were presented for dramatic entertainment alone, whereas from the 1710s onward Soga plays were written and staged to be part of a yearly ritual. *Kanadehon Chūshingura* was performed repeatedly and is still presented, with variations, in Kabuki and Bunraku. Many of the best Edo-period Soga plays were lost to the Kabuki repertoire of performable plays because the tradition of writing original New Year's plays discouraged repeat performances of even the best plays, and because first-month Kabuki required felicitous works of short duration, not long, dramatic pieces. When screenwriters and directors adapt the story of the forty-seven retainers for film and television, they have a familiar story and fine literary texts readily available to draw on for their work. Today there is no familiar, definitive version of Soga drama. Powerful and exciting *ko-jōruri* puppet plays, as well as works by the great Chikamatsu, lie buried after two centuries of celebrational New Year Kabuki.

Present-day Kabuki is the most exciting theater to be seen in Japan. Soga plays are still performed, and dances based on *Gorō* and *Kusazuribiki* (The Armor-Pulling Contest) are among the staples of modern *buyō*. *Sukeroku,* tangentially a Soga play, is also a favorite today. Three Soga Kabuki classics, *Ya no ne* (see pp. 202–17) for a translation), *Kotobuki Soga no taimen* (The Festive Soga Meeting), and *Uiro uri* (The Medicine Peddler), are presented relatively often, usually during one of the ceremonial occasions that still exist in Kabuki, such as *kaomise* (the gala opening month of the Kabuki season), *shumei* (performances to commemorate an actor's succession to a higher rank or new stage name), *tsuizen* (memorial plays), or, rarely, in performances that celebrate the New Year in something resembling Edo-period style. In the 1992–93 season, for example, *Ya no ne* was performed for the Kyoto *kaomise* at the Minami Theater, *Kotobuki Soga no taimen* was presented to celebrate the reopening of Tokyo's Meiji Theater for Kabuki performances, and Danjūrō XII performed Gorō in *Uiro uri* at Tokyo's Kabuki Theater in May to celebrate the eight-hundredth anniversary of the deaths of the historical Soga brothers.

Kabuki presents felicitous, exaggerated, and ritualized Soga plays, but the four Noh plays that are currently performed dramatize the martial prowess and filial devotion of the Soga brothers, and their dedication to a righteous but seemingly hopeless task. This is the essence of the medieval story of the Soga brothers.

CONTINUITY AND TRANSFORMATION

Japan is famous for its preservation of ancient traditions, and claims of fidelity to orthodox artistic and ceremonial practices have carried such weight that "devoted preservation of ancient traditions" has become part of the "Japanese myth," the body of "truths" that all Japanese hold about their country and their culture. Japan's master craftsmen and artists like to claim that their arts are the same now as they were centuries ago, or at least the same as when their grandfathers practiced them. A close look at the Soga tradition, however, shows that many playwrights and actors chose not to leave the tradition exactly the same as they had found it. Understanding how and why they changed the plays and stories they inherited will help us break through the myth of "tradition preserved" to see artistic innovation at work in a constantly changing social and artistic environment.

Because Soga lore was so often retold, either as narrative or on the stage, and because so much textual material remains, the examination of changes wrought over time in Gorō, Jūrō, Tora, and other characters illuminates many of the forces that induced Japanese artists to do things differently than they had been done before. The dynamics of literary and theatrical change, as revealed by the transformations of characters in the Soga story, are complex. At any given time in Japan different and often conflicting value systems guided the lives and beliefs of people of many ranks and stations: the warrior elite, the clergy, the merchants, and so on. Furthermore, ways of life and ideologies for each of these groups changed over time. The nature of the characters of the Soga story was always connected to the ideology of presenters and receivers of the story, and was further modified by the technical requirements of specific performance forms.

A study of the Soga theatrical tradition is especially exciting because Soga plays were often on the leading edge of cultural transformation. Many changes that would affect all of Japanese drama are found first in Soga plays. For example, two of the earliest surviving Noh plays with Kabuki-like plots and characters were Soga plays, and they represent a whole new direction of development in Japanese drama. These plays represent a kind of "active transformation" in which an unprecedented change in character or plot is made, and the impact of the change is so significant that it inspires a wide range of imitation and refinement.

Why were Soga plays so often at the forefront of change in Japanese drama? One reason is that from the early fifteenth century until the end of the nineteenth century there was continuous and simultaneous work being done on new Soga pieces for several literary and theatrical genres. During the fifteenth and sixteenth centuries playwrights of Noh and *kōwakamai* ballad drama as well as reciters of the oral tale were actively creating works about the Soga vendetta. Although each genre required different treatment of source material, aspects of one genre often inspired creative new approaches in others. The sheer breadth of resources in the Soga tradition made innovation easier for reciters and playwrights alike.

As the moral and cultural values in Japanese society evolved, playwrights and actors were inspired to modify the characters and plots of plays about the Soga brothers in keeping with popular taste. For example, as Japan entered the Edo period, feminine archetypes changed as merchant society and culture flourished. Evidence of the new archetypes is seen first in the visual arts, fiction, and skits for the early Kabuki stage, all of which portrayed and idealized contemporary women. Some decades later playwrights and actors began to recast Tora, a historical figure, to conform to these new ideals. By 1683, in Chikamatsu's puppet play *Yotsugi Soga* (The Soga Heir), the transformation was complete: Tora speaks in the jargon of a contemporary courtesan, performs all of the popular dances of the day, and is devoid of a religious dimension. Because Tora's transformation in drama was accomplished three to four generations after the first appearance of the archetypical Edo-period courtesan, it is clear that Tora was not a model for the new archetype. She was recreated to fit it. This change was imposed on the Soga story by new trends in fashion, entertainment, and drama—it was a kind of "passive transformation."

By the mid-sixteenth century *The Tale of the Soga Brothers* was, along with the story of Yoshitsune and *Heike monogatari* (The Tale of the Heike), one of three best-known historical tales in Japan. When playwrights and actors used a completely familiar story, such as the Soga revenge, they could experiment with new themes, plots, characters, and performance styles without fear of disorienting their audience. This is a well-known practice today in the West: contemporary directors eager to do radical experiments with Shakespeare are much more likely to choose the best-known plays, such as *Hamlet* or *King Lear*, and not relatively unknown plays like *Titus Andronicus* or *King John*. It is no surprise that Chikamatsu used the Soga theme in *Yotsugi Soga*, which launched both his own career and the new puppet drama.[5] In Kabuki the Soga story was an important vehicle for experimentation in thematic structure and acting techniques. Roles in Soga plays figured importantly in the careers of the two outstanding acting innovators of the Genroku age (1688–1703), Ichikawa Danjūrō (1660–1704) and Sakata Tōjūrō (1647–1709).

What remained constant from the 1300s to 1900 was the appeal of the main characters of the Soga saga. During those six centuries there was never a time when Soga stories and plays fell out of vogue. Given the thoroughness of some transformations in plot and character, on the surface it might appear that a coherent Soga tradition existed in name only. The story line of the dance play *Gorō*, after all, has virtually nothing to do with the original revenge tale, and Gorō in the dance play seems nothing at all like Gorō in the epic. Nevertheless, certain social and literary values link the many incarnations of the main characters over the centuries. In every version of the Soga tale, whether drama or narrative, Jūrō, Gorō, and Tora were exemplars of virtue and heroism, although the nature of virtue and

5. See chapter 5 for the dramatic innovations Chikamatsu made in his first play, *Yotsugi Soga* (The Soga Heir).

heroism changed over time. Tora, for example, was a heroine in medieval works because after suffering the degradation of working as a prostitute, and after losing Jūrō, the only man who had ever loved her, she devoted the rest of her life to the propagation of the Buddhist faith and to the saving of souls. From the 1500s to the late 1600s Tora was gradually transformed into a more secular hero, a beautiful and charming professional entertainer who nevertheless epitomized the virtues of a samurai wife: total dedication to her husband and a willingness to sacrifice herself for a higher good.

The Soga brothers remained heroes over the centuries onstage and in fiction because the historical brothers had given up their lives for a universally accepted righteous cause: serving the honor of their family name. The high moral stature of avengers resulted from the vertical bonds of samurai society, which operated like an extended family structure, and from the loyalty and self-sacrifice that subordinates owed their superiors. Japanese concepts of filial duty and the moral imperative of revenge were supported by Chinese stories of exaggerated acts of filial piety and outlandish Chinese vendetta tales. Many of these found their way into the oral Soga epic.[6] For real-life samurai, blood revenge acquired almost sacred status in the Edo period. At that time it was the explicit duty of a samurai whose father, elder brother, or uncle had been killed to register with the authorities his intentions of carrying out a vendetta, and then to track down and kill the murderer.[7] Vendetta registration was not kept a secret, so the avenger would be known to his quarry and could legally be killed by him. It is difficult to determine why this single aspect of samurai justice was not settled in the courtroom and instead required mortal combat on the streets. Perhaps the influence of the Soga story and other revenge tales was so strong that government officials deemed the vendetta a crucial test of persistence and devotion, in short, of samurai manhood, and therefore blood revenge could not be relegated to rhetorical debate and institutionalized punishment. In the Edo period many playwrights experimented with the portrayal of Jūrō and Gorō, but the brothers' moral rectitude as loyal avengers was never questioned.

6. Indian and Chinese tales of loyalty and filial piety are featured in books 1, 3–7, and 9 of the *rufubon* version of *Soga monogatari*, and Chinese revenge tales in books 4, 5, and 7 of the same text.

7. Douglas Mills, "Kataki-uchi: The Practice of Blood Revenge in Pre-modern Japan," *Modern Asian Studies* 10.4 (1976): passim.

The overall structure of the Soga revenge story was another unchanging element in the tradition: a quest for revenge. The narrative tale that by the early sixteenth century was most widely known took the form of a loosely connected series of episodes. The core focused on the doings of the Soga brothers or members of their immediate family, while short stories featuring the Buddha and his disciples and accounts of Indian, Chinese, and Japanese religious and lay heroes were inserted to provide commentary on the core story, and to add a loftier tone and a didactic element. Nevertheless, listeners' interest must have been held by the main story of the Soga brothers' difficult and dangerous quest to righteously murder a man much richer and more powerful than themselves. The brothers' heroic and tragic end three-fourths of the way through the tale was followed by a women's spiritual quest, led by Tora and Shōshō, to win salvation for the Soga brothers' souls, to console and enlighten the brothers' surviving female relatives, and to attain enlightenment for themselves.

Before the seventeenth century, playwrights had ignored the women's spiritual activities and tangential tales. They devoted all of their resources to adapting the core of the Soga story to the stage. Medieval Noh and *kōwakamai* plays were short works, so each could tell only a small part of the Soga epic, but spectators knew how these short, dramatized episodes fit into the whole revenge story. In the 1400s and 1500s, while playwrights were paring the story down to its essence as short, dramatic encounters featuring the brothers and Tora, reciters of the narrative tale were doing just the opposite: they were adding more tangential material, and occasionally even inventing new episodes featuring the main characters of the story. By the early 1500s some playwrights began to experiment with works that depicted the brothers and Tora in episodes that were considerably removed from their traditional quests for revenge and salvation.

With the central tale of the tragic vendetta so well implanted in the Japanese imagination, plot digressions and radical reinterpretation of characters were the main features of Soga plays in the middle of the Edo period. Kabuki and puppet plays were presented by and for the new urban commoner classes, and the values and tastes of this new social group influenced the changes in the Soga story and its characters. From the 1680s onward, novel approaches to old characters and plots became a de facto requirement of new Kabuki and puppet plays. It is in Edo-period theater that the most variation in character and plot exists from play to play, but the quest motif remained as a deep structural feature unifying all work in the Soga tradition, and newly fashioned plots of the Soga story still used this motif. Often, especially in Kabuki, a short-term quest for a sword, scroll, or other family heirloom was used to motivate the action of new Soga plays. The logic of the search for an heirloom was that the larger pursuit of revenge could not be continued until the short-term problem was solved. Audiences steeped in stories of the vendetta understood even short, felicitous pieces and essentially plotless dance dramas as digressions from a road to revenge and self-sacrifice. Even in the most festive Soga Kabuki plays, the awareness of inevitable tragedy confers an evanscent quality on scenes of celebration or triumph.

Innovations in plays about the Soga vendetta were necessitated by changing relationships between dramatic texts and their performance contexts. Performance is fluid and ephemeral. Every performance is different because no two audiences are the same and no actor plays exactly the same role twice. Until the age of film and video, an essential characteristic of live performance was its ephemerality. When performances were lost to human memory, they were gone. Play texts, by contrast, were quite durable. As soon as a Soga play was written down, it became a link in the chain of the Soga literary tradition. Many links, if not the entire chain of the tradition, were available to playwrights from Noh through Kabuki. Playwrights and performers could confidently borrow and use extant works almost exactly as they stood when contexts of performance changed little over time. Until the late nineteenth century, copyright and royalty laws did not exist to hinder such activity. The separately published but identical texts for the seven-day Soga *ko-jōruri* puppet drama[8] are examples of repeated use of identical texts.

When performance conditions changed rapidly, so did the content of plays about the Soga brothers. Playwrights and directors (usually the leading actor) used audience tastes and their collaborators' skills and performance techniques as essential parameters when creating new plays, but they also added their own convictions, talents, and inspiration to the creative mix constituting a new Soga play. Chikamatsu contributed his own convictions to the Soga tradition in his conversion of Tora and Shōshō into secular rather than religious paragons of virtue. The first Ichikawa Danjūrō forever changed the

8. *Ko-jōruri* is a term used to designate the "old puppet theater." See chapters 4 and 5 for a discussion of *ko-jōruri* and *jōruri*, the "mature" puppet theater.

Soga tradition in Kabuki with his religiously inspired *aragoto* (wild acting) protrayal of Gorō, and Danjūrō's son, responding to the growing pride of his commoner audience, created an immensely popular "gentle *aragoto*" tradition for Soga Gorō, which depicted Gorō as a heroic townsman.

The heroes of the Soga story proved extremely malleable characters onstage. In every genre of traditional Japanese theater the depiction of character is based heavily on acting styles and presentational techniques. Until the late seventeenth century, performers wrote their own play texts, and after that playwrights collaborated closely with performers, writing to meet the specific requirements of leading actors and puppet chanters. The heroes of the Soga story proved durable and flexible, favorite characters for actors and presenters working in a wide range of styles. In Kabuki, in fact, two Soga plays (*Kotobuki Soga no taimen* and *Uiro uri*) are used today to showcase in a single short play a wide variety of acting styles. Thanks to the continuity and durability of the Soga dramatic tradition, when we travel through time with Jūrō, Gorō, and Tora and witness their multiple incarnations on the Noh, puppet, and Kabuki stages, we gain a new understanding of the dynamics of innovation and conservatism in traditional Japanese theater.

Chapter Two: Origin and Development of the Soga Story

Before the Soga brothers made their appearance on Japan's theatrical stages, their tale had been told for several centuries by minstrels who traveled the length and breadth of Japan. The Soga story became part of Japan's "national literature," known by all Japanese of every rank and station, from lowly farmers to the samurai barons who ruled the land. Playwrights and dramatists who turned to the story for inspiration had surely heard several different recitations of the tale. No study of dramatic representations of the Soga story can begin without an examination of the epic *Tale of the Soga Brothers,* the font of all knowledge about the brothers and their heroic vendetta.

The latter part of the twelfth century, when the historical vendetta occurred, was a time of war, upheaval, and changing social and political values. In modern history books the Soga brothers rarely merit even a footnote in the chapter on the shogun Yoritomo, yet in medieval and Edo-period Japan their story was known to every Japanese. A better understanding of the original facts of the story and the hearts and minds of the Japanese of the medieval era will explain this discrepancy.

The first mention of the Soga brothers is found in a medieval chronicle called the *Azuma kagami* (A Mirror of the East), compiled by an unknown author or authors. It covers eighty-five years, from 1180 to 1265, and its main purpose was to legitimize the Hōjō Regency and its usurpation of shogunal power and prerogatives.[9] *Azuma kagami* is in three parts; though it purports to be a daily record, only the third part was so recorded. The first part, which covers the Genpei War (1180–85) and the period of the Soga story, was reconstructed sixty

9. Yoritomo's two sons succeeded him as shogun. Then the Hōjō family took power, leaving the shogun, like the emperor, a figurehead. *Azuma kagami* exposes the errors and indiscretions of Yoritomo and his successor shoguns but always treats the Hōjō family with the highest respect. Kadokawa Gen'yoshi, *Katarimono bungei no hassei* (Tōkyō-dō, 1975), 417.

years after the events described, using court diaries, official documents, and popular tales.[10]

Several entries in *Azuma kagami* record events found in *The Tale of the Soga Brothers.* The entry for the seventh day of the ninth month of 1190 states that Hōjō Tokimasa (1138–1215) took the role of "cap father" in Soga Gorō's coming-of-age ceremony.[11] The truth of Tokimasa's role poses an interesting problem. In every version of *The Tale of the Soga Brothers,* Tokimasa is described as Gorō's "cap father," but his role remains hidden from the shogun and from society at large until the shogun interrogates Gorō after the vendetta. Gorō's mother had sent him at age eleven to Hakone Temple to become a priest, and he was supposed to devote his life to prayer for his father's salvation (as a priest he would have been unable to participate in a vendetta). Gorō fled the temple just before his investiture and became a samurai for the express purpose of avenging his father. The compiler of *Azuma kagami,* well aware of the apotheosis of the brothers, may have wished to give the Hōjō family some of the credit for Gorō's first valiant act. If Tokimasa did in fact cap Gorō and give him his adult name, Tokimune, he would have had good reason to keep his actions secret—as a samurai Gorō posed a threat to the shogun himself, for Yoritomo had ordered the execution of Gorō's grandfather. Tokimasa was a cunning politician. One recent theory suggests that he planned the Soga vendetta, using the brothers as his pawns in order to eliminate Kudō Suketsune, an important rival in the highest circle of the shogunate.[12]

Azuma kagami covers the events of the hunt on Mount Fuji in some detail. A summary follows (direct quotes are indicated with quotation marks):

> The Soga brothers, grandchildren of Itō Sukechika, broke into Kudō's lodge on the plain at Mount Fuji and killed him and his attendant, Ōtōnai. Ōtōnai was Kudō's vassal, and Kudō had just helped him to win a lawsuit in Kamakura.

10. Ibid., 406. For the role of *Heike monogatari* in the compilation of *Azuma kagami,* see Kenneth Butler, "The Textual Evolution of the *Heike Monogatari,*" in *Harvard Journal of Asiatic Studies* 26 (1966): 95.

11. The "cap father" (*eboshi oya*) placed samurai headgear on a child's head in the *genbuku* or coming-of-age ceremony. The child was normally about thirteen years old, but, because Gorō had planned to be a priest, he was seventeen for his *genbuku.* The cap father usually gave part of his name to the child. The *toki* in Tokimune reputedly derives from Hōjō's given name, Tokimasa.

12. Okami Masao and Kadokawa Gen'yoshi, *Taiheki, Soga monogatari, Gikeiki* (Kadokawa Shoten, 1960), 212.

Two women entertainers, who had been summoned to perform for Kudō and Ōtōnai, screamed when they saw the men killed, and the brothers raised a great victory cry. These shouts created an uproar in the camp. The shogun's guards ran out, unaware of what was happening. "Rain and thunder pounded like beating drums, torches were extinguished in the dark night, and the samurai were in such confusion that they could not tell east from west. This worked to the advantage of the brothers, who wounded many of them." (The casualties arc named—the brothers killed one and wounded nine.) Jūrō was slain by Nitta no Shirō Tadatsuna. Gorō, after penetrating the shogun's camp in the hopes of taking on Yoritomo, was captured by the shogun's attendant, Gosho no Gorōmaru.

The next day the shogun interrogated Gorō. Gorō expressed his anger and resentment, speaking of his family's fall in fortune after the death of his grandfather. Gorō said that he killed Kudō to "wash away the shame from his father's corpse." Gorō informed the shogun of the vows he and Jūrō had made as children and of their unremitting dedication to those vows. He declared that he had attacked the shogun to avenge his grandfather; now that he had failed, he requested permission to commit *seppuku.* Gorō identified Jūrō's severed head, brought in by Nitta. Kudō's wife and son requested and were given permission to arrange Gorō's execution. Messengers brought the brothers' last letter, intended for their mother. Its tone was proof of the brothers' noble characters, and the shogun was so impressed that he said it would be kept in the archives forever.

Three weeks after the vendetta, Jūrō's mistress, a prostitute from Ōiso, was interrogated but released after her innocence was ascertained. Kudō's widow and son accused the youngest Soga brother, the monk Onbō (1177–93) (he was born shortly after his father's death), of complicity in the murder of Kudō. Onbō's stepfather denied the charge, but a messenger was sent to bring Onbō to Kamakura.

Jūrō's mistress performed memorial services for him twenty-one days after his death. She offered sutras and presented a horse to the temple. It had been a gift from Jūrō. She took the tonsure the same day and became a nun. "Observing her in black and white robes, many must have wiped away tears of regret."

Onbō was brought to Kamakura and was informed that he would be beheaded. He requested permission to read the sutras and to commit *seppuku.* He reiterated his family's hatred of the shogun, and then committed ritual suicide.[13]

13. Horida Kasau, *Yakubun azuma kagami hyōchū* (Meicho Kankōkai, 1979), 309–16.

How much of the above account is history and how much is embellishment? We can accept the identities of the Soga brothers, the men they murdered, and the men who killed and captured the brothers. The number of men killed and injured by the brothers after the vendetta is certainly closer to reality than the fifty killed and three hundred and eighty wounded as described in the popular version of *The Tale of the Soga Brothers.* It is likely that the shogun interrogated Gorō, and Gorō's defiant attitude is believable. Yoritomo's brutally effective elimination of political enemies is well attested by other sources, and so the arrest and execution of Onbō are probably accurate.

There is convincing evidence, however, that a fictionalized account of the Soga brothers was already being recited by the mid 1200s and that the compiler of *Azuma kagami* used it as a source for his description of the Soga events. The dramatic style of the "rainy night" section of the vendetta description (quoted above) differs conspicuously from the more common, short, matter-of-fact entries. *Azuma kagami* is written in Chinese, but many sections of the text, when converted back into Japanese and read aloud, seem to derive from oral literature.[14]

The most conclusive evidence for the prior existence of an oral tale or tales about the Soga brothers is the particular interest shown in Jūrō's mistress. In general, *Azuma kagami* is concerned with political and military events; the activities of an entertainer rarely enter its purview. Wandering nuns, many of whom were also former entertainers and prostitutes, were important reciters of oral tales, and in the sections of *Azuma kagami* that derive from oral tales, nuns and prostitutes are prominent characters.[15] Jūrō's mistress in *The Tale of the Soga Brothers* is Tora Gozen, a prostitute of Ōiso village (near present-day Odawara). Nuns who narrated the Soga tale often called themselves "Tora" and were known as *tora goze.*[16] The character Tora, Jūrō's mistress, was embellished, or even created by these reciters—it lent immediacy and pathos to a tale if the listeners believed that the narrator herself had been an actual participant in the events described. The lines from *Azuma kagami*, "Observing her in black and white robes,

14. Kadokawa, *Katarimono bungei no hassei,* 415.

15. Ibid., 420. For example, in sections referring to Yoshitsune, his mistress Shizuka Gozen is described.

16. *Goze* now means "a blind, female reciter." *Gozen* is a polite form of address corresponding roughly to "lady."

many must have wiped away tears," seem to come straight from an oral recitation.

APOTHEOSIS OF THE BROTHERS AND ORIGINS OF THE ORAL EPIC

It is clear that some sixty years after the assassination of Kudō Suketsune the story of the Soga brothers was being recited in eastern Japan. In an era of so many heroic and tragic martial deeds, how was it that these militarily and politically insignificant brothers came to be immortalized in legend? The answer lies in popular religious beliefs and in practices concerning violent death.

The deaths of the Soga brothers aroused real emotions of fear and compassion in Japanese of high and low station living in the Mount Fuji region. Medieval Japanese relied on religion to ease their fears and to bestow compassion on the Soga brothers' spirits. Shinto and Buddhist responses to emotions of fear and pity explain why *The Tale of the Soga Brothers* came into being.

In every culture rituals of death—funerals, wakes, elegies, dirges, laments—"universalize, and stabilize the original quality of sorrow (*and fear*) and transmute them to a historical past."[17] From these rituals in ancient Greece tragic literature was born, and in ancient and medieval Japan there was also an intimate connection between literary creation and the spirits of the dead. The great elegies of *Man'yōshū* (A Collection of Ten Thousand Leaves), Japan's first poetic anthology compiled in the mid-eighth century, were written to tell the dead that they were remembered, respected, and sorely missed. These sentiments were partly motivated by love or respect for the deceased, but they were also meant to prevent the spirits of the dead from causing harm in the world of the living.[18]

According to Shinto belief, men can become gods (*kami*) after their death. The earliest historical sources tell us that ancestors whom the Japanese recognized as the founders of clans or families were worshipped as *kami*. Belief in another kind of human god, *goryō* (revered spirit) or *arahitogami* (wild man-god), derived from the fear of unappeased ghosts. *Goryō* and *arahitogami* were the spirits of politically or militarily powerful men who died with their aims unfulfilled:

17. T. R. Henn, *The Harvest of Tragedy* (London: Methuen and Co. Ltd., 1956), 267.
18. For a discussion of the theme of death in *Man'yōshū* and the ritual role of elegies, see Umehara Takeshi, *Koten no hakken* (Kōdansha, 1973), 29–35.

> They were associated with disasters, epidemics, and wars through divination by shamans or priests. The belief was influenced by the Chinese idea that if the spirits of the dead did not have memorial services performed for them by their descendants they would become evil spirits or demons (*kuei*) or be transformed into locusts or other harmful insects.[19]

By the mid-Heian period (A.D. 900 onward), belief in *goryō* was very strong. Huge exorcism ceremonies, *goryō-e*, were held in Kyoto after natural disasters and epidemics if Shinto diviners decided the calamities had been caused by angry *goryō*. The most important *goryō* of the Heian period was Sugawara Michizane (845–903), a courtier and scholar unjustly banished to Kyushu in 901 as a result of court intrigues. Five years after his death, lightning struck the imperial palace, starting a fire, and killing by electrical shock several courtiers who had opposed Michizane.[20] Priests determined that the disasters had been caused by Michizane's vengeful spirit. To placate the spirit, his imperial rank was posthumously restored, and he was deified as a god of learning in the Kitano Tenmangu Shrine in Kyoto. Reverence for Michizane's spirit (called Tenjin) is still strong today throughout Japan.[21] The medieval Japanese understanding of who the Soga brothers were and what they had become was strongly influenced by the story of Michizane.

The death of wrathful warriors often inspired fear of their *goryō*—in this the Soga brothers were hardly unique. The tenth-century rebel Taira no Masakado (d. 940) and the Genpei War generals Kiso no Yoshinaka (1154–84) and Saitō Bettō Sanemori (1111–83) are a few defeated war leaders who were deified by people living near the places they were killed. The story of Masakado is told in *Shōmonki* (The Chronicle of Masakado), and Yoshinaka and Sanemori figure prominently in *Heike monogatari*.

At several points in *The Tale of the Soga Brothers*, when Soga Gorō is frustrated by his inability to come to grips with Kudō, he declares that he will commit suicide, become an angry *goryō*, and kill Kudō in that way. In each instance, the older and wiser Jūrō calms his

19. Hori Ichirō, *Folk Religion in Japan: Continuity and Change* (Chicago: University of Chicago Press, 1968), 43.
20. Ibid., 28.
21. Students pray for success in school and on entrance examinations at Tenjin shrines all over the country. At examination time the crowds at these shrines are impressive.

brother and saves him from committing suicide. Even in the earliest versions of the tale (the *manabon* version, see p. 39), Gorō has a more headstrong character, and Jūrō never threatens to become a *goryō*. Gorō's intemperate vows and his violent disposition were probably attributed to him because the sound of his name, Gorō, suggested *goryō*.[22]

In all versions of *The Tale of the Soga Brothers* the spirits of Jūrō and Gorō begin to wreak havoc soon after the vendetta. In the earliest versions of the tale, Gorō's executioner, who beheaded him painfully with a dull sword, dies insane seven days after the execution. In later versions the executioner is disgraced, exiled, and dies of disease four months after the vendetta. A half-brother who had refused to support Jūrō and Gorō is killed three months after the vendetta while fighting rebellious samurai in Kamakura. Other minor enemies of the brothers are disgraced and exiled. All of these misfortunes are attributed to the wrath of the brothers' spirits.[23]

According to early versions of the Soga story, Tora erected a shrine near the site of the brothers' deaths and waited there seven days for a visit from their spirits. Finally Gorō's voice responded to a poem she recited.[24] Subsequent versions stated that the spirits of the brothers lingered near the site of the vendetta, and at night the sounds of combat could be heard, along with shouts, "I'm Jūrō Sukenari! I'm Gorō Tokimune!"[25] Travelers who heard the *goryō* either died on the spot or went mad. The records of the founding of the Soga Hachiman Shrine state that Yoritomo was troubled by nightmares about the brothers.[26] According to most versions of the tale, the shogun summoned a wandering priest, Yōgyō Shōnin, and asked him what to do about the brothers' spirits. Yōgyō Shōnin told Yoritomo the story of Sugawara Michizane and said that he and other *goryō* had been pacified by erecting shrines to honor them as gods. Yoritomo followed the priest's advice. He ordered a shrine to be built, and he donated estates to finance its operation. The shrine was to placate the Soga spirits by means of *kagura* performances and other rites. The depredations of the Soga spirits ceased, and a priest witnessed the brothers'

22. For a discussion of the connection between the name Gorō and *goryō* beliefs, see Ōshima Tatehiko, "*Soga monogatari* no keisei," *Kokugo to kokubungaku* 37.4 (1960): 107.

23. Ichiko Teiji and Ōshima Tatehiko, eds., *Soga monogatari*, vol. 88 of *Nihon koten bungaku taikei* (Iwanami Shoten, 1966), book 10.

24. Ōshima, "*Soga monogatari* no keisei," 108.

25. Ichiko and Ōshima, *Soga monogatari*, 405, book 11.

26. Ōshima, "*Soga monogatari* no keisei," 109.

attainment of Buddhist salvation in a dream. The tale goes on to state that "even now, those who intend vengeance upon their enemies come from provinces far and near to worship the gods of this shrine. Thus the brothers' spirits are revered by all, high and low."[27]

The shrine to the Soga brothers still exists today, although the building is not the original one (see figs. 4–6). The transformation of the Soga *goryō* from dangerous spirits into gods to be entreated for assistance follows the pattern of Sugawara Michizane. Of course, relatively few pilgrims would have visited the shrine to pray for assistance in vendettas, but the Soga gods also played an important role in the religion of local farmers. Initially, the brothers' spirits had to be appeased since farmers believed the spirits would assume the form of harmful insects and destroy the rice crop.[28] Medieval Japanese believed that even malevolent gods, if shown the proper respect and given suitable offerings, might use their strength in behalf of supplicants to protect them from lesser spirits of ill-fortune and disease.[29] The season of the vendetta and Gorō's name apparently accounted for his *goryō* coming to be worshiped as a thunder god. Thunder is represented onomatopoetically in Japanese by the sound *goro, goro, goro*,[30] and all versions of the tale agree that the first rain of the monsoon fell on the night of the brothers' raid. Early summer rains are crucial to the success of Japanese agriculture, and many prayers and rituals are devoted to ensuring their timely arrival. In the area around Mount Fuji, and later in the whole Kantō region, the first monsoon rains came to be called *Soga no ame* or *Tora ga ame* (Soga or Tora rain),[31] and festivals are still held on the anniversary of the vendetta at Soga shrines and temples to console the brothers' spirits and to pray for rain.[32]

27. Kitagawa Hiroshi, trans., *The Tale of the Soga Brothers* (Hikone: Shiga University Press, 1984), 2:144. In the tale, the name of the shrine is Shōmyōkō Jingu, and the village assigned to support it is called Matsukaze. *The Tale of the Soga Brothers* and the shrine records are in agreement on the particulars of the founding of the shrine.

28. Ōshima, "*Soga monogatari* no keisei," 107.

29. For a detailed discussion of the Soga brothers in local folk religion, see Masaya Akira, "*Soga monogatari* no minzokuteki kiban," *Kokugakuin zasshi* 69.4 (1968): 41–49. Masaya discusses the religious observances of the late fifth month, Soga exorcism rituals, and the process by which dangerous gods can be turned into helpful ones.

30. Aoe Shunjirō, "Nihon geinō no genryū," *Minzoku mingei* 61 (1971): 152.

31. See Ōtō Tokihiko, "Tora ga ame," *Minzokugaku kenkyū* 7.2 (1951): passim.

32. Miyano Shigeo, ed. *Nihon sairei gyōji jiten* (Shudōsha, 1968), lists all the major festivals still performed in Japan, including several festivals devoted to the Soga spirits. A well-known festival is celebrated in the village of Shimo Soga in Kanagawa Prefecture on 28 May.

Fig. 4. Memorial markers to the spirits of the Soga brothers on a cedar-covered knoll at the southern base of Mount Fuji, where the brothers were killed. Photo by author.

Fig. 5. Soga Hachiman Shrine, on the southern slope of Mount Fuji. Photo by author.

Fig. 6. Painting of Gorō in the inner sanctuary of Soga Hachiman Shrine, normally not open to the public. Other sanctuary paintings depict Jūrō and Tora. The painting of Jūrō features a much gentler facial expression than that of Gorō here. Photo by author.

Many medieval Japanese were not certain that the brothers had in fact achieved Buddhist salvation and had thus become benevolent spirits. Medieval accounts record reappearances of the brothers' spirits near the site of their death.[33] Annual festivals in the Mount Fuji area continued to honor the brothers (see figs. 7–8); recitation of the brothers' exploits was one part of the ritual, for nothing angers a *goryō* as much as ignorance of its deeds. Japanese believed that the recitation of a narrative text could pacify real and dangerous spirits.

The witnesses of the reappearance of the spirits were often *nenbutsu* priests (*nenbutsu hijiri*), *nenbutsu* referring to the Buddhist litany *namu amida butsu* (hail Amida Buddha). *Nenbutsu* priests told Japan's masses of the all-embracing compassion of the Amida Buddha.[34] They taught that faith in Amida's compassion and recitation of the *nenbutsu* assured rebirth in Amida's Paradise. But victims of violent death rarely had the time or will to compose their minds in an attitude of faith and recite the *nenbutsu*. Their spirits were therefore condemned to suffer in the Asura Hell of strife and combat, with only occasional night visits to the world of the living. *Nenbutsu* priests, through the power of their own faith, could release these tormented souls and send them to Paradise. In times of war these priests traveled to battle sites and conducted services to rescue the spirits of slain soldiers. Local residents feared the restless spirits of slain warriors, but it was pity and compassion that motivated the priests to pray for the salvation of souls in torment.

Some who listened to the Soga story feared the Soga spirits, but most lived far from Mount Fuji, and their strongest feelings were compassionate identification with characters in the tale. Although many early reciters cast themselves as fellow sufferers in the actual Soga tragedy, by the mid-thirteenth century the pity aroused by the Soga story, as in Western tragedy, was experienced at an aesthetic distance.

Pity and compassion are central themes in all versions of *The Tale of the Soga Brothers*. Several important feudal lords secretly support the brothers throughout their quest. The efforts made by virtuous

33. The most important account is in *Jizō bōsatsu reigenki*, written in 1512. The account is summarized in Ōshima, "*Soga monogatari* no keisei," 111. The same article discusses other accounts of the appearance of the spirits of Tora or the Soga brothers.

34. Hori, *Folk Religion in Japan*, contains an excellent chapter on the beliefs and practices of the *nenbutsu* faith.

Fig. 7. Two boys dressed as the Soga brothers for the annual Soga festival held 28 May at Kōzenji in Shimo Soga village. Photo by author.

Fig. 8. The "umbrella burning," the central event at the annual Soga festival held 28 May at Kōzenji in Shimo Soga village. Photo by author.

characters to save or aid the Soga brothers certainly strengthened listeners' compassion for the heroes. In all its narrative forms the medieval Soga story was used to teach Buddhist compassion; scenes of cruelty or brutality are described with disapproval by the narrator and are sometimes set against Indian or Chinese stories of compassion.

Religious responses to violent death gave rise to *The Tale of the Soga Brothers*, but the impact of the Soga story went beyond the demands of Shinto propitiation of the gods and Buddhist compassion. The tale portrayed a struggle between conflicting positive values.[35] The Soga brothers faced a conflict in loci of duty. The shogun's order and law are always praised, in *Azuma kagami*, and in all versions of the tale, yet the brothers are praised for breaking this law (in their case, the law against private vendettas at public events).

The most common conflict in values in traditional Japanese literature is *giri* versus *ninjō*. *Giri* is duty to family honor, to one's lord, or to the state; *ninjō* is love, or human feelings. In *The Tale of the Soga Brothers* the mother suffers the greatest conflict of values; she wishes to spare the lives of her sons, yet she knows that her husband's honor can only be upheld by a vendetta that will certainly bring about her sons' deaths. For her, parental love and family duty are entirely irreconcilable. As dramatic as such conflicts in values may be in stories or on the stage, it is unfortunate for individuals in a society if its main values contradict one another, as they sometimes did in medieval Japan. The contradiction between the harsh warrior code and the compassion of Buddhism was a source of doubt and anguish for medieval samurai, particularly in times of strife. *The Tale of the Soga Brothers* demonstrates that literary creation combined with religious rites was one means to resolve conflicting social, political, and spiritual values after real-life tragedies.

The simplest and most primitive tragic situation "is one in which the hero provokes or inherits a situation of enmity and the

35. According to Lionel Abel, "Is There a Tragic Sense of Life?" in Robert Corrigan, ed., *Tragedy: Vision and Form* (New York: Harper and Row Publishers, 1981), 58, this is an essential element of the "tragic vision." In Greek tragedy the conflict is often between duty to family or to the gods, as opposed to duty to the state. The emotions of fear and compassion that engendered *The Tale of the Soga Brothers* and that figure importantly in the Soga story are common to the romantic and tragic traditions of several cultures and ages. Unfortunately, a serious study of intercultural parallels is beyond the scope of this book.

return of the avenger constitutes the catastrophe."[36] *The Tale of the Soga Brothers* is not the first or most primitive Japanese revenge story. Japanese myths portray revenge situations, and in folk tales revenge is a common and simple form of justice. Folk tale revenge pits unmistakable and immaculate good against cruel or covetous evil, and the outcome is invariably a victory for the good.[37] It is romantic, not tragic revenge.[38] The Soga brothers' revenge, suggesting a romance, takes the form of a quest,[39] but the Soga tale, as we have seen, is more complex than a folk tale or a romance. Not only are two positive values in opposition, but the outcome is unclear; the brothers "lose in the winning and win in the losing."[40] Although the brothers are innocent and courageous, in the manner of romantic heroes, they have none of the magical and fantastic powers of such heroes. "Emphasis is thrown on their success, the completeness of their achievement, and the paradox of victory within the tragedy."[41]

FORMATION AND SPREAD OF THE ORAL TALE

Little evidence remains telling us when, where, and by whom *The Tale of the Soga Brothers* was recited. Literary historians who investigate the origins of the tale rely on analyses of the earliest recorded texts and conclude that during the first two centuries after the vendetta priests and nuns from temples in the Hakone region (southeast of Mount Fuji) spread *The Tale of the Soga Brothers.*

36. Northrop Frye, *Anatomy of Criticism, Four Essays* (Princeton: Princeton University Press, 1947), 208.
37. *Setsuwa* tales such as "The Monkey and the Crab" epitomize romantic revenge. A cruel monkey gratuitously murders a crab, and the crab's son valiantly sets out to avenge his father. Along the way he acquires various improbable allies (they vary depending on the version of the story but include a mortar, a wasp, and other animate and inanimate creatures). Together they kill the evil monkey, and all the good creatures survive a victorious battle with the monkey's kin.
38. See Frye, *Anatomy of Criticism*, 27, 186–90 for characteristics of the romantic.
39. Ibid., 219–22, esp. 220. The Soga story falls in the romantic portion of the continuum of tragedy that has as one pole romance and as the other pole irony.
40. Robert Corrigan, "Tragedy and the Tragic Spirit," in Corrigan, *Tragedy: Vision and Form*, 9.
41. Herbert Muller, *The Spirit of Tragedy* (New York: Alfred A. Knopf, 1956), 22, emphasizes the importance in tragedy of the hero's choice of his tragic fate and his acceptance of the full consequences of that choice. In the Soga story the brothers make their tragic choice as children (Gorō is older, seventeen, when he renounces the priesthood). The brothers' dedication to their heroic and tragic goal receives more emphasis than the process of making the choice.

The *manabon* version of the tale, dating from approximately 1350, is the earliest surviving written text of *Soga monogatari* (see p. 39). The content and style of parts of the *manabon* text indicate that they were used in sermons by Amidist or Shingon priests of Hakone Temple.[42] In *The Tale of the Soga Brothers,* Buddhist morality is embodied either in the actions of the main characters or in inserted Buddhist and Chinese tales. These stories were widely known to Japanese and were used by entertainers and by priests of many sects to embellish their rhetoric. The characters in the Soga tale also use these rhetorical techniques: for example, Gorō cites *Ninnōgyō* (The Benevolent Kings Sutra) when trying to persuade his mother to forgive him, and Tora's mother, urging Tora to be filial and obedient, takes her precedents from Buddhist commentary to the *Mahābhārata.*[43]

We have seen that itinerant *nenbutsu* priests were important disseminators of the Soga story. After the establishment of the Jishū *nenbutsu* sect[44] in the middle of the thirteenth century, members of that sect became important leaders of the religious life of the lower

42. Amano Fumio, "Miyamasu Sogamono kō," *Geinōshi kenkyū* 60 (1978): 30–31. The work of Amidist priests included *shōdō* (chant leading) and *sekkyō* (sutra explanation), activities that were virtually the same in the early medieval period. According to Ōshima, "*Soga monogatari* no keisei," 116, and Douglas Mills, "Soga Monogatari, Shintōshū, and the Taketori Legend," *Monumenta Nipponica* 30.1 (1975): 43–47, the *manabon* text of *The Tale of the Soga Brothers* is linguistically and thematicaly related to *Shintōshū* (A Collection of Shinto Tales), a collection of fifty religious stories and accounts of the origins of shrines and temples. The compilers of *Shintōshū* were Agui priests. The Agui was a temple in the Atago region of Kyoto, originally affiliated with Enryakuji, the great Tendai monastery on Mount Hiei. The Agui monks rejected the Tendai sect in favor of Amidism and moved to the east in the late Heian and early Kamakura periods. They administered important Jōdō temples in the Kantō, including Hakone Temple.

The memorial services for the Soga brothers that appear in the narrative tale probably derive from actual services performed by Buddhist priests, and in their sermons priests associated with the Hakone Temple doubtlessly emphasized the divine aid given the brothers by the Hakone Gongen, the chief deity of the temple. The prominent role of the Hakone abbot is testimony to the close connections between the temple and the Soga story. For a discussion of the relationship between religious sermons and the Soga story, see Fukuda Akira, "Soga katari to shōdō," *Ritsumeikan bungaku* 1 (1977): 119–22.

43. See Ichiko and Ōshima, *Soga monogatari,* book 6, "Benzaiten," and book 7, "Hanzokuō."

44. The Jishū sect was founded in 1275 by Ippen Shōnin (1239–89). Ippen was also called Yōgyō or Yūgyō Shōnin. He received training at Mount Hiei and later embraced the Amidist faith.

classes. They performed annual services on such occasions as rice-planting time when, in the Kantō, observances to pacify the wrathful spirits of the Soga brothers would have been important. The shrine-founding episode in *The Tale of the Soga Brothers* provides evidence of the Jishū sect's connection to the Soga tale: Yōgyō Shōnin, who in that chapter lectures Yoritomo on the history of *goryō*, was the founder of the Jishū sect. Jishū reciters of the tale probably added this episode to enhance their own prestige and authority despite the fact that Yōgyō Shōnin was born forty-five years after the Soga vendetta and could not possibly have met Yoritomo.[45]

The preaching of popular Buddhism had always involved an element of entertainment, but the Jishū sect expanded the role of this element in religion.[46] The religious tales recited by Jishū priests took on many characteristics of popular stories and folk tales, and *nenbutsu hijiri* sought to make their audiences identify with the characters and situations in the stories they recited as parables. Local geography was accurately described in the early versions of *The Tale of the Soga Brothers*, and local families and heroes were introduced into the narrative. Sometimes the reciters cast themselves as characters of the story, following the tradition of *The Tale of the Soga Brothers* that states that the brothers' two faithful retainers became monks and roamed the country performing memorial services.[47] These former Soga retainers purportedly founded several Soga shrines and temples in areas far from the Kantō.[48]

While no medieval historical sources actually survive that describe priests or monks reciting the Soga story, they do for women entertainers, and in fact wandering nuns and female minstrels were

45. Medieval Buddhism, and *nenbutsu* sects in particular, were markedly syncretic. Native Shinto beliefs were incorporated rather than disproved or opposed, so it is not surprising that a Buddhist priest should preside over the dedication of a Shinto shrine. See Hori, *Folk Religion in Japan*, 92, on syncretism in the *nenbutsu* faith.

46. The Jishū sect introduced *nenbutsu odori* (dances) and *nenbutsu kyōgen* (pantomimes) as entertaining yet spiritual activities. According to popular belief *nenbutsu odori* was founded by Ippen at Zenkōji, a major temple in Shinano Province (the site of present-day Nagano City, Nagano Prefecture). Today *nenbutsu odori* and *nenbutsu kyōgen* seem more entertaining than instructive, but they remain popular festival events.

47. Ichiko and Ōshima, *Soga monogatari*, book 10, tells us that they became *kōya hijiri* (wandering priests). Ippen was known by the appellation *kōya hijiri* or *kūya hijiri* (Hori, *Folk Religion of Japan*, 103).

48. Okami and Kadokawa, *Taiheki, Soga monogatari, Gikeiki*, 248–50.

even more important than Buddhist priests in the nationwide dissemination of *The Tale of the Soga Brothers*.[49] They were known by various names. One general appellation was *goze*:

> The *goze* grew out of a magico-religious tradition in which mediums held a prominent position. Mediums, as the spiritual ancestors of the *goze*, would reproduce the scenes of battles by allowing angry spirits who had taken part in them to recall the events as they had happened. In this way the spirits would be appeased. The *goze* were not satisfied merely to tell a tale. Their work, both for status and for dramatic effect, was to recreate an event, and this required them to possess an aura of "being there."[50]

As we have seen, the most important *goze* reciter was Tora Gozen, Jūrō's former mistress. It is impossible to determine whether or not she really existed, but the original home of women called "Tora" is the temple of Kōraiji in Sagami Province (present Kanagawa Prefecture).[51] Kōraiji was a convent with a close affiliation to the Hakone Temple. Many stories in *Shintōshū* (A Collection of Shinto Tales) describe the repentance of performing girls who later became Kōraiji nuns.[52] Tora Gozen's life story fits the pattern perfectly, and in later versions of *The Tale of the Soga Brothers* Tora spends her final years in a hermitage at Kōraiji.

According to all versions of the Soga tale, Tora Gozen traveled to various religious institutions where she conducted memorial services for Jūrō and Gorō or attempted to commune with their spirits (see fig. 9). In the medieval period the nuns of Kōraiji and other

49. Medieval sources that refer to women reciting the Soga tale include: (1) *Shichiju-ichiban shokunin uta awase* (Matched Poems on the Seventy-One Occupations) by Sugawara Kazunaga (1460–1529), with illustrations by Tosa Mitsunobu (1434?–1525?). An illustrated text describes a blind woman with a *biwa* (the same lute used by the blind, male *biwa hoshi*, itinerant "monks" who recited *Heike monogatari*). A reproduction is available in Hanawa Hokinoichi, ed., *Zoku zoku Gunsho ruijū* (Kokusho Kankōkai, 1904), 18:65–207. (2) The Noh play *Mochizuki*, in which a woman impersonates a blind reciter of the Soga story (called a *mekura goze* in the play) in order to approach her husband's murderer to take revenge. *Mekura* means "blind person." The use of the word *mekura* to modify *goze* may indicate that in the medieval period all *goze* were not blind.

50. Kitagawa, *The Tale of the Soga Brothers*, xi.

51. The word *tora* is also associated with *miko* (Shinto mediums) of the Hakone and Kamakura regions. Kadokawa, *Katarimono bungei no hassei*, 263.

52. Ibid., 429.

Fig. 9. Tora weeps at the site where the Soga brothers died. From "Tora Visits Ide (Mount Fuji)," book 12, chapter 2 of *The Revenge of the Soga Brothers.* Japanese, seventeenth century, Sumiyoshi School. Courtesy of the Philadelphia Museum of Art, The J. Stogdell Stokes Fund and the George W. B. Taylor Fund.

women calling themselves Tora *bikuni* (nuns) traveled all over Japan conducting services for the brothers and reciting the story of the Soga vendetta. It is Tora's activities after the vendetta that differ most in variant versions of the tale.[53] The route of her travels, her companions, and the temples and saints she visited vary depending on religious biases.

In the early stages of the development of *The Tale of the Soga Brothers* the story of Tora Gozen was as important, or even more important, than the story of the Soga brothers.[54] It was her story, not the accounts of the vendetta, that first spread on a wide scale. The story of Tora described her birth and youth, her relations with Jūrō, her life of religious devotion, and finally her death.[55] The Tora *goze* and Tora *bikuni* left their mark on the landscape of Japan—there are temples and shrines dedicated to Tora or the brothers all over the country.[56] Tora appears in local folklore,[57] and there are some eight hundred graves around the country that are claimed to be hers.

The women reciters of the Soga story made significant contributions to the character of the tale. In many episodes the events and the moral thrust of the tale seem to reflect a woman's point of view. The brothers' relationship to their mother is a central theme in all versions. They are as devoted and sympathetic to her as their duty to avenge their father allows them to be. Jūrō is faithful and sensitive to Tora. The brothers respect women in a way uncharacteristic of ac-

53. All versions of the Soga tale say that Tora visited Zenkōji after the vendetta to perform memorial services for the brothers—the only site for a pious act in which all versions are in agreement. For a detailed discussion of Tora's motives in going to Zenkōji, see Kondō Yoshihiro, "Bungaku to josei to shinkō," *Shintō gaku* 5 (1958): 30–31.

54. Kadokawa, *Katarimono bungei no hassei*, 436.

55. The *Ōiso Tora monogatari* survives in documents belonging to temples. In some cases the tale goes beyond Tora's death. According to a version belonging to the Zenpukuji, a temple near Ōiso, Tora had a son by Jūrō, conceived on the day of the vendetta. This son, Sukewaka, later took the tonsure and founded the Zenpukuji. In Shizuoka Prefecture many people claim to be the descendants of Jūrō and Tora. Ibid., 435.

56. See Kondō, "Bungaku to josei to shinkō," 42, for a list.

57. There are several religious and magical sites associated with Tora. One example is the "Tora Stone" (*Tora ga ishi*) at Ōiso. It is a rock that is said to have jumped up and deflected an arrow aimed at Jūrō. In the Edo period it was said that it still bore the mark of the arrow, and legend said that only good and kind men could lift the stone. For this and other stories, see Kadokawa, *Katarimono bungei no hassei*, 435–36.

tual medieval morality and practise.[58] Before the vendetta Jūrō cautions Gorō to be careful not to harm the prostitutes who are spending the night with Kudō and Ōtōnai; it would be a sin to kill innocent women. However, the brothers think nothing of slaughtering numerous samurai, even men who are not related to their enemy. In *Heiji monogatari* (The Tale of Heiji), a war tale that was not disseminated by female reciters, the treatment of women is markedly different: court ladies are stabbed, burned to death, and otherwise molested by ruthless samurai.

The women of *The Tale of the Soga Brothers* are its most virtuous and sensitive characters. Women are loyal and devoted to their lovers and husbands as long as these men are alive, and even after the men they love die, the women remain saintlike in their devotion to their men's salvation. Tora's companion, Shōshō, delivers the longest sermon in the popular version of the tale by way of instruction to the mother of Jūrō and Gorō. Shōshō says that she is repeating the sermon that the priest Hōnen (1133–1212) gave when she and Tora visited him.[59] Shōshō's sermon reveals the misogynistic nature of the pre-Amidist Buddhist sects and the new hope that Amidist belief afforded women:

> According to one sutra, "Even though the eyes of all the Buddhas of the three periods may fall to the earth and decay, women may not attain Buddhahood." According to another sutra: "Women are the couriers of hell and often destroy the seeds of Buddhahood. Although a woman may resemble a bodhisattva, her heart within is like that of a demon." Women are disparaged in both the Buddhist and Confucian canons. Amida Buddha pledged, however, that the

58. See Kondō, "Bungaku to josei to shinkō," 32–33, for a good account of the low and sinful reputation women were accorded by medieval Japanese society and by Buddhist thought. Nevertheless, many medieval tales idealize women. In tales recited by women, the heroes are often warriors who are devoted to entertaining girls or prostitutes, not to women of the samurai class. These girls are portrayed as models of virtue. In *Gikeiki* (The Chronicles of Yoshitsune), for example, a dancing girl named Shizuka Gozen, is an important heroine.

59. Hōnen (1133–1212) was the founder of the Jōdō sect. He trained in Tendai Buddhism on Mount Hiei but abandoned esoteric practise and wandered the country teaching that one could enter Amida's Paradise (Jōdō) by means of faith and repeated prayer.

> most evil of men may achieve salvation merely by chanting his name; he also vowed that women may attain Buddhahood.[60]

The last lines of *The Tale of the Soga Brothers* consist of the reciter's explanation of the lessons to be learned from the story. The admonitions apply to all listeners but are directed especially toward women:

> In this world death may come to the old or to the young; no one, be he noble or low born, can escape the law of impermanence. In the end wealth and jewels are like pleasures experienced in a dream. Women, you are especially deep in sin—you should do nothing but chant the *nenbutsu*. The words of this tale have power and all who understand this story will be able to open up their evil hearts, turn toward the true path, and seek Buddhahood. But those without the will to attempt this will not benefit even though they hear my words. So listen carefully, let the story permeate your hearts, and you will escape the sufferings of this world and be reborn in the Pure Land Paradise.[61]

The Tale of the Soga Brothers is in fact an important piece of feminine literature. The last chapters in particular seem to have been recounted by women for the benefit of women. In them we do not find the world of exquisite taste and sensibility of the Heian court ladies, but instead the world of the oppressed women of the medieval period. Tora is an archetypical medieval heroine. She suffered as much as the brothers did, yet she and other women had long been denied even the hope of Buddhist salvation after death. Amidism gave women religious hope, a chance to attain the spiritual peace that was within the reach of men, and medieval women became important teachers of the faith. The quiet last books of *The Tale of the Soga Brothers,* populated by gentle and devout ladies, make a stark contrast to the first ten books, dominated by men and their greed, passion, and righteous violence.

RECORDING THE TALE

The Soga story was first set down on paper in the mid 1300s, about a century and a half after the brothers' vendetta.[62] Priests and

60. Thomas J. Cogan, trans., *The Tale of the Soga Brothers* (Tokyo: University of Tokyo Press, 1987), 292.
61. Ichiko and Ōshima, *Soga monogatari,* 425–26.
62. See ibid., 8–12, for a textual history of the narrative.

monks transcribed every extant version of the tale, and its religious and moral character was maintained, or even strengthened by the process of recording. There were probably almost as many oral Soga tales as there were reciters. All surviving texts of *The Tale of the Soga Brothers* are episodic and contain long tangential stories. There are few attempts to create effective transitions between the episodes, but in most cases there is a clear connection between the story of the brothers and accompanying Chinese or Indian tales. The recorders of the tale were inclusive rather than exclusive in their selection of episodes. Over the next several centuries transcribers modified old episodes and added new ones, but rarely deleted anything. The final "popular tale" is a product of accretion and is full of inconsistencies.[63]

The surviving texts of *The Tale of the Soga Brothers* are divided into two major lines: the ***manabon*** line and the ***kanabon*** line.[64] The ***manabon*** line is the earlier. It includes four texts, three recorded in Chinese and one in Japanese. The oldest text is written in Chinese, and the other three texts closely resemble it. Even though the texts were recorded using Chinese characters only, and in Chinese word order, they were taken from Japanese oral tales, and the words of the Japanese oral recitation could be reconstructed by readers who were skilled in translating Chinese texts into Japanese as they read them. The oldest text, often called "the ***manabon***," was probably written in the Nanbokuchō, the period of the Northern and Southern Courts (1336–92),[65] by a Hakone priest. It emphasizes the divine aid of the Hakone Gongen, manifested in the actions of the abbot of Hakone Temple. The Kantō roots of the ***manabon*** are apparent in its accurate geographical descriptions and detailed portrayals of Kantō warriors—their names and homes, their accoutrements and attire, and their feats of valor or cowardice in the Genpei War, at hunts, and in combat with the Soga brothers.[66] Deeply rooted in the oral tradition, the

63. According to Araki Shigeru, "Sogamono no kōwaka bukyoku to *Soga monogatari*," *Wakō daigaku jinbungaku kiyō* 12 (1977): 121, two episodes—"Yui ga hama" (Yui Beach) and "Wada sakamori" (Wada's Banquet)—originated in independent oral traditions and were added to later versions of the tale. The former episode describes the near execution of the brothers at the order of Yoritomo. In it Kajiwara, usually an enemy, supports the brothers. In the latter episode, the warlord Wada Yoshimori, usually a staunch supporter of the the brothers, loses his temper at a banquet, and his men very nearly attack Jūrō.

64. The ***mana*** of ***manabon*** indicates that the text was recorded in Chinese characters, with few or no ***kana***.

65. Kitagawa, *The Tale of the Soga Brothers,* 1:xiii.

66. Tsukazaki Susumu, "Kyōdō bungei to shite no *Gikeiki, Soga monogatari*," *Kokubungaku* 11.2 (1966): 66–67.

manabon retains a Kamakura-period "spirit of gloom" not found in other hero and war tales.[67] This "spirit of gloom" is characterized by the tale's emphasis on morality, repentance, and *goryō* belief.

The *kanabon* line contains two main texts, the *Taisanjibon* and the *rufubon* (the "popular" or "vulgate" version), both recorded in Japanese in the sixteenth century.[68] The *Taisanjibon* was recorded earlier, probably by a priest from Mount Hiei; the *rufubon* later, by a Jōdō (Pure Land) priest. Each priest (or group of priests) added the religious biases and formulae of his doctrine and a chapter promoting his sect; one describes the founding of the Tendai monastery on Mount Hiei, and the other a meeting between the Jōdō saint Hōnen and the nuns Tora and Shōshō.

THE POPULAR VERSION

By the fifteenth and early sixteenth centuries it appears that the *rufubon* version had become the most commonly recited version of the tale. It is unclear how widely each of the earlier versions had circulated, but the *rufubon* became part of Japan's "national literature," a story known by Japanese of every class and every geographical region. More medieval Soga plays have links to the *rufubon* than any other version of the tale, and it was the *rufubon* that was published again and again in the Edo period.

The *rufubon* was formed between the mid-1300s and early 1500s, and over those two centuries the story took on many of the characteristics of popular Muromachi-period (1336–1575) fiction. The evolution of *Gikeiki* (The Chronicles of Yoshitsune) and stories tangential to the central account of Yoshitsune show us that Muromachi-period listeners were very interested in the romantic adventures of traditional martial heroes.[69] The theme of romance is more important in the *rufubon* than in the *manabon*: in the latter Gorō is devoted only to his mother and to the Hakone abbot, and he expresses disdain for women;

67. Ōshima Tatehiko, "*Soga monogatari* no sekai," *Rekishi kyōiku* 15.8 (1967): 30. "Spirit of gloom" in Japanese is *inki no kibun*.

68. Ichiko and Ōshima, *Soga monogatari*, 6–8.

69. For an excellent account of the characteristics of popular Muromachi-period tales, see Helen Craig McCullough, *Yoshitsune: A Fifteenth-Century Japanese Chronicle* (Tokyo and Stanford: University of Tokyo Press and Stanford University Press, 1966), introduction. See also Hayashiya Tatsusaburō, *Kabuki izen* (Iwanami Shinsho, 1954), on *machi shu bunka*.

in the former he is given a mistress, a woman entertainer.[70] The *rufubon* also devotes considerably more attention to the romance of Jūrō and Tora than do the texts of the *manabon* tradition.

The *rufubon* delights in the drama of argument, confrontation, and combat. Until after the vendetta, when the heroines become religious exemplars, women are beautiful creatures to be won or possessed, unimportant in their own right but often objects of heated contention between men.[71] Contrasts in character among the male heroes become more pronounced—Gorō is stronger and more headstrong, and Jūrō is more prudent and circumspect.

The *rufubon* also borrowed motifs from *Heike monogatari*, the most influential war tale of the medieval period. Most notable is the influence of the last chapter of *Heike* on the last chapter of the *rufubon*. The story of the tragic court lady Kenreimon-in set the tone for the conclusion of the Soga story so that the *rufubon* comes to a close in a mood of wistful longing and Buddhist consolation for the painful loss of loved ones.[72]

Despite the aristocratic quality of its last chapter the recorders of the *rufubon* preserved the tale's character as rustic, oral literature. In this regard the *rufubon* reflects a process of compilation and development different from its literary cousin, *Gikeiki*, which was carefully refined and edited. The *rufubon* retains many of the formulaic expressions used in oral recitation[73] as well as the tangential parables and stories characteristic of oral tales, but it lacks certain important thematic and plot devices characteristic of Muromachi-period narrative literature. In the central story there are no fantasy elements; the brothers encounter no monsters, or, for that matter, helpful supernatural creatures. Standard motifs, such as the stealing of

70. Neither in the *rufubon* nor in any other version of the narrative Soga tale is Gorō's lover Shōshō. In the *rufubon* Gorō's mistress is a prostitute whose name we never learn. She is merely called "a prostitute from Kewaizaka." She becomes a nun in book 5. Tegoshi no Shōshō is present at the vendetta and becomes a nun with Tora some time after the vendetta. In later incarnations of the Soga story, Gorō's lover becomes "Kewaizaka no Shōshō."

71. For specific episodes see Cogan, *The Tale of the Soga Brothers*, 101, 107, 108, 129, 148. All of these episodes of conflicts over women are found only in *kanabon* texts.

72. See ibid., xxx–xxxii for a discussion of the influence of *Heike monogatari*.

73. Kitagawa, *The Tale of the Soga Brothers*, xi. Examples inlcude such lines as: "pray for happiness in the world beyond" (*gose bodai o toburau*); "to die old or young is a whim of fate" (*rōsho fujō nari*); and "how tragic!" (*muzan nari*).

crucial instructions to a secret art, or the winning of a fair princess by means of one's musical talent, which figure prominently in *Gikeiki*, are conspicuously absent from *The Tale of the Soga Brothers*. The postvendetta chapters, with their emphasis on repentance and devotion, were lengthened in the *kanabon* tradition and given even broader religious appeal. The "spirit of gloom" persists in Gorō's determination to become a *goryō*, even more strongly expressed in the *rufubon* than in *manabon* texts. The activities of the brothers' unappeased, avenging spirits are thoroughly documented in the *rufubon*.[74]

Significant changes in the main characters took place during the development of the Soga story from a local tale to a national legend. In the *manabon* the brothers are equally virtuous and dedicated to their mission. Jūrō, clearly the leader and decision maker, is faithful to Tora but does not let his love for her interfere with the revenge. The headstrong and emotional Gorō often relies on his brother's guidance. The extent of Gorō's fiery determination is revealed when he vows to commit suicide and become a vengeful *goryō* if that is necessary to avenge his father.

In the *rufubon* Gorō's character remains the same, but he emerges as a man of almost superhuman strength thanks to new scenes of combat and confrontation that demonstrate his prowess. His most important rival is the other renowned strongman of the period, Asahina (d. 1213), son of Wada Yoshimori (1147–1213), an influential feudal lord. Asahina has no special role in the *manabon*, but he became a major character in one episode of the *rufubon* ("Wada's Banquet"; see fig. 10) in order that the listeners or readers might better appreciate Gorō's tremendous power. In situations of potential conflict Gorō is almost always eager for a fight, but usually Jūrō restrains him. On one occasion only does Gorō choose to accept humiliation rather than engage in a fight that might make his revenge impossible.[75]

Jūrō in the *rufubon* is the embodiment of patience, prudence, and forethought. In situations of potential conflict he always "swallows his shame" to further his greater cause. Jūrō, the more sensitive brother, does not conceal his emotions: he pines for his sweetheart

74. Cogan, *The Tale of the Soga Brothers*, 253–56, 262–63, 279–80.

75. In *Soga monogatari rufubon*, book 5, Gorō refuses to fight with Kajiwara Kagesue over who will get a prostitute. Although Gorō is described as much stronger than Kajiwara, at the time Gorō was alone and Kajiwara was accompanied by many retainers.

Fig. 10. Wada's banquet. Wada Yoshimori is infatuated with Tora, but she angers him by serving sake first to Jūrō, the man she loves. Yoshimori is at the top. Jūrō, wearing a robe decorated with a plover motif, has a cup of sake on the mat in front of him. Tora is immediately below Jūrō, and Asahina, wearing a robe decorated with a crane motif, is near the bottom of the picture. Gorō has not yet appeared on the scene. From "Benzaiten (Banquet Scene)," book 6, chapter 2 of *The Revenge of the Soga Brothers.* Japanese, seventeenth century, Sumiyoshi School. Courtesy of the Philadelphia Museum of Art, The J. Stogdell Stokes Fund and the George W. B. Taylor Fund.

and weeps openly after leaving his mother for the last time. On the latter occasion Gorō laughs harshly to conceal his tears. When the brothers leave their mother for the last time, she contrasts them in these terms: "Gorō was educated in a temple, but with his dark skin he looks like a commoner. Jūrō lived in the country as a child, but he is fair and looks so elegant."[76]

We find a similar creation of opposing heroic character types in the development of the "gentle Yoshitsune/wild Benkei" pairing in *Gikeiki*, a phenomenon entirely absent from the earliest accounts of Yoshitsune's exploits. The gentle hero/wild hero partnership and dichotomy became essential to the Soga story in the late medieval period and would reach its fullest development on the Kabuki stage.

In the *manabon* Tora is a model wife and daughter-in-law despite the fact she is not actually married to Jūrō. Nevertheless, her most important characteristic is her saintlike spiritual activity after the vendetta. In the *rufubon* she is made more clearly feminine, and her life as a courtesan is emphasized. She is reputed to be the most beautiful prostitute at any of the stops along the Tōkaidō. The portrayal of Tora as a saint after the vendetta is not weakened by the earlier treatment of her romantic relations with Jūrō; in fact, the contrast between her two lives, as prostitute and nun, is essential in the *rufubon*. Tora's early life was romantic but full of tears and oppression: as a prostitute she was at the beck and call of the proprietress who ordered her to entertain men whom she loathed. As a nun Tora is able to give complete expression to her religious devotion, both to Jūrō's spirit and to the religious practices necessary for her own salvation.

The saintly quality of the ladies in the *rufubon* is still their essential attribute, and Tora is the most important of several prostitutes who become nuns. Gorō's lover (we never learn her name) takes the tonsure to escape the advances of Kajiwara Kagesue, a minor villain, and to prove her fidelity to Gorō. She then disappears from the tale. Tegoshi no Shōshō, a prostitute sympathetic to Jūrō, witnesses both his meeting with Kudō and the vendetta itself. She is persuaded by Tora to become a nun, and the two become faithful companions.

Changes in the roles of the women in the Soga story from *manabon* to *kanabon* versions point to the earliest traces of an impor-

76. Ichiko and Ōshima, *Soga monogatari*, 290.

tant new mood in the story: the addition of feelings of pathos. Pity and compassion had moved *nenbutsu* priests to succor the tragic Soga spirits, but the *rufubon* began a tradition of humanizing the brothers, returning them, in some scenes, to everyday life. It is in the *rufubon* that the brothers and their mother first complain of their poverty, a form of suffering that most listeners would have known all too well. "Sympathy for the underdog" attained its definitive form in medieval tales.[77] The Yui Beach scene, featuring the cruel mistreatment of the Soga brothers when they were little boys, was added to the *kanabon* texts, providing additional pathetic moments. More tearful parting scenes were added to the *rufubon* version of the tale.

The language of the *rufubon* reflects the social class of its heroes: it is more straightforward and less allusive than the major works of the aristocratic tradition. There are relatively few poems for a work of its length—30 as against 93 in *Heike monogatari*, and 784 in *Genji monogatari*, which is about twice as long. Jūrō and Tora convey their love for each other mainly in prose. Poetry, however, had its functions in the life of the provincial samurai, and the tale demonstrates the kind of occasions on which poetry was composed: the morning after a night of love, partings, as a spontaneous reaction to natural beauty, in jest (on some obviously vulgar topic), at the command of one's lord, and, in one case, as a secret code.[78] The poetry in the tale suits its composers. It is either totally derivative or else brash and original. The original poems state their intent clearly, with little use of wordplay or allusions to classic poems.

The Tale of the Soga Brothers as it was told to the people was, in the language of Northrop Frye, a kind of "sacred and religious auto."[79] The "auto" presents a powerful focus for the community, and it creates in audiences more a sense of communality than an individual awakening or catharsis.[80] The "auto effect" is important to audiences

77. See Ivan Morris, *The Nobility of Failure* (London: Secker and Warburg, 1975), 67–105. The Japanese term for sympathy for the underdog is *hogan biiki*, literally, "sympathy for Yoshitsune," the hero of the *Gikeiki*. *Soga biiki* was a less-used term with similar meaning.

78. In book 9, "The Fuji Plain," Hatakeyama Shigetada (1164–1205) recites a nature poem to the brothers. Its real meaning is, "today is the last day of the hunt, so you must strike immediately."

79. Frye, *Anatomy of Criticism*, 283.

80. Ibid.

who see tragic or heroic plays based on the history of their own country—for example, ancient Greeks watching Greek tragedy or Elizabethan audiences watching Shakespeare's history plays. The audience leaves the performance feeling that "because of what these people did the world is as we know it today." *The Tale of the Soga Brothers* and many other Japanese literary works contain formulaic expressions of communality. They open with expressions of thankfulness for peace and prosperity achieved by the current political regime if the work has a contemporary setting, or by an ancient emperor if it is set in the past. In longer works, such as *The Tale of the Soga Brothers*, the first chapter or chapters may consist of an account of the origins of the nation and the imperial dynasty. Many works conclude with the word *medetashi*, expressing blessing or congratulation and implying satisfaction with a good or just conclusion.[81]

In its form as "national, popular" literature *The Tale of the Soga Brothers* is a rich and complex work reflecting its varied roots. Its appeal is mixed: it contains romance, martial conflict, and expressions of pathos. Its messages are contradictory: "a good person is filial and kind," or "a good person loves honor above life and law," or "a good person recognizes that life is but a dream of suffering and renounces it for Amida's Paradise." The tale is a jumble of episodes, and its conflicting appeals and moralities are not integrated into a literary unit that expresses a coherent philosophy. It is true that the last lines by the narrator affirm the compassion of Amida and condemn avarice and lust, but they do not address the problems presented by the acts of love, honor, and violence that form the core of the story.

The thread that holds the narrative together is of course the story of the Soga brothers with its tragic conclusion. We shall see that it was the dramatic and emotional power of the central story that inspired the first playwrights to turn the Soga brothers into heroes on the stage.

81. Almost all Noh plays end in this way.

Chapter Three: Fragmenting the Story to Focus on the Heroes

THE NOH OF KAN'AMI AND ZEAMI

Noh was Japan's first important indigenous theater, and it has been performed continuously from the fourteenth century until today. Some two hundred years after the deaths of the historical Soga brothers, the heroes of the story were once again given corporal form, this time by actors on the Noh stage. Noh plays about the Soga vendetta were very different in structure from orthodox Noh plays, and the Soga brothers were very different sorts of characters than those who usually took center stage in Noh drama. To appreciate how unorthodox, and even experimental, many Soga Noh plays were, and to understand why this was the case, we must turn our attention briefly to the conditions that led to the development of Noh as the finest literary and stage art of Japan's medieval period.

Noh was created through a complex process of selection and integration of elements from various popular and religious performing arts.[82] Most early performances were held outdoors, on temple and shrine grounds, as festival events or as subscription performances (large-scale, long-running public performances sponsored by religious

82. For a detailed discussion of the characteristics of three kinds of early Noh (*ennen, dengaku,* and *sarugaku*) see Inoura Yoshinobu and Kawatake Toshio, *The Traditional Theater of Japan* (New York and Tokyo: Weatherhill and The Japan Foundation, 1981), 40–80. For an institutional history of early Noh, including performance records, see P. G. O'Neill, *Early Nō Drama: Its Background, Character, and Development, 1300–1450* (London : Lund Humphries, 1958). For a good short discussion of the characteristics and importance of early *sarugaku, dengaku,* and *ennen*, see Donald Keene, *Nō: The Classical Theatre of Japan* (Tokyo: Kōdansha, 1966), 28–31. The direct ancestor of Noh was *sarugaku,* and Noh retained that name long after its content had become more sophisticated than the acrobatics, skits, and animal tricks of early Kamakura-period *sarugaku.* The word Noh was appended to all three of the early arts; it literally means "talent" or "skill."

institutions as money-raising ventures).[83] Nobles or powerful samurai who saw or heard about interesting public performances often summoned entire troupes to perform privately at their mansions. Theatrical performances became more elaborate and sophisticated as more patrons sponsored entertainment at social rather than religious gatherings. The development of Noh into a sophisticated and powerful stage art was closely linked to the patronage of the aristocracy.

The creation of mature Noh was largely the work of two great actor-playwrights, Kan'ami and Zeami, father and son and founders of the Kanze Noh troupe. Kan'ami (1333–84) was a performer from the province of Yamato, present-day Nara. He studied under the best performers of various arts and integrated what he had absorbed into his Noh drama.[84] The essence of his art was mimicry and dance.

In 1374, toward the end of Kan'ami's career, the shogun Ashikaga Yoshimitsu (1358–1408) saw Kan'ami and Zeami at a public performance in Kyoto. The shogun was so impressed that for the rest of his life he became a generous patron of Kan'ami's troupe. Zeami (1363–1443) was eleven years old then, and he spent much time in the shogun's palace after 1374. There he received a first-rate formal education worthy of a nobleman.[85] Although Zeami, like his father, performed at certain shrine and temple festivals, his aristocratic and noble patrons were far more important in the development of his art.

Zeami is the greatest figure in the history of Noh drama. During the early part of his stage career he was the most highly acclaimed actor in Kyoto, and his plays and treatises have achieved canonical status.[86] Over the centuries his ideas about Noh drama have become

83. For a detailed account of the organization, significance, and performance records of subscription (*kanjin*) *sarugaku* and *kanjin dengaku*, see O'Neill, *Early Nō Drama*, 66–77.

84. Kan'ami studied under master performers of *kusemai*, *dengaku*, and other, quite different, schools of *sarugaku*.

85. See Thomas B. Hare, *Zeami's Style: The Plays of Zeami Motokiyo* (Stanford: Stanford University Press, 1986), 11–38 for the best biography of Zeami in English. Zeami's personal tutor was Nijō Yoshimoto, the leading poet of his day and perhaps the most thoroughly educated man of his age.

86. Zeami is credited with having written as many as one hundred and as few as twenty plays. Donald Keene, ed., *Twenty Plays of the Nō Theater* (New York: Columbia University Press, 1970), 4. Thomas Hare (see previous note) has done an excellent analysis in English of Zeami's plays and his art of play writing. Zeami's treatises have been translated by J. Thomas Rimer and Masakazu Yamazaki in *On the Art of the Nō Drama: The Major Treatises of Zeami* (Princeton: Princeton University Press, 1984).

an orthodox creed for actors, educated audience members, and critics of Noh. The single most remarkable feature of all the Noh plays written about the Soga brothers is their nonadherence to every salient feature of Zeami's prescriptions for the writing and performing of Noh. For this reason it is important here to reexamine briefly the purpose of and standards of excellence in Noh drama according to the treatises and practice of Zeami.

Zeami established *mugen* (dream) Noh as the most respected variety of Noh play. In dream Noh plays the main character is not a living person but the ghost of a person long dead, or the disembodied spirit of a person or inanimate object. The ghost or spirit appears before an observer, usually a priest, and sings and dances unforgettable moments of suffering or resentment. In most dream Noh plays, the observer's (the *waki* role) prayers subdue, appease, or enlighten the ghost or spirit, who after a final dance disappears once again, this time for eternity. In dream Noh the character played by the *shite* (the main actor) dominates the play. It is the heart and mind of this one character that are to be revealed to the audience through the work of the playwright, the *shite,* and the entire ensemble. Zeami created a new kind of dream Noh based on medieval war tales. In his "warrior Noh" (*shuramono*) the ghost is usually a warrior who died violently and was condemned to the Asura Hell of perpetual strife. Such ghosts return from time to time to the sites of their deaths and must be helped to break their attachment to the world by the intercession of a priest.[87]

Zeami sought, using various means, to impart aristocratic dignity to Noh. Most important was his emphasis on the aesthetic ideal of *yūgen.* The term had been used for several centuries, first in the criticism of court poetry, later entering the critical vocabulary of *renga* poetry and Noh. Its meaning differed depending on the period and artistic medium. Interpretations of *yūgen* include: "dark, phantasmal beauty," "mysterious or poignant beauty," and "grace, elegance, and

87. Noh plays are traditionally divided into five categories: (1) god plays: ceremonial or congratulatory plays showing the manifestation of a Shinto god; (2) warrior plays; (3) woman plays: the ghost of a famous woman appears and recounts the powerful feelings of love resentment that tied her spirit to the world; (4) miscellaneous plays, usually about living persons; and (5) demon plays, about violent gods or demons, or other supernatural creatures. Sometimes demon plays feature particularly barbaric human beings.

charm."[88] Today the play *Matsukaze* (originally by Kan'ami, but almost totally rewritten by Zeami) is considered an archetypical *yūgen* play. It features the poetic and melancholy longing of the ghosts of two fisher girls for an elegant courtier who once loved them. Zeami wrote that plays about women were the best vehicles for creating *yūgen*, but he held that all main characters should have something of the quality of *yūgen* to them.

In his first treatise, *Kadensho* (The Transmission of the Flower), Zeami wrote that the structural basis of Noh should be the *jo-ha-kyū* progression of "introduction, development, climax" that had been introduced to Japan in the seventh century in Chinese court music. The *jo-ha-kyū* structure gave a new unity to Noh, and it was applied to such diverse elements of the art as play writing, musical composition, and the basic tempo of the actor's movements on stage.[89] Zeami's critical writings also demonstrate his understanding of the importance of the relationship between the performer and his audience. He wrote that the actor must alter his performance to suit the tastes and moods of his patron or audience. Zeami believed that better performances could be achieved before a knowledgeable and critical audience.[90]

Zeami's immediate ancestors had in fact been of very low social status—Noh performers were often called "river bank beggars"—but aristocratic lineage was important in gaining respect in medieval Japan. Even low-ranking samurai families found it essential to forge exalted family pedigrees in order to increase their power and influence. In his history of Noh as presented in *Kadensho*, Zeami created a distinguished ancestry for his art. He cited the goddess Ame-no-

88. See Keene, *Nō: The Classical Theatre of Japan*, 22–26 for Zeami's *yūgen* and *yūgen* in Noh.

89. Zeami's plays that best fit his *jo-ha-kyū* model are divided into five *dan* or sections. In the first, or *jo dan*, the subordinate actor introduces himself and explains the setting of the play. Three *ha dan* follow, including the appearance of the *shite*, or main actor, and some interaction between the main and subordinate actors. In the last *ha dan* the main character reveals his or her deepest feelings, usually in a dance. In the *kyū dan* the main character's suffering is usually resolved, and the main character leaves after a concluding dance, the most lively dance of the play.

In the Noh walk the actor starts to move almost imperceptibly but moves gradually faster and faster so that his stop seems abrupt. This is one example of *jo-ha-kyū* in stage movement.

90. Jacob Raz, "The Actor and His Audience, Zeami's Views on His Audience," *Monumenta Nipponica* 31.3 (Autumn 1976): 251–74, has an excellent treatment of the subject.

Uzume-no-Mikoto as the founder of Noh (many Japanese arts make the same claim),[91] and a disciple of the Buddha, a Chinese emperor, and the Japanese sage-prince Shōtoku Taishi, as early contributors to Noh.[92]

As in many other traditional Japanese arts, it was only after a code of rules to guide performers had been created that the humble Noh theatricals could be transformed into artistic presentations of the highest quality and dignity. In medieval Japan serious art was accompanied by a body of criticism dealing with aesthetic goals and methods of study; for Noh this meant the creation of a critical vocabulary, methods for actor training, and rules for performing and writing plays. In his treatises Zeami provided all of these, as well as secret instructions for worthy successors, an important requirement for any art in the medieval period.[93]

The changes wrought by Zeami were reinterpreted and institutionalized in the Edo period by artists whose main function was to provide the ruling warrior elite with ceremonial music and theater. Viewing Noh plays was largely prohibited to commoners.[94] In the Edo period the repertory of plays was considerably reduced. Plays of various types were performed, but Zeami's aristocratic ideals were firmly established as canon. From the Edo period until today Japan's upper classes have patronized Noh, but it is important to remember that in the Muromachi period it was popular in every region of the country and with all classes.

FIFTEENTH-CENTURY SOGA NOH PLAYS

Soga Noh plays present a picture very different from the usual Noh drama that centers on the career and the aesthetics of Zeami.

91. It was the dance of this goddess that brought the Sun Goddess, Amaterasu Ōmikami, out of the rock cave after her humiliation at the hands of her brother, the god Susano-o, thereby bringing light to the world once again. The Shinto dance *kagura* claims to descend from this dance; the claim is stated clearly in the Noh play *Miwa*.

92. Zeami Motokiyo, *Kadensho*, translated by Sakurai Chūichi et al. (Kyoto: Sumiya-Shinobe Publishing Institute, 1968), 61.

93. McCullough, *Yoshitsune*, 38, discusses how important it was in the medieval period for serious arts to possess a tradition of secret instructions of "deep knowledge," a tradition that derives from the practices of esoteric Buddhism.

94. At most only one or two subscription performances per year were open to the general public in major cities.

Only two of the thirty-four Soga Noh plays written during the Muromachi period have been attributed to Zeami,[95] but both attributions are dubious, and neither play is performed today. All the other plays are either anonymous or are attributed by at least one medieval source to a playwright named Miyamasu. Miyamasu was a contemporary of Zeami[96] and the head of a small *za* (medieval guild or troupe) based in the Nara area. There is no evidence that Miyamasu ever went to Kyoto or ever performed for the nobility or aristocracy. *The Tale of the Soga Brothers* was a product of the common people, and Soga Noh plays by Miyamasu and by unknown authors give us a glimpse of Noh as popular theater. They show us what form Noh might have retained had the shogun Yoshimitsu not been attracted to the art by the skill of Kan'ami and the charm of the young Zeami.

Zeami wrote that the playwright should remain true to the spirit and language of his sources, even using poems and quotes from the original work. Soga Noh plays take their basic plots from narrative sources but do not borrow lines from any extant version of *The Tale of the Soga Brothers.* The plays were written at a time when the narrative was first being transcribed but was still alive as oral literature. Zeami generally drew his inspiration from written literature, or from oral literature that had been set down and canonized by the time he took up his brush (*Heike monogatari*, for example). Miyamasu and other writers of Noh plays about the Soga brothers probably did not have access to manuscripts. The *manabon* manuscripts were kept in Hakone area temples, and even if Kansai playwrights had traveled to Hakone, it is unlikely that they would have been allowed access to temple archives. Therefore, the sources for most Soga plays were likely to have been oral recitations. Not every version of the tale was written down, and the unique episodes found in Noh plays may have been

95. See appendix C for a list of Muromachi-period and Edo-period Soga Noh plays. See Kobayashi Shizuo, *Yōkyoku sakusha no kenkyū* (Maruoka Shuppansha, 1942), 236, for attributions based on two medieval documents, the *Jika densho*, a sixteenth-century Konparu School document, and the *Nōhon sakusha chūmon*, compiled in 1524. For a discussion of these two documents, see O'Neill, *Early Nō Drama*, 102.

96. The biographical material available for Miyamasu is very scanty. The two most important modern works on him are Kobayashi (see previous note) and Kitagawa Tadahiko, "Yōkyoku sakusha Miyamasu o meguru shiron," *Kokugo kokubun* 26 (May 1957): 323–37. Kobayashi believes that Miyamasu's period of activity extended from about 1429 to 1467; Kitagawa estimates that he was born some time between 1378 and 1389.

taken from oral recitations that were never recorded, or may have been invented by the authors of Noh plays. Oral reciters took considerable liberty in expanding or modifying certain elements of their tales,[97] and Noh playwrights likely exercised the same freedom when using oral source material.

Few Soga plays correspond closely to any extant version of *The Tale of the Soga Brothers.*[98] The brevity of a Noh play (about ten to fifteen pages in English translation) entailed major modifications in presenting the long narrative story. Only one episode could be used in a play, and even it had to be cut to its essentials. Soga Noh plays are thus more concise than the original story, sometimes concentrating in a single gesture or phrase action that is described at length in the narrative.[99] Although Miyamasu and other playwrights changed the dialogue and action in their plays, they remained faithful to the spirit of their sources. They never used episodes from a source tale to explore new religious, moral, or aesthetic territory as Zeami sometimes did.[100]

The four currently performed plays, *Youchi Soga, Genbuku Soga* (The Adulthood Rites of Gorō Soga), *Chōbuku Soga* (The Soga Vengeance Ritual), and *Kosode Soga* (The Sogas and the Robe) were all written in the fifteenth century and seem related to the *manabon* in their emphasis on themes of filial piety, parental devotion, and the divine power of the Hakone Gongen. In all but *Chōbuku Soga*, the

97. See Butler, "The Textual Evolution of the *Heike Monogatari.*"

98. Most articles on Soga Noh plays or on Miyamasu include a discussion of plays and sources. Enami Yoku, in "Sogamono yōkyoku no genkō," *Kokugakuin zasshi* 32.12 (1926): 37–52, makes a play by play investigation of sources for Soga Noh plays. He concludes that most plays are based on the *rufubon* and have little relationship to the *manabon* or to *kōwakamai* plays. According to Enami, the plays that Amano classifies as *manabon*-related plays are linguistically related to the *rufubon.* My division of plays into *kanabon*- and *manabon*-related groups follows Amano, "Miyamasu Sogamono kō."

99. An excellent example can be found in the play *Chōbuku Soga.* When Gorō is still a young temple page (he still goes by his boyhood name of Hakoō), he meets Kudō for the first time when Kudō visits Hakone Temple. In *The Tale of the Soga Brothers* there is a long dialogue in which Kudō attempts to ingratiate himself with Hakoō. Hakoō suppresses his tears of rage and frustration and goes away with even stronger feelings of hatred. In the Noh play the same feelings are communicated in a brief verbal exchange during which Kudō affectionately places his hand on Hakoō's shoulder, only for Hakoō to shrink away in loathing. See Laurence Bresler, "Chōbuku Soga: A Noh Play by Miyamasu," *Monumenta Nipponica* 29.1 (Spring 1974): 74–76 for this passage.

100. Zeami's play *Nue* (based on *Heike monogatari*) is a good example. In *Nue*, a monster that figures merely as the target of a hero's arrow in the original narrative takes on an autonomous and sympathetic existence.

main role (*shite*) is one of the Soga brothers, but unlike typical Noh plays in which the *shite* role alone is paramount, in these plays the other brother, as "companion" (*tsure*), is virtually equal to the *shite* in importance. The fact that by the fourteenth century the brothers were perceived as an inseparable pair of heroes encouraged playwrights to depart from Zeami's precept that strong plays have only one important character. As in all fourteenth-century versions of the narrative tale, both brothers are brave and virtuous.

The plot in each of the four plays, however, differs significantly from corresponding episodes in either *manabon* or *kanabon* versions of the tale. The second half of *Chōbuku Soga*, for example, presents an absolutely unique episode in the legend of the Soga brothers: Fudō Myōō, a violent manifestation of the Dainichi Buddha (see fig. 11), appears in response to Gorō's prayers (Gorō is still a boy, known by his childhood name of Hakoō) at a ceremony performed by the abbot of Hakone Temple. Fudō chops off the head of an effigy of Kudō (see fig. 12). It is a demonstration of the will of the Hakone Gongen and an augury of success for the brothers.[101] The play emphasizes a special relationship between Gorō and Fudō that is not part of any narrative version of the tale but that is a logical one because all versions of the Soga story tell of Gorō's training at Hakone Temple, and Fudō is one of the temple's deities.

All four plays emphasize the brothers' separation from their parents, an important theme in *manabon* texts,[102] but in three of the four plays exciting visual entertainment is just as important: Ōtōnai's cowardly behavior and the fight scenes in *Youchi Soga*, the spectacular rampage of Fudō Myōō in *Chōbuku Soga*, and the brothers' danced duet in *Kosode Soga*. Zeami wrote that spectacular plays were the lowest form of entertainment,[103] but Miyamasu's Soga plays demonstrate the effectiveness of visual spectacle in plays for commoners.

The most important thematic difference between all the Soga Noh plays and every version of the narrative is the nonreligious nature of the former. Sugawara Michizane appears as a compassionate

101. Amano, "Miyamasu Sogamono kō," 21.

102. Amano states that in these four plays Miyamasu chose to present precisely those elements from the *manabon* tradition that *shōdō-shi* would have emphasized in their sermons. The didactic intent of *shōdō-shi*, however, is not found in these Noh plays.

103. In his treatise entitled "Kakyō" Zeami compares "*nō* of sight, *nō* of sound, and *nō* of heart." Zeami, "Kakyō," in Rimer and Yamazaki, *On the Art of the Nō Drama*.

Fig. 11. The deity Fudō (Kita Minoru) in *Chōbuku Soga*. Photo by Morita Tōshirō.

Fig. 12. The deity Fudō (Kita Minoru) prepares to behead an effigy of Kudō Suketsune in *Chōbuku Soga*. Photo by Morita Tōshirō.

god in *Aisomegawa* (The Aisome River) and as a violent thunder god in *Raiden* (Thunder and Lightning), but there are no references to *goryō* in Soga Noh plays. Numerous accounts of the appearance of the brothers' ghosts were recorded from the fourteenth through the sixteenth centuries, but contrary to our expectations the brothers are portrayed as ghosts in only one Muromachi-period play.[104]

The most important Buddhist theme in *The Tale of the Soga Brothers* is the repentance and devotion of the various women after the vendetta, but not a single Noh play is based on the last books of the narrative. Noh has often been characterized by its ritual and religious nature and by the importance of Amidist and Zen theological and aesthetic elements. Theology and salvation, however, are almost entirely lacking in Soga Noh plays, though the Buddhist belief in the impermanence of all things is emphasized, and the ill-fated brothers are compared to falling flowers, short-lived insects, and the smoke of Mount Fuji.[105]

The heroines of the Soga story are conspicuous in their absence from the Noh stage. Tora is featured in four of the Soga Noh plays written in the medieval period but in none of the currently performed plays. In Noh plays Tora appears not as a pious nun but as a woman entertainer in love with Jūrō. In the two plays in which the mother of the Soga brothers appears, she embodies the suffering and pain that parents endure when they lose their children. None of the Soga plays about women, or any other Soga plays for that matter, attempt to create a mood of *yūgen*. It would seem that *yūgen* was too subtle for commoner audiences. Plays relying on spectacle, the sadness of parting from loved ones, and conflict between good and evil must have been far more effective.

The most basic structural feature of Soga plays is their reliance on plot. Miyamasu and other authors of Soga plays did not use the *jo-ha-kyū* sequence favored by Zeami as the framework of Noh. In

104. *Fushiki Soga* (Soga and the Fallen Tree) is the closest Soga Noh play to a narrative source—the *rufubon*. The play has been attributed to both Miyamasu and Zeami, but to neither convincingly. It takes the brothers to the early stages of the Fuji hunt and describes how at the moment Jūrō let an arrow fly to shoot Kudō, his horse stumbled over a fallen log and the arrow flew wildly astray.

105. For examples see: (1) *Youchi Soga* in Laurence Kominz, "The *Noh* as Popular Theater: Miyamasu's *Youchi Soga*," *Monumenta Nipponica* 33.4 (1978): 452, 457; (2) *Fumisaki Soga* in Tanaka Makoto, ed., *Bangai yōkyoku shū* (Koten Bunko, 1950), 2:95; and (3) *Hitsukiri Soga*, in ibid., 483–92.

the absence of any formal unifying structure, temporal progress alone moves Soga plays to their conclusions. In many plays the plot centers on the resolutions of conflicts, whether verbal exchanges or martial combat. Many plays feature as many as two or three dramatic climaxes. Conflict scenes are dramatically portrayed when performed today, and they feature more physical contact between actors than they do in most Noh plays. In Soga plays the subordinate roles are often more important than in more orthodox Noh, if only because dramatic conflict requires at least two substantial characters pitted against each other. This is not true of conflict in Zeami's plays. In his "warrior plays," for example, combat either is between the protagonist and invisible demons in the Asura Hell or is a reenactment of old memories of war from another life. The importance of conflict in most plays by Zeami is not the outcome, which is preordained, but rather what that struggle tells the audience about the character of the protagonist and about his spiritual condition and possible Buddhist salvation.[106] In Soga plays, conflicts and their resolutions are important in and of themselves and are the essence of the appeal of many plays.

In plays without a central conflict motif, the sadness of parting is often the main theme. The brothers' partings from their mother and from the Hakone abbot and Jūrō's last meeting with Tora form the core of three Noh plays. Plays featuring child actors (***kokata***), usually as victims of evil adults, were similarly calculated to provoke strong feelings of sympathy for the protagonists. In ***Chōbuku Soga*** Kudō drives Hakoō to tears, and in ***Kirikane Soga*** (Reluctance to Slay the Soga Brothers) the brothers, as children, are nearly put to death by Yoritomo's samurai. The motif of good children fighting evil adults is still a mainstay of popular entertainment all over the world.

Although conflict and parting form the thematic foundations of Soga Noh, and the processes of conflict and parting give the plays a simple temporal structure, the stage appeal of Soga Noh plays is often based on spectacle. Since one simple way to create a theatrical spectacle is to fill the stage with actors, most Soga plays have more characters than is typical for Noh.

Dance is another form of spectacle. Zeami used dance in a very sophisticated way, as a vehicle to express through abstract and symbolic

106. Watsuji Tetsurō, "Yōkyoku ni Arawareta Rinri Shisō—Japanese Ethical Thought in the *Noh* Plays of the Medieval Period," translated by David A. Dilworth, *Monumenta Nipponica* 9 (1969): 483-92.

means the deepest feelings of his main characters, but the dance in Soga plays is meant to be enjoyed as visual entertainment and is rarely burdened with embedded symbolic meaning. Combat scenes include spectacular *hataraki* dances with difficult jumps and falls. These and other kinds of dance provide entertainment on an immediate level. In many Soga plays a character calls for a dance as part of the festivities during a party; these dances are often used to close plays on a celebratory note.

SOGA NOH AT ITS BEST: *YOUCHI SOGA*

In the currently performed repertory of Noh plays, *Youchi Soga* is the most frequently presented, and it displays almost all of the characteristics of mid-Muromachi-period Soga Noh plays. Two conflict situations lead to dramatic crises: a test of wills between the brothers and their retainers in part one (see fig. 13), and a martial combat between Gorō and the shogun's soldiers in part two. Between the two conflicts is a tearful parting between the brothers and their retainers. It contains a *kuse* section (musically and poetically the most expressive segment of Noh plays), which describes the brothers' love for and devotion to their mother. The language of this section of *Youchi Soga* is lyrical and moving, and the brothers display their learning as they describe the reasons they are choosing specific objects as keepsakes to have their retainers carry back to their mother (see fig. 14).

This emotional parting is followed immediately by a very funny, fifteen-minute-long *kyōgen* interlude featuring Kudō Suketsune's companion Ōtōnai. In every version of the the Soga story except as it is told in this play, the brothers kill Ōtōnai and Kudō at the same time, during the night raid. In *Youchi Soga*, however, the audience learns that Ōtōnai has escaped, and he gives a vivid account of the brothers' raid (see fig. 15). Ōtōnai is a great coward. He made no move to defend Kudō during the brothers' raid, and he appears on stage wearing a woman's kimono and carrying a flute instead of his sword. The Soga brothers' attack came while he was asleep after a night of revelry with courtesans. Ōtōnai runs off when the other character in the *kyōgen* interlude tells him that the Soga brothers are coming to kill him.

Spectacle is crucial to the appeal of *Youchi Soga*. The small Noh stage is filled with gorgeously clad actors portraying samurai, creating a vivid visual spectacle that is enhanced by some of the most excitingly

Fig. 13. Gorō (Matsuura Shin'ichirō) prevents the retainers Oniō and Danzaburō from committing double suicide in the Noh play *Youchi Soga*. Osaka, 1982. Photo by author.

Fig. 14. Jūrō (Hatano Shin) hands a letter to his retainer Danzaburō to deliver to Jūrō's mother in the Noh play *Youchi Soga*. Osaka, 1982. Photo by author.

Fig. 15. Ōtōnai (Shigeyama Akira) wearing a prostitute's robe, tells how the Soga brothers almost killed him in the night raid in the Noh play *Youchi Soga*. Osaka, 1982. Photo by author.

choreographed fight dancing used in Noh drama. The choreography at the conclusion of the play includes the spectacular death fall of a samurai slain by Gorō, Gorō's search in the darkness for the shogun (whom he intends to kill), hand-to-hand grappling pitting Gorō against the shogun's retainer Gorōmaru (see fig. 16), whom Gorō throws using a judo technique, and, finally, the shogun's guards binding Gorō in ropes.

The division of roles in *Youchi Soga* is highly unorthodox. The play uses a *shite* (Gorō), seven *tsure*, two *kyōgen* actors, and no *waki* at all. The *tsure* range in importance from Soga Jūrō, who in the first half of the play has a higher stature and more important role than the *shite*, to samurai guards who have only two lines of text to deliver. The unconventional assignment of roles in *Youchi Soga* and its heavy reliance on conflict and spectacle indicate that the author, most likely Miyamasu, sought to craft a very different kind of drama from what Zeami was creating at the same time; and indeed, on today's Noh stage, *Youchi Soga* and Zeami's warrior plays seem to have little in common.

SOGA NOH PLAYS AS PRECURSERS TO KABUKI THEATER

Two late Muromachi-period Noh plays, *Hitsukiri Soga* (A Soga Slices the Packing Chest) and *Fumisaki Soga* (The Soga Letter) are theatrical "missing links" that provide new insight into the process of the development of Kabuki theater. They demonstrate that many of the stage devices that were mainstays of Edo-period theater have clear roots in the most dramatic and experimental works of Noh. Prototypes of Edo dramaturgy that appear in these two Soga plays include: (1) characters in outlandish and improbable disguises, (2) *shukō*—intriguing and often highly unlikely modifications of traditional story plots, (3) stark juxtapositions of martial and romantic male heroes, (4) erotically appealing gender confusion, and (5) bombastic martial superheroes.

These and other transitional Noh plays have been missing from theater histories because in the Edo period they were cut from the repertory of performed plays, and only a few manuscripts survived. It stands to reason that the ruling warrior elite, seeking to distinguish itself from the lower classes, would encourage the elimination of plebeian Noh plays from the repertory. This was especially true of Noh plays that resembled Kabuki, which the samurai authorities regarded

Fig. 16. Gosho no Gorōmaru (Yamamoto Akihiro) seizes Gorō (Matsuura Shin'ichirō) from behind at the end of the Noh play *Youchi Soga*. Osaka, 1982. Photo by author.

as morally corrupt. *Youchi Soga,* which is still performed by all schools of Noh, is as visually exciting as *Hitsukiri Soga,* but its content would have been much more acceptable to samurai. *Youchi Soga* is morally uplifting in Confucian terms. It shows a younger brother obeying his older brother, and it celebrates two sons' love for and devotion to their mother. *Hitsukiri Soga* idealizes the love of a samurai and a prostitute and shows a younger brother physically attacking his older brother, albeit in ignorance of his brother's true identity.

Along with *The Tale of the Soga Brothers, Gikeiki* inspired the creation of several unorthodox Noh plays. Unlike the third great medieval war tale, *Heike monogatari,* which by the fourteenth century had a standardized version that reciters adhered to, recitation about the Soga brothers and Yoshitsune was characterized by the continuous creation of variant versions of episodes and stories that supplemented and expanded on the bodies of Soga and Yoshitsune lore. Perhaps the tradition of narrative experiment and creativity in Soga recitation inspired the same attitude in playwrights working in the same thematic tradition.

It is not known who wrote *Hitsukiri Soga* and *Fumisaki Soga,* but the plays were certainly in existence by 1528 because they appear in *Jika densho,* a document handed down in the Konparu family of Noh actors. The plays have original, spectacular scenes completely unrelated to any version of the narrative tale, and complex, heterogeneous plots that sometimes test the viewers' credulity. In the terminology of Edo-period theater, a unique twist in the plot of a play is called a *shukō,* and scholars use the same term to describe the plots in these two plays. In *Hitsukiri Soga* Jūrō is with Tora in her brothel when they hear loud noises outside. Suspecting that the noises are being made by Kajiwara, a minor enemy, Jūrō grows anxious and afraid. Tora tells him to hide behind a large Chinese chest. The intruder is in fact Gorō, who, peeping into the room just in time to see someone dash toward the chest, storms inside, upsetting dishes and *sake* bottles. He berates Tora for betraying Jūrō and harboring an enemy. With a mighty blow of his sword he slices the packing chest in two, only for Jūrō to emerge unharmed from behind. The brothers are happily reunited, and they celebrate their departure with a banquet.

The play has several innovative aspects that mark it as a transitional work, a very Kabuki-like Noh play. The first act shows Tora alone, waiting for Jūrō to visit her. She is angry at him for his long absence and criticizes his insensitive behavior. When Jūrō at last arrives, she is happy and resentful at the same time. This concern with Tora's feelings, as a prostitute in love, links the play with the *rufubon* tradition, particularly the episode "Wada's Banquet." Most of the play takes place in a brothel, an unusual setting for a Noh play, which *Hitsukiri Soga* shares with the Noh and *kōwakamai* plays entitled *Wada sakamori* (Wada's Banquet). Brothels were the settings for the earliest Kabuki skits, and brothel scenes continued to be important throughout Edo-period theater.

In *Hitsukiri Soga* Gorō rudely interrupts the farewell scene between Jūrō and Tora (the two lovers are alone in all narrative versions of the story). Gorō rashly and mistakenly rebukes Tora, and he takes violent action before he even knows whom he is attacking. Gorō wears a very long sword, a characteristic mark of *kabukimono*[107] and, later, of *aragoto* (wild acting) roles in Kabuki (see chapter 6). In the play Jūrō is Gorō's opposite. He is determined to avenge his father, but his love for Tora pulls him inexorably to Ōiso, where she lives. He dispels Tora's resentment with sensitive words but is upset and frightened when he hears a supposed enemy approach. He obeys Tora and hides where he is told; it never occurs to him to fight. Gorō almost kills Jūrō, but Jūrō does not rebuke his brother.

Their different personalities are depicted in other plays as well. In *Youchi Soga*, Gorō is quicker to act than his older brother even though, as in all versions of the narrative tale, Gorō respectfully obeys Jūrō, and Jūrō makes the important decisions about the vendetta. The beginnings of the delight in vividly contrasting portrayals of the brothers, which was to be so pronounced in Edo theater, are evident in *Hitsukiri Soga*.

Fumisaki Soga is set after the vendetta. Oniō and Dōsaburō, the brothers' faithful retainers, bring keepsakes they received on Fuji Plain back to the mother of the Soga brothers. Not wishing to upset her, they do not reveal that the brothers have been killed but assure her instead that they will be returning soon. Tora and Shōshō appear; they too intend to give the mother keepsakes of her sons, but Oniō tells them not to inform the mother directly of her sons' deaths. He suggests that instead they wear the brothers' caps and robes and delude her into thinking that her sons have returned. The women, obeying

107. *Kabukimono* were dandies and ruffians, often masterless samurai, who wore exotic clothes and frequented the pleasure districts in late Momoyama and early Edo-period cities. For information on *kabukimono* and their role in the cultural life of Japan, see Moriya Takeshi, *Kabuki no jidai* (Kikan Ronsō, 1976).

instructions, describe in song and dance the Fuji hunt and vendetta, revealing only at the end that the brothers are dead. Of course, it is highly unlikely that a mother could mistake two dancing girls for her own warrior sons, but *shukō* often demand considerable suspension of disbelief.

In both plays, touching scenes are juxtaposed with exciting, though silly, ones. The first halves of both plays seriously explore women's feelings of neglect and anxiety, and the second halves entertain with dances and spectacle. In *Fumisaki Soga* there is no suggestion of the shock and chagrin the mother would inevitably experience upon discovering the deception; she loses all importance in the play when Tora and Shōshō put on the brothers' clothes and begin to dance. The appeal of this section of the play is threefold: (1) the technical difficulty and uniqueness of dancing in pairs, (2) the contrasting decorative and combat descriptions, and (3) the erotic interest of watching men playing women impersonating men. We will see that this threefold appeal—pair or group dances, clashing rather than harmonious moods, and erotic cross-gender performance—were central to early Kabuki performance. *Fumisaki Soga*, like *Hitsukiri Soga*, has a distinct proto-Kabuki flavor, and there exists in *Fumisaki Soga* for the first time in the Soga tradition clear evidence of a romantic connection between Gorō and Shōshō. In Edo-period drama the Gorō-Shōshō relationship became as important as the love between Jūrō and Tora.

While *Hitsukiri Soga* and *Fumisaki Soga* are clearly forerunners of Edo-period Kabuki and puppet plays about the Soga story, they were very rarely performed, and it is difficult to know how influential they were as texts. Although "hiding in chest" scenes became stereotypical to Kabuki, there is no way to know if early Kabuki and puppet playwrights were actually influenced by *Hitsukiri Soga*. Chikamatsu used a "hiding in chests" scene in his first play, *Yotsugi Soga*, and it is almost certain he had access to a text of *Fumisaki Soga* because the major *shukō* in *Yotsugi Soga* follows the plot of *Fumisaki Soga* exactly.

Five Muromachi-period Soga plays not attributed to Miyamasu—*Zenji Soga* (The Soga Priest), *Kirikane Soga*, *Wada sakamori*, *Hakone Soga* (The Sogas at Hakone), and *Jūban giri* (Fighting Ten Men)—feature violent physical combat, tearful scenes of parting, and confrontations between innocent children and samurai villains. *Wada sakamori* is the most interesting play of the group. Its plot follows the *rufubon* quite closely, and it is almost as dramatic as *Hitsukiri Soga*.

And although almost every Noh play is composed of speech and song in a formal balance, *Wada sakamori* is totally dominated by dialogue. The chorus sings only one line before the song that concludes the play. The highlight of the play is a dramatic tug-of-war between Gorō and Asahina. The playwright's movement away from music and dance toward reliance on dialogue and, presumably, pantomime, presages developments that would take place on the Kabuki stage in the mid to late seventeenth century.

Zenji Soga, like *Wada sakamori*, is by an unknown playwright.[108] It is filled with pathos and conflict and is marked by a highly unorthodox allocation of roles.[109] Most of the play centers on the attempted arrest of Zenji (Onbō), the youngest Soga brother, born after his father's death. In a strange twist of the original story, his foster father is made the arresting official. Yet Zenji resists arrest skillfully, killing one of his assailants. The play is remarkably short (only sixty-six lines) but highly repetitive—a lengthy description of the vendetta is repeated three times in exactly the same words. The dialogue, which could carry the play effectively as it does in *Wada sakamori*, is very stilted in *Zenji Soga*. The author's sole innovation consisted in portraying the normally passive Zenji as a fierce and accomplished warrior.

The spectacle, martial conflict, and improbable *shukō* of *Hitsukiri Soga*, *Fumisaki Soga*, and *Zenji Soga* make these plays seem ludicrous because they are so different from what we feel is appropriate to the Noh stage. The austere stage and properties of Noh, its economy of movement, and its strong, monotonous chant and relentless rhythms can concentrate the focus of performer and audience to penetrate to the depths of the human soul. The presentational techniques of Noh were not suited to the kind of entertainment offered by Soga Noh plays: interaction or conflict between characters and the juxtaposition of a variety of scenes and moods. The authors of plays like *Hitsukiri Soga*, *Fumisaki Soga*, *Wada sakamori*, and *Zenji Soga* were attempting to create a new kind of drama but were limited by the

108. The *Jika densho* credits the play to Zeami, but all other medieval sources state that the author is unknown. The reader of the play would never associate it with Zeami.

109. Three *tsure* appear in the first half, and the *shite*, *kyōgen*, *waki*, and five *waki tsure* appear in the second half. In Noh plays, *tsure*, or companions to the *shite*, virtually never appear without the *shite* being present. In most two-part plays the *shite* appears in both parts since his is by far the most important role, and the *kyōgen* appears in the interlude between the parts and has no interaction with the *shite*.

musical structure of Noh and by the physical size and shape of the stage.

The Edo period was an important time of refinement and standardization for Noh theater, but dramatic innovation passed to other theatrical genres. Noh plays written in the Edo period were hardly ever performed, and none are in the current repertory. Two types of Soga Noh plays were written: plays deriving from popular Edo drama, which were ineffective because they were restrained by the rigorous rules of Edo-period Noh performance; and plays following orthodox patterns of dream Noh as it was standardized according to Edo-period concepts of the well-crafted Noh play. In these plays the brothers first appear as residents of the Mount Fuji area and later as ghosts. They were simply fitted into the mold of dream Noh; the development and language of the plays are stereotypical, and the characters lack passion and conviction.

KŌWAKAMAI

Noh was the dominant dramatic genre of Japan's medieval age, but many other performing arts flourished throughout the period. *Kōwakamai*, the strongest rival of Noh drama, was a direct descendant of *kusemai*, solo dances performed by women to the accompaniment of simple percussion and chanted texts. *Kōwakamai*, like Noh, developed by borrowing from other forms, most notably Noh and *heikyoku* (the recitation of *Heike monogatari*).[110]

James Araki, author of the definitive work in English on the art, calls *kōwakamai* the "ballad drama" of Japan. It was performed on stage, but its accompanying texts were narratives. Performers sang or declaimed the texts and illustrated them with movements that have been lost to us. Historical sources show clearly that rhythm was the central element of *kusemai*, and stamping and walking are the only movements in the *kōwakamai* as it survives today.[111] The episodes chosen for *kōwakamai* plays were among the most dramatic and spectacular in their source stories, but there is no way to know how the dramatic

110. James Araki, *The Ballad Drama of Medieval Japan* (Tokyo: Charles Tuttle Co., 1964), 19–79.

111. *Kōwakamai* is performed today in Ōe village in Kyushu. Araki believes that the artistic and dramatic quality of the surviving performance has declined considerably since the early 1600s. See ibid., 80–107 for a detailed analysis of *kōwakamai* as it survives today.

narratives were enacted. The costumes, movement, and music of today's *kōwakamai*, performed at just one shrine in Kyushu,[112] are simple and monotonous with little change from play to play. There is no indication that a single dancer ever represented a single character in a play. Today one performer sings and "dances" all the solo sections, and two others join in choral sections or participate in dialogues. *Kōwakamai* performance in the latter half of the sixteenth century must have been more interesting than that performed today because it rivaled Noh in attracting powerful warrior patrons and large audiences of commoners.

Kōwakamai texts were printed and published in the early Edo period in two forms, either as librettos with musical notation resembling that of Noh or as prose stories meant to be read. The latter are somewhat longer and more cohesive than the former, but even the librettos read as narratives. Fifty texts have survived to the present day. Forty of them retell popular episodes from *Gikeiki, Soga monogatari, Heike monogatari*, or other accounts of the Genpei War era.[113] Scholars are highly skeptical of the "official" history of *kōwakamai*, which asserts that all of the plays were written by the supposed founder of the art, Momonoi Naoaki (1405–70), a samurai from Echizen Province (present Fukui Prefecture) and a descendant of Emperor Seiwa (r. 858–76).[114] Just as Zeami glorified the lineage of Noh, so *kōwakamai* performers invented a geneology for their ancestors that would justify their being treated with respect. Literary historians now agree that most plays must have been written in the fifteenth century, but that they were not used as librettos for stage performance until the sixteenth century. The stylistic uniformity of most of them suggets that they were written within a short period of time by a single author or a single troupe.[115]

Kōwakamai themes emphasize loyalty, honor, and military prowess. There are numerous portrayals of *giri-ninjō* conflicts, and *giri* is given the greater moral value. In many plays heroes and heroines sacrifice their own lives or their children's lives to fulfill the

112. For a description of *kōwakamai* as it is performed today at the village of Ōe in Kyushu, see ibid., 80–99.

113. For plot summaries of all extant *kōwakamai* plays, see ibid., 125–49.

114. See ibid., 19–26 for a discussion of the official *kōwakamai* history and its inconsistencies.

115. Ibid., 76.

stern demands of samurai *giri*. Only one of the fifty plays is a romance, and in it the main character sacrifices his life for love.[116]

Although *kōwakamai* plays include dream premonitions, magic implements, and encounters with supernatural creatures, they are essentially nonreligious. Heroes do not dedicate their lives to spiritual enlightenment or rebirth in Amida's Paradise, but rather strive for achievements attainable in their mortal lives. Like most worldly men, they concern themselves with the next world only when faced with death.

Kōwakamai reached its height of popularity in the sixteenth and early seventeenth centuries. Most contemporary Japanese know little about the art except that the warlord Oda Nobunaga (1534–82) danced a *kōwakamai* just before he led his small army to its stunning victory at Okehazama, the victory that began Oda's spectacular rise to national power. This incident, the "official" history of *kōwakamai*, and the predominance of plays with martial themes persuaded early scholars that *kōwakamai* was an art performed for and by the warrior class. In fact, however, in the sixteenth century it enjoyed the patronage of all classes. There were subscription *kusemai* and *kōwakamai* performances that attracted large crowds,[117] and *kusemai* and *kōwakamai* were performed before warlords and the nobility.

Kōwakamai, like Noh, was appropriated by the military class after the establishment of the Tokugawa Bakufu.[118] Noh actors were officially classified as performers, but, perhaps thanks to the convincing genealogy of the Kōwaka family, *kōwakamai* performers were accepted as true samurai—they were given lands to administer and were permitted to wear two swords.[119] Scholars still debate the reasons why *kōwakamai* declined and died when so many other arts survived, even those patronized only by a small fragment of society. Araki suggests that as *kōwakamai* performers became more accustomed to their samurai status, "they may have felt it beneath their dignity to perform on stage."[120] Samurai patronage of Noh was assured in the Edo period, but it was the artistic commitment of actors and troupe leaders that

116. The play is *Shinkyoku* (literally, "New Piece"). For a summary, see ibid., 147–48.

117. Asahara Yoshiko, "Kōwaka bukyoku kokō Sogamono o megutte," *Bungaku* 35.10 (1967): 38.

118. *Bakufu* literally means "tent government" and was the term used to designate the shogun's military government.

119. Araki, *The Ballad Drama*, 78.

120. Ibid.

maintained the vital force of the art. Without an example like that of Zeami to follow, *kōwakamai* performers may not have considered their art a sacred calling; their obligations as samurai were more important to them than the careful preservation of their theater.

SOGA *KŌWAKAMAI* PLAYS

Seven of the fifty extant *kōwakamai* plays are based on the Soga story (see appendix D). The sources of Soga Noh plays are diverse and difficult to locate, but the Soga *kōwakamai* plays clearly demonstrate the emergence of the *rufubon* in the fifteenth and sixteenth centuries as the national version of *The Tale of the Soga Brothers.* All plays are close to the *rufubon* in thematic emphasis, characterization, and literary style.

Several Soga *kōwakamai* and Noh plays have the same or very similar titles, but the language and structure of the *kōwakamai* plays are unrelated to their corresponding Noh plays although the same or similar events are described. The unique plot twists found in Noh, such as Jūrō's cap-father role in *Genbuku Soga*, the appearance of the divinity Fudō Myōō in *Chōbuku Soga*, the survival of Ōtōnai and his comic role in *Youchi Soga*, are all absent from the Soga *kōwakamai* plays that describe the same sections of the Soga story. The *kōwakamai* plays follow the plot of the *rufubon* in each of the above episodes. These Noh plays are older works, likely to have been written before the *rufubon* emerged as the dominant version of the Soga tale.

Soga *kōwakamai* plays conform more to narrative sources than do Soga Noh plays partly because the former are considerably longer works. They cover from four to twenty-three chapters of the *rufubon* and thus required less cutting of the source tale. *Kōwakamai* plays and the tale shared a similar narrative structure, so *kōwakamai* plays needed less rewriting than Noh plays, which required considerable modification of narrative sources to conform to the formal musical and structural patterns of Noh.[121] It does not appear that the music of *kōwakamai* prescribed set patterns for dialogue and monologue, prose and poetry, in the same way that the musical structure of Noh dominated the writing of most Noh plays.

Soga *kōwakamai* plays resemble Soga Noh plays in their lack of concern with religious themes; *goryō* belief and the religious

121. Araki, "Sogamono no kōwaka bukyoku," 122–23.

activities of the women after the vendetta are never mentioned. In *kōwakamai* plays religious stories serve as rhetorical tools, but they are different and considerably shorter than those of the narrative, and they never form long, separate episodes as in *The Tale of the Soga Brothers*.[122]

Kōwakamai plays gave greater emphasis to dramatic events than did the *rufubon*. The authors of Soga *kōwakamai* did not invent new dramatic episodes such as we find in some Noh plays; instead, scenes of conflict and confrontation from the tale were often made more elaborate. Noh dramatists deleted long passages of dialogue and description, sometimes replacing them with movement on the stage. In *kōwakamai*, however, dialogue and description were often more exhaustive than in *The Tale of the Soga Brothers*, and in some cases *kōwakamai* authors added dramatic action to narrative explanation.

Wada sakamori is the most exciting Soga *kōwakamai* play. Although the play deletes two Buddhist tales that appear in the *rufubon*, the play is longer than the corresponding episode in the tale. Almost every dramatic section of the story is expanded in the play. A comparison of the climax of the episode in each version demonstrates how one *kōwakamai* author modified his source material for the stage. The situation is as follows: Wada Yoshimori and Jūrō are about to fight because Tora has served sake first to her lover, not to Yoshimori. A premonition of danger has brought Gorō to the scene, and he stands outside the banquet room, holding his sword hilt. Asahina notices Gorō's shadow on the *shōji* screen and begins to dance. He wants to approach Gorō in a nonthreatening manner. The following is the *rufubon* version of *Kusazuribiki* (The Armor-Pulling Contest):

> He slid open the *shōji* and, just as he expected, there stood Gorō in a powerful posture, as impressive as a guardian king.[123] Asahina went right up to him and spoke to him

122. Three examples include *Ichiman Hakoō* (Ichiman and Hakoō), *Kosode koi*, and *Jūban giri*. In *Ichiman Hakoō* Sukenobu recites a relatively long (eight lines) description of the road to Hell in order to delay the execution of the Soga boys and give the petitioners more time to win an amnesty from Yoritomo. "Ichiman Hakoō," in Sasano Ken, ed., *Kōwaka bukyoku shū* (Rinsen Shoten, 1974), 2:450–51. In *Kosode koi* Gorō tells of the origins of Hakone Temple, and in *Jūban giri* he explains the Lotus Sutra as part of his final *nenbutsu* prayer. "Kosode koi," in ibid., 489, and "Jūban giri," in ibid., 528.

123. *Funjikatte tatta* refers to the basic posture of traditional martial arts and the martial dance of Noh. Gorō is standing with his knees bent slightly, creating a low center of gravity, and with his feet pointing away from each other.

> in the style of a comic play, "Why, here is another guest. Please come in."[124] Asahina seized several of Gorō's armor plates and gave a great pull, but Gorō did not budge. Asahina thought, "I can move great stones with these arms—how can Gorō resist me?" He pulled with all of his strength, "Eiya! Eiya!" Gorō thought nothing of these efforts and stood unmoving, laughing mockingly at Asahina. The armor straps could not stand the great strain and suddenly snapped, sending Asahina backward, crashing onto the floor.[125]

Now let us examine the *kōwakamai* version:

> Asahina opened the *shōji* with a slam. When he looked inside he saw a stranger—a great robust man, seven feet tall. His breastplate was completely white, and his great sword, more than five feet long, was pulled six or seven inches out of its sheath. He looked like he would be a dangerous foe if it came to a sword fight, and even the demonlike Asahina stood with shaking knees. "So, are you Gorō? Your elder brother, Jūrō, is in the room. Why don't you come in and join the party?"
>
> "I'd like to but as you can see I'm not dressed for the occasion."[126]
>
> Asahina thought to himself, "I've heard that Gorō boasts he is such a fine horseman he could put reins on a great snake and ride it. It's an amusing story, but I'd like to see his real strength." Saying, "You really won't join us?" he ran up to Gorō, took hold of two or three plates of armor at the waist, and pulled forward with an "Eiya!" Gorō didn't budge. Asahina thought to himself, "He really is very strong. I am Kobayashi no Asahina, champion among 480 men, including the 93 warriors of the Miura house. If I don't pull Gorō into the banquet room, I will be disgraced." One after another rippling muscles bulged on Asahina's arms, evidence of his great strength.[127] The thick hair that grew on his chest bristled like bronze needles from the surface of a *go* board. His muscles rippled from his body to his forehead and back again. He looked just like a pine entwined in wisteria

124. There is nothing in the way the phrase is couched that makes it resemble *kyōgen*, but any sentence can be delivered using *kyōgen*'s vocal rhythm and pitch.
125. Ichiko and Ōshima, *Soga monogatari*, 257.
126. Gorō is wearing a white warrior's robe (*hitatare*) and armor.
127. "Power sinews" (*chikara suji*) appear as sinews or veins on the faces, chests, arms, and legs of Buddhist statues of Guardian Kings.

> vines or a griffin standing on its hind legs.[128] It was a remarkable scene.
>
> Gorō thought, "In the three manors of Usami, Kuzumi, and Kawazu[129] I am known to be strong enough to ride wild horses. If a small man like Asahina pulls me into the room, I'll be disgraced before everybody. If he really pulls hard, one of three things will surely happen: either the armor plates will tear off, or I'll break my knee joints, or the floor boards on which we are standing will crash to the ground." So Gorō stood in a powerful posture with knees bent and legs apart.[130]
>
> Asahina, his sideburns wildly awry,[131] pulled forward, "Eito!" and pulled backward, "Eitono!" and the armor plates ripped off. Gorō did not budge and stood as before.[132]

The theatricality of the *kōwakamai* version is apparent in its use of onomatopoetic words (*eito, eitono*) and in the descriptions of Asahina's movements and physical strain. The thoughts of the protagonists do not enter into the simple description in the tale, but we enter the minds of Asahina and Gorō in the *kōwakamai* play. *Wada sakamori* expands and dramatizes its source more than do most *kōwakamai* plays, but the above example is representative of the kinds of modifications to *The Tale of the Soga Brothers* that can be found in *kōwakamai.* "The Armor-Pulling Contest" became one of the best known episodes in the whole Soga story thanks to energetic presentations in *kōwakamai* and in the Noh play *Wada sakamori.* The scene was staged frequently in Edo-period drama and inspired a whole range of tug-of-war dances and playlets.

We find important structural development in the Soga story as it is presented in *kōwakamai* texts. The basic progression of events is the same in *kōwakamai* plays and in the *rufubon*, but *kōwakamai* authors addressed the problem of temporal transition. Little attention was paid to stylistic and temporal transitions in any version of

128. Both are impressive and solid.

129. These three manors were the objects of dispute in the Itō family for three generations. At the time of the Soga revenge, Kudō Suketsune held title to them. *Soga monogatari*, book 1, states that the Itō estate of Kusumi comprised three manors: Usami, Kawazu, and Itō.

130. This is *funjikatte tatta*; see n. 123.

131. "Sideburns awry" (*basshin o irarage*) describes the appearance of a warrior when his hair begins to come undone as a result of strenuous physical activity. One can see in Kabuki today how hair sticks out to the side first.

132. "Wada sakamori," in Sasano, *Kōwaka bukyoku shū*, 2:476–77.

the tale; instead, the reciters and authors strove to put each trial the brothers faced into a historical or religious context. *Kōwakamai* playwrights deleted or abbreviated tangential stories that interrupted the plot, and added transitional scenes. In the narrative tale, with the exception of the brothers' final journey to the Fuji hunt, the various episodes take place in a set location. In *kōwakamai*, travel scenes were often added to provide transitions for episodes set in different locations. While the *rufubon* tells us nothing of the brothers' journey to Hōjō Tokimasa's residence for Gorō's coming-of-age ceremony, in the *kōwakamai* version the brothers quarrel over who is to ride their only horse—each wants to allow the other to ride. Finally they decide to ride double. The journey to Tokimasa's house is used not only to link scenes in two separate geographical settings but also to further demonstrate the brothers' love and respect for each other.

Soga *kōwakamai* plays, unlike Soga Noh plays, may have been meant to be performed (or read) in sequence, creating, in effect, a long "Soga revenge tale." Two of the seven *kōwakamai* Soga plays, *Kosode Soga* and *Tsurugi sandan* (Praising the Swords), are linked by a travel sequence that occurs at the end of the former and that takes the brothers from the village of Soga to Hakone Temple, where *Tsurugi sandan* begins.

CONTRIBUTIONS OF MEDIEVAL DRAMA TO THE SOGA STORY

The *rufubon* version of *The Tale of the Soga Brothers* was created by a process of accretion, with little or no cutting or selectivity involved. Reciters of the popular tale inherited the secular and religious episodes in older versions, and some of them added their own, new, religious material, or new episodes that described the exploits of the Soga brothers. In Noh drama, however, we see the beginning of the creative deconstruction of the narrative tale. Noh playwrights were not trying to improve or add to the narrative tale. Instead they endeavored to takes bits of it and craft those bits into exciting and moving moments of human drama.

Because Noh and *kōwakamai* plays about the Soga brothers are short works divided into several contrasting scenes, medieval drama reinforced the episodic nature of the Soga story. The focal point of each episode in the plays was a scene of conflict or suffering. In most plays the vendetta itself, the brothers' final goal, recedes from the consciousness of the reader or viewer as the brothers become entangled in a preliminary struggle or emotional crisis. Within the plays the brothers usually concentrate on their immediate goals or problems, rarely pausing to reflect on the conflict that looms before them. Noh and *kōwakamai* end with a sense of *medetasa*, a celebratory mood, often expressed in music or dance, which reflects the brothers' feelings after they have passed safely through some danger or have overcome a difficult obstacle. In the parties and celebrations that conclude these plays there is rarely any hint of a future tragedy.[133] The use of celebration and dance as conventions of closure is part of the process of deconstruction and modification of a narrative source tale essential to making plays effective on stage. The process necessarily fragments the larger story and diminishes its tragic character in episodes other than the final attack on Kudō Suketsune.

Some of the tangential Chinese and Indian stories that appear in narrative versions of *The Tale of the Soga Brothers* were as long as corresponding episodes about the brothers themselves. There was simply no way to accommodate such lengthy digressions in short Noh and *kōwakamai* plays. It was these digressive stories that gave the lives of the brothers religious significance, but they disappeared from the Soga tale as it was presented on the medieval stage. Most Noh playwrights lived in the Kansai, where the Soga brothers were relatively unimportant as deities. The absence of religious themes in Noh and *kōwakamai* indicates a secular appeal to the Soga story even though in the medieval period reciters all over the country were recounting a tale that had significant religious content. Stripped of its Amidist didacticism and tangential cautionary tales, in medieval drama the Soga legend emerged as a story of human suffering, dedication, and heroism, intended primarily to entertain, not to teach.

Noh plays about the Soga brothers were never intended to be performed in sequence. We have no idea whether or not the seven Soga *kōwakamai* plays were meant to be performed in chronological sequence, but when they are read in chronological order the story becomes more focused and coherent than any version of the narrative tale. The story in all medieval drama is centered clearly on the Soga brothers themselves;

133. The conclusion of *Ichiman Hakoō*, however, does make reference to the brothers' vendetta. The last line reads: "so the brothers were able to attain their great goal." "Ichiman Hakoō," in ibid., 457.

there are no Soga plays about the brothers' father, their grandfather, or Yoritomo's rise to power. The lack of interest in Yoritomo reflects the villification of him that took place during the Muromachi period.

No medieval plays present the religious activities of the women after the Soga vendetta. In the case of *kōwakamai* this reflects the largely secular and martial values of the entire corpus of these texts. In the case of Noh, the fact that Tora does not appear as an important heroine reflects the difficulty of writing plays about a woman hero if there is not a body of surviving poetry associated with the woman. According to the practice of Zeami, poetry is the key to the soul in the best Noh plays about women heroes. Presenting women as professional entertainers was another approach to the creation of women characters on the Noh stage, an approach favored by Kan'ami. This is how Tora and Shōshō are portrayed in *Fumisaki Soga,* the one play that describes their activities after the vendetta, but in focusing on the women as entertaining and skillful dancers, their religious activities are largely ignored.

The brothers' filial piety and devotion to honor are emphasized throughout the *kōwakamai* Soga story, and although their suffering is deep and real, the absence of references to *goryō* belief deprives the story of some of its power. Gorō becomes stronger and wilder in some *kōwakamai,* but he never exhibits the righteous, godlike wrath we find occasionally in the narrative tale.

Soga Noh and *kōwakamai* plays are very different, but they shared the same audience—the common people of medieval Japan. This audience enjoyed Soga plays for their visual spectacle, their sympathetic heroes who suffer for a righteous cause, and their conflict between good and evil that ends in the triumph, albeit the tragic triumph, of good. The commoner audiences of the early Edo period shared the same cultural and moral values as their ancestors of a few generations before, so it is no surprise that Soga plays appealed to them as well. Soga *kōwakamai* plays were put to use as recitation texts for the puppet stage—some Soga puppet texts are virtual word-for-word copies of *kōwakamai* plays. When Kabuki producers first put historical characters on stage, they too turned to the Soga story and to Soga Noh and *kōwakamai* for inspiration.

Chapter Four: Epic Reconstruction and Parodic Deconstruction

Noh and *kōwakamai* came under direct government control in the early seventeenth century. During the Edo period, a 250-year time of peace, prosperity, and national isolation, two new theater forms, Kabuki and *jōruri* (puppet theater) brought brilliant innovations to the Japanese stage. A complex interdependant relationship existed between the two arts for most of the period, a relationship so important that it precludes the study of either in isolation. Both were commercial urban theaters, and their vitality was one expression of the new wealth and creativity of the merchants and craftsmen in the three great cities of Edo, Kyoto, and Osaka. It was in Kabuki and the puppet theater that the story of the Soga brothers reached its pinnacle of popularity and status, but the characters of the tale, their motivations and appearances, and even the basic plot of the Soga vendetta were dramatically changed. The story acquired new ritual significance in the world of Edo Kabuki, which led to further modifications of the traditional story.

Early *jōruri* (called *ko-jōruri*) integrated three separate arts: puppetry, chant, and the accompaniment of the three-stringed *shamisen*. For many centuries in Japan, puppets had been used in theatrical presentations, from skits depicting fighting or amorous scenes, to Noh plays, to religious displays intended to instruct the audience.[134] The puppets of *ko-jōruri* were manipulated by one man each. Operators held puppets above their heads so the puppets' skirts or feet trailed along the top of the curtain or wall that concealed the puppeteers from the audience's view. Some theaters used marionettes controlled from above by strings.[135] Puppeteers sometimes spoke the lines of their

134. See Charles J. Dunn, *The Early Japanese Puppet Drama* (London: Luzac and Co. Ltd., 1966), and Donald Keene, *Bunraku: The Art of the Japanese Puppet Theatre* (Tokyo and New York: Kodansha International, 1965), for more detailed discussion of the origins of the puppet theater.

135. See Dunn, *Early Japanese Puppet Drama*, 59–69 for detailed descriptions of puppetry in the early Edo period.

puppets, but by the early 1600s the independent chanter was becoming more important for the vocalization of plays.

The term *jōruri* derives from *Jōruri hime monogatari* (or *Jūnidan zōshi*, The Tale of Princess Jōruri), one of several tangential tales to *Gikeiki*. The tale's heroine, Princess Jōruri, is Yoshitsune's faithful mistress, and she sacrifices her life to help Yoshitsune on his path to greatness.[136] The story was very popular in the late medieval period and was recited to the accompaniment of the *biwa* in a vocal style closely related to *heikyoku*. In the first decades of the seventeenth century the style of *jōruri* recitation varied depending on the individual performer, but the influence of *heikyoku* remained strong.[137] The *shamisen*, a three-stringed instrument with a sounding box covered in cat or dog skin was a modification of a smaller, snake-skin-covered instrument imported from the Ryukyu Islands in the mid-sixteenth century. By about 1580 it had become well established in Japan and was used to accompany singing of all kinds. It replaced the *biwa* as a popular instrument because of its romantic, even erotic, tones. The adoption of puppets and the *shamisen* to accompany the recitation of the story of Princess Jōruri signified the birth of *ningyō jōruri* (puppet *jōruri*) as a stage art. *Jōruri* came to refer to both the music of the puppet theater and to the puppet theater as a whole. *Ko-jōruri* (old *jōruri*) refers to the puppet theater prior to Chikamatsu. In 1600 the puppet theater had an exciting new form, and performers were searching for literary texts and technical innovations that could bring them wealth and fame in a highly competitive theater environment.

Paintings depicting city life and a few diary entries about trips to the puppet theater tell us something about *ko-jōruri* presentations in the early 1600s, but our knowledge of the art is based primarily on the study of play texts; about 350 remain, or one-third of the estimated total number of *ko-jōruri* plays presented.[138] The texts and titles that survive tell us that *ko-jōruri* retained a strong narrative flavor.

136. See Keene, *Bunraku*, 25–26, for the development of *The Tale of Princess Jōruri* in the medieval and Edo periods. See Dunn, *Early Japanese Puppet Drama*, 7–13, 109–11, for a discussion of the term *jōruri* and earliest accounts mentioning the story, and 14–17 for a discussion of the musical accompaniment and recitation of the story. See McCullough, *Yoshitsune*, 47–50 for a brief summary of the tale and a short discussion of its origins.

137. See Dunn, *Early Japanese Puppet Drama*, 16. A tradition of *sekkyō jōruri* has survived until the present, and its recitation and use of the *shamisen* retain several distinctive features of *heikyoku*.

138. Ibid., 72–75.

Most early *ko-jōruri* pieces were long tales: the story of Princess Jōruri or stories deriving from *sekkyō,* tales of Buddhist virtue and salvation that in the medieval period had been recited to the accompaniment of simple percussion.[139] Shorter, more dramatic pieces were also performed in *ko-jōruri.* Several early play titles correspond exactly to *kōwakamai* titles, and texts survive that are direct copies of *kōwakamai* plays. Some *ko-jōruri* were borrowed from Noh.[140]

The *ko-jōruri* program plan resembled Noh, with *kyōgen*-like skits interspersed between the acts of serious plays. In the first decades of the Edo period, *kyōgen* interludes were performed by actors, not puppets, but later in the century comic puppets were introduced.[141] The program of alternating comic and serious plays was so popular and so well established in Japan's theatrical tradition that *ko-jōruri* included comic interludes until about 1700.[142]

The founder of Kabuki was Okuni, a Shinto shrine dancer (*miko*) from Izumo, on the western coast of the Sea of Japan. In 1596 she brought a group of dancing girls to Kyoto where they perfomed "Kabuki dance" (Kabuki *odori*). Okuni's dance was probably a variation of *nenbutsu odori,* and paintings depicting Okuni and her troupe indicate that her dance was also related to *fūryū odori.*[143] The word Kabuki derives from the verb *kabuku,* which in the late sixteenth cen-

139. See Susan Matisoff, *The Legend of Semimaru: Blind Musician of Japan* (New York: Columbia University Press, 1978), 50–52 for medieval *sekkyō,* and 118–22 for *ko-jōruri* and *sekkyō jōruri* in the early Edo period.

140. Dunn, *Early Japanese Puppet Drama,* 43.

141. See Shinoda Jun'ichi and Saitō Seijirō, *Noroma soroma kyōgen shusei* (Daigakudō Shoten, 1974), 513–38, for the development of comic puppet interludes.

142. See ibid., 526–31, for performance programs in the last three decades of the seventeenth century. C. Andrew Gerstle reaches the same conclusion in his work, *Circles of Fantasy: Convention in the Plays of Chikamatsu,* vol. 116 of Harvard East Asian Monographs (Cambridge, MA: Council on East Asian Studies, Harvard University Press, 1986), basing his information on Mori Shū, *Chikamatsu Monzaemon,* vol. 4 of *Koten to sono jidai* (San'ichi Shobō, 1959), 66–70.

143. *Fūryū odori,* which became popular in the medieval period, refers to folk dances involving large numbers of participants. They were performed as festival events by members of the rural and townsman classes. *Fūryū odori* costumes were elaborate and gorgeous, often colorful modifications of every-day clothing, supplemented with flower hats, lantern hats, or other fanciful decorations. In the late medieval period *fūryū odori* sometimes became the catalyst for demonstrations or even uprisings of peasants or townsmen. For further information on relationships between *nenbutsu odori, fūryū odori,* and early Kabuki dance, see Hattori Yukio, *Kabuki seiritsu no kenkyū* (Kazama Shobō, 1968), 145–62, and Mary Elizabeth Berry, *The Culture of Civil War in Kyoto* (Berkeley, CA: The University of California Press, 1994), 248–54.

tury carried the meaning "to speak or act in an ostentatious, antisocial, eccentric, or erotic manner." Surviving lyrics from Okuni's Kabuki attest to its erotic appeal,[144] as do paintings that show Okuni and other dancing girls dressed in men's attire. *Kabukimono* (literally, "Kabuki people") referred to young dandies and ruffians, often masterless samurai, who frequented the pleasure districts of the cities in great numbers in the first decades of the Edo period. There were many *kabukimono* in the early Edo period because the wars of 1600 and 1614–15 had created numerous masterless samurai, many of whom gravitated to the pleasure districts that were becoming havens for outcasts or those wishing to remain anonymous and outside a rapidly hardening class system. *Kabukimono* wore outlandish clothing, often of European origin, carried very long swords, and spoke in a special jargon. From Okuni's time, *kabukimono* and people like them have been prominent in the milieu of the Kabuki theater.

Okuni's Kabuki was all the rage in Kyoto. She performed regularly for the public, at special festivals, and even in a private show for Toyotomi Hideyoshi (1536–98), the ruler of Japan.[145] During the several years that she appeared regularly at a permanent stage at Ukon no Baba near Kitano Shrine, Okuni was so popular that she was called "the lord of Kitano." In 1608 she was summoned to Edo Castle to perform for the shogun.[146] Other women formed Kabuki troupes in imitation of Okuni. Many Kabuki dancers were prostitutes, and an important purpose of women's Kabuki was to display prostitutes to prospective customers. The brothel and theater districts were in different parts of Kyoto, and accounts of the early 1600s describe troupes of prostitutes parading daily from Rokujō Misuji (Sixth Avenue and Misuji) to perform at theaters on the Shijō (Fourth Avenue) riverbank, Kyoto's fast-growing entertainment district.[147]

Women's Kabuki was a mixture of popular entertainments: dances, skits, and *misemono* (shows). *Misemono* included demonstrations of unusual talents, exotic clothing, or bizarre physical features.[148] Kabuki seems to have included short skits and mimicry in Okuni's

144. Earle Ernst, *The Kabuki Theatre* (Honolulu: The University Press of Hawaii, 1956), 165.
145. Dōmoto Kansei, *Kamigata geinō no kenkyū* (Kyoto: Kawara Shoten, 1954), 41.
146. Ibid., 41–43.
147. Ibid., 43.
148. Suwa Haruo, *Genroku kabuki no kenkyū* (Kasama Shoin, 1967), 2–4. Examples of early Kabuki *misemono* include: animal tricks, dancing with a long pole held on the nose, balancing a cup on the pole, dancing on a bed of sword points, acrobatics and martial dances, displays of exotic European clothes, and so on.

time. The setting for skits was invariably the pleasure quarter. Two of the most common motifs were *keisei kai*, in which an amorous man procures and converses with a courtesan, and *furo agari*, in which a brothel guest comes out of the bath, converses with bathhouse girls, and calls for a courtesan. Records tell us that Okuni played the man's role in *keisei kai* skits. *Keisei kai* and *furo agari* presentations showed the audience an exotic yet accessible demimonde, and much of their attraction lay in the audience's recognition of or introduction to the customs and vocabulary of the pleasure quarter. The contemporaneity of the material stood in contrast to the traditional performing arts, including *ko-jōruri*. Kabuki dancers sometimes portrayed living celebrities—well-known courtesans, Okuni herself, and Okuni's reputed lover, the famous *kabukimono*, Nagoya Sanzaemon (dates uncertain).

Legend has it that Nagoya Sanzaemon was a former samurai who had studied Noh; he likely taught much of what he had learned to Okuni and her troupe. *Kyōgen* actors participated in Kabuki performances, sometimes doing complete *kyōgen* plays, and Okuni and Sanzaemon reputedly performed comic plays together.[149] In women's Kabuki, dance was the most important form of entertainment, and all the dancers appear to have been women. The skits and *misemono* between the dances included both male and female performers. The following is an example of a women's Kabuki program: "(1) Opening dance, (2) Okuni dance, (3) Narihira dance (Ariwara no Narihira, the hero of *The Tales of Ise*, was a famous poet and lover from the Heian period), (4) Okuni and Nagoya love scene, (5) Kabuki dance, (6) *Furo agari*, (7) Closing song, and (8) Finale."[150] This record, and others like it, make it clear that women's Kabuki was much like a vaudeville or burlesque show.

Women's Kabuki remained popular until 1629 when it was banned by the shogunate. The action followed repeated fights at Kabuki performances between samurai over who was to purchase which dancer. After 1629 women were banished from the stage, and prostitutes and courtesans were confined to the licensed quarters. The Tokugawa government could tolerate or even use licentiousness, but

149. *Tōkaidō meisho ki* states that an actor named Sanjūrō performed *kyōgen* for Okuni's troupe, and that Sanzaemon performed with Okuni (ibid., 8). Nagoya Sanzaemon's relationship with Okuni (and even his existence) is still disputed by scholars. For a good discussion of the issue, and the significance of the Okuni-Sanzaemon legend, see Hattori, *Kabuki seiritsu no kenkyū*, 259–309.

150. Suwa, *Genroku kabuki no kenkyū*, 7.

it could never condone disorder.[151] Following the government ban, Kabuki was performed by young boys (*wakashu*). Boys' Kabuki had much the same content as women's Kabuki, and the boys, like the women before them, used the performances partly to advertise sexual services. The quality of Kabuki improved gradually during the first half of the seventeenth century because experienced Noh and *kyōgen* actors whose troupes had not been officially sanctioned by the government entered the Kabuki world as teachers of dance and mime. Records tell us that the *wakashu* performed some Noh and *kyōgen* dances, but beginning with Okuni, most Kabuki dance has derived from a mixture of folk dance and contemporary, popular dance. Boys' Kabuki was banned in 1652 for the same reason that brought the government's censure of women's Kabuki.

SOGA PUPPET PLAYS: RECREATING THE EPIC ON STAGE

In the 1630s and 1640s, while the Kabuki *wakashu* were charming audiences with their dancing, chanters of *ko-jōruri* were searching for stories that would form the nuclei of exciting or moving puppet performances. *Ko-jōruri* texts were published under the chanter's name, and he attested their accuracy as certified "true versions" (*shōhon*) of his plays.[152] The uninitiated reader of an early *ko-jōruri* text would never suspect he is reading drama; texts are in purely narrative form, with no stage directions or divisions of lines according to roles. The narratives are accompanied by many large illustrations depicting characters as humans in natural settings, not as puppets on the stage. Whatever the source material, *ko-jōruri* plays are divided into six sections of roughly equal length, each section beginning with the same formulaic narrative phrases used to open *kōwakamai* plays and oral tales.[153] *Ko-jōruri* texts were published in large numbers; spectators read them before or during performances, or they could be read as illustrated story books.[154]

151. Donald Keene, *World Within Walls* (New York: Holt, Rinehart, and Winston, 1976), 234.

152. Dunn, *Early Japanese Puppet Drama*, 70.

153. The *kōwakamai* play *Wada sakamori* was the only Soga *kōwakamai* play that did not begin with a formulaic phrase. The *ko-jōruri Wada sakamori*, however, begins, "And after that" (*Sate mo sono nochi*), and the following five acts begin with similar formulaic opening phrases.

154. See ibid., 70–71, for information on early *ko-jōruri* texts.

The first *ko-jōruri* chanters whose names we know were raised and trained in Kyoto from about 1600 through the 1620s. For reasons that remain unclear, their livelihood became difficult in Kyoto and all moved to Edo.[155] *Ko-jōruri* texts of the 1630s and 1640s were taken from other literary genres and used exactly as they were, or sometimes slightly modified. Typical stories included Buddhist tales of the origins of sects and temples (*honjimono*), *kōwakamai* plays, and tales of "troubles in great families" (*ōie sōdō*), which derived from *sekkyō* stories such as *Sansho dayū*.[156]

Episodes from the Soga story had just the right length and complexity for the early puppet stage. In 1643 Satsuma Jōun (?–1669) performed the first Soga puppet play, using for his text the *kōwakamai* play *Kosode Soga*.[157] The most didactic and least dramatic of the *kōwakamai* Soga plays, Jōun's choice of this play indicates that the religious themes of *honjimono* and *sekkyō* stories were still important in *ko-jōruri*.

Jōun soon moved away from puppet plays with moral and religious appeal toward a theater that placed greater emphasis on the unique presentational possibilities of puppets: the imitation of a large variety of human actions and the portrayal of supernatural creatures and events. Hayashi Razan (1583–1657), a Confucian scholar and advisor to the shogun, left this description of Jōun's puppet theater:

> Puppets were dressed as men, women, monks or laity, immortals, soldiers, horsemen, and porters. There were dancers and those who raised fans and beat drums. Some leapt about and some rowed boats and sang. Some had been killed in battle, and their heads and bodies were separated. Some were dressed in the clothes of the gentry. Some shot arrows, some waved sticks, and some raised flags and bore aloft parasols. Some were dragons and snakes, and some were birds. Some were foxes and carried fire in their tails, at which all the spectators marveled. The performance began at eleven in the morning and lasted until three that afternoon.[158]

155. Ibid., 78.
156. Ibid., 83–84.
157. Wakatsuki Yasuji, *Ko-jōruri shin kenkyū (Keichō kanbun hen)* (Shingetsu Sha, 1958), 295.
158. Donald Keene, *The Battles of Coxinga* (London: Taylor's Foreign Press, 1951), 20.

From this account it is clear that Jōun sought to dazzle his audience with a spectacular puppet theater.

Jōun also performed the second Soga puppet play, *Youchi Soga*, whose text is virtually identical to the *kōwakamai* text of the same name.[159] *Youchi Soga* is the longest Soga *kōwakamai* play, and it has numerous scenes that could have been excitingly portrayed by puppets: the grandeur of the Fuji hunt, Nitta no Shirō's wild ride on the back of a huge boar, the tumble of Jūrō's horse over a fallen tree just as Jūrō let fly an arrow at Kudō, and the murder of Kudō.

The changes that Jōun and others made in *ko-jōruri* both reflected and stimulated Edo audiences' interest in exciting puppetry. Texts taken from traditional literary sources, however, soon proved inadequate to provide enough spectacular effects for Edo audiences. Jōun's successors in Edo were the first to write completely original *ko-jōruri* plays, and they wrote plays with themes of warfare and violence. The most important and representative of these were the *kinpira* plays, and they not only would lead to the first revisions of the Soga story in *ko-jōruri* but also would inspire new developments in Edo Kabuki. *Kinpira* plays described the exploits of the four fictional sons of the "Four Guardian Kings," or Shitennō. The Shitennō were valiant retainers of Minamoto Yorimitsu (944–1021), and medieval folklore and literature immortalized their heroic fights with demons living in the Kyoto area.[160] In *kinpira jōruri* the sons of the Shitennō continued their fathers' exploits, fighting against the mortal and supernatural enemies of their lord, Minamoto Yoriyoshi (995–1082). The leader of Yoriyoshi's faithful band was Sakata Kinpira, "a daredevil warrior, youthful and short tempered but brave and persistent."[161] "The language of *kinpira* plays became extremely simple and the action, too, became less complicated than that of their predecessors. Every character behaved in the way that was expected of him, no emotions of pity, love, or sympathy were aroused, there were no tragic moments."[162] Violent presentation accompanied light-hearted stories of

159. The play was published under the name Satsuma Koheita (Wakatsuki, *Ko-jōruri shin kenkyū*, 384). Koheita was either Jōun's name early in his career or the name of his teacher.

160. The Shitennō kill the demon Shūtendōji in the Noh play *Ōeyama* and the great earth spider in the Noh play *Tsuchigumo*, and they encounter the demon of the Rashōmon gate in the Noh play *Rashōmon*. These stories were also told as folk tales and are still performed as pantomime in *mibu kyōgen*.

161. Fujimura, ed., *Nihon bungaku daijiten 1* (Shinkōsha, 1934), 828.

162. Dunn, *Early Japanese Puppet Drama*, 88–89.

combat: the *kinpira jōruri* chanter Izumi Dayū (dates uncertain), for example, beat an iron bar to accompany his chant and used it to smash puppets in combat scenes.

In Edo, *kinpira jōruri* reached its height of popularity from about 1658–72. *Kinpira* plays were performed at the same time in the Kansai, where they probably revived the puppet theater in the region,[163] but their popularity was short-lived; Kansai audiences wanted more from their plays than violenceand martial heroics. *Kinpira jōruri* nevertheless had an important impact on the development of the art. Even in non-*kinpira* plays, audiences expected to be entertained with exciting puppetry and stage effects, called *karakuri*. The unique advantage of puppets is their artificiality. On the puppet stage a monster is as real as a man so their interaction is more authentic than it can be on the human stage. Supernatural creatures, superhuman abilities and feats, and strange transformations have remained a part of the puppet drama throughout its history.

When the *kinpira* mania began to fade, chanters needed stories that were complex and interesting, that provided a wide range of human emotions, and that included dramatic scenes suitable for *karakuri*. It was only natural that they turned for inspiration to the great war tales of the medieval period: *Heike monogatari*, *Gikeiki*, and *Soga monogatari*. It was as *ko-jōruri* that the traditional Soga story reached its definitive form as a coherent story with a unified literary style and a logical, uninterrupted progression of events.

The entire Soga story was presented on the puppet stage in a one-week, seven-play series, perhaps as early as 1670. The plays were published over a forty-year period—each play was published several times, often with different titles. The two oldest surviving texts date from 1660 and 1675. Four plays were published as the *shōhon* of the Osaka chanter Harima no Jō (1632?–85),[164] but the authors of the rest are unknown. The frequent republication of identical plays using different titles shows that chanters other than Harima no Jō also presented the seven-day Soga series,[165] and it indicates that the Soga story

163. Ibid., 91–93.

164. See Yokoyama Shigeru, ed., *Ko-jōruri shōhon shū* (Kadokawa Shoten, 1964), 2:489–95, and Wakatsuki, *Ko-jōruri shin kenkyū*, 165, for attributions to Harima no Jō.

165. See Yokoyama, *Ko-jōruri shōhon shū*, 2:489, for a list including some titles, and Wakatsuki, *Ko-jōruri shin kenkyū*, 718, 1,191–95, 1,300–3 for a discussion of identical plays with different titles in the seven-day series.

as it appeared in the seven-play series had become the theater's canonical Soga text by the late 1660s. The plays of the series constitute by far the most comprehensive treatment of the Soga story in Japanese drama (see appendix E for a list of plays and acts).

Yokoyama Shigeru in his *Ko-jōruri shōhon shū* states that the Soga series is "one of the best thematic groups in *ko-jōruri*."[166] In his comparison of the *rufubon* and the seven-day *ko-jōruri* series, he makes the following points:

1. There are no tangential tales in the *ko-jōruri*. There are no stories of temple origins and no Chinese tales. There are only a few short Buddhist stories.
2. The plot is tighter and better structured in the *ko-jōruri* than in the narrative tale.
3. *Ko-jōruri* sentences are "more stylistically fluent."
4. The *ko-jōruri* story is popularized and conventionalized.
5. In the *ko-jōruri* there are numerous progressions leading to dramatic peaks. Dramatic episodes are more frequent and more effective than in the *rufubon* or *kōwakamai*.[167]

The five points cited by Yokoyama represent a continuation of the process of change in the Soga story that began in Noh and *kōwakamai*. The list of plays and acts in appendix E shows that *ko-jōruri* playwrights had turned to the *rufubon* as their major source for writing Soga plays. The period of slavish imitation of *kōwakamai* texts had ended. In the medieval period playwrights had based their works on oral tales, but in the Edo period, printed editions of various versions of the Soga story were readily available.[168] The fidelity of early *ko-jōruri* Soga plays to *kōwakamai* plays was made possible by the publication of printed *kōwakamai* texts beginning in 1635.[169] Many editions of the *rufubon* were published in the Edo period; the first edition came out in 1605, and subsequent editions were published in 1627, 1646*, 1663*, 1671*, 1687, 1698*, and 1701* (* indicates an illustrated edition).[170]

166. Yokoyama, *Ko-jōruri shōhon shū,* 2:490.
167. Ibid., 490–91.
168. See Keene, *World Within Walls,* 1–6, for a brief discussion of the impact of printing on early Edo-period literature.
169. Takano Masami, "Chikamatsu Sogamono kō," *Kokugo to kokubungaku* 10.4 (1933): 473.
170. Ichiko and Ōshima, *Soga monogatari,* 13.

The seven-day *ko-jōruri* Soga story is more complete than any previous dramatic version of the story. The first three plays, which describe events before Jūrō and Gorō enter the tale, derive from the *rufubon* and from tales of Yoritomo.[171] No medieval play had ever treated this material. The next three plays focus on the brothers' vendetta: borrowings from *kōwakamai* are numerous, but some passages derive from sections of the *rufubon* that were never used in *kōwakamai*. Tora, Zenji, and the Soga mother are the principal characters of the last play, which has no precedent in *kōwakamai*. The first two acts of this play depict Zenji's heroic resistance and death and seem to take their inspiration from the Noh play *Zenji Soga*, but the last three acts are scenes of nostalgia and religious devotion based closely on the last two books of the *rufubon*.

Ko-jōruri chanters invented new scenes, often dramatic confrontations that would have required *karakuri* manipulations in their presentatation. An analysis of motifs and plot structure in *Kosode Soga*, also published separately as *Tsurugi sandan*, demonstrates the eclectic sources of inspiration for the seven-day *ko-jōruri* series. The two completely original episodes, indicated by italics, depict martial confrontation, and one is also a "special effects" scene:

Summary	Sources and Commentary
Act 2. Jūrō goes to Ōiso and then sets out for home, bringing Tora with him.	This section derives from the *rufubon* and is not found in any *kōwakamai* play.
On the way home from Ōiso, Kudō's men waylay Jūrō and Tora, but Soga Sukenobu and his retainers come up just in time to chase Kudō's men away.	This incident was invented for this play.
Act 3. Tora and Jūrō spend their last night together at his house. The next day Jūrō and Tora travel together as far as Yamabikoyama, where they exchange sake cups in a farewell party. Gorō joins the couple.	Gorō's participation in the farewell party may derive from the Noh play *Tora okuri* (Parting from Tora). Tora's thoughts and feelings are better developed in the play than in the tale, but as a whole this section is close to the *rufubon*. The *kōwakamai* does not show the farewell party at Yamabikoyama.

171. Harima no Jō wrote one of the few *ko-jōruri* plays about Yoritomo, *Yoritomo shichiki ochi* (early 1680s?); see Wakatsuki, *Ko-jōruri shin kenkyū*, 165, for attribution. The Noh play *Shichiki ochi* and several editions of the story of Yoritomo published as fiction may have provided Harima no Jō with material for his Soga plays.

Gorō goes to the Kewaizaka pleasure district to visit his mistress. He stays briefly, leaves her a letter, and sets out for home. The letter tells the girl of his imminent death. She runs away and becomes a nun. Kajiwara Kagesue loves the girl too, and he is angry at Gorō for causing her to leave her profession.	This incident is drawn from the *rufubon*, where it takes place earlier in the story. Gorō's visit to his mistress is found in neither Noh nor *kōwakamai.*
Kajiwara wants to attack Gorō, but Gorō declines to fight over women.	This follows the *rufubon.*
Gorō tries to flee. Kajiwara is so angry that he leads fifty men in pursuit. The pursuit is so swift that Gorō is forced to take action. He fells a great tree on top of all fifty men, killing them. Kajiwara alone escapes, and runs away as Gorō laughs at him derisively.[172]	This is a *karakuri* section invented for the puppet play, and it demonstrates the kind of exaggerated violence that *kinpira jōruri* brought to the puppet stage. The scene parallels Jūrō's predicament in act 2 above. Jūrō's passive response and Gorō's active one stand in clear contrast.

The characterizations and motivations of the heroes of the *ko-jōruri* Soga story remained much as they had been in *kōwakamai*, but the brothers' enemies began to be transformed into villains typical to melodrama. The simplification of the villains resulted from the demand for scenes of violence following *kinpira jōruri*, and from the mechanics of puppet drama that require a greater stereotyping of roles than was present in *kōwakamai* or Noh. There were a limited number of puppet heads, including several types of villains. Puppet movements and vocal representations were set by character type. The Kudō of the puppet stage had to use the head of the typical arch-villain. The brothers' blood enemy simply could not be shown as a different or more complex character. Beginning with *ko-jōruri*, Kudō Suketsune becomes a more active character in the story. He or his retainers seek out the brothers and try to kill them before the Fuji hunt. Dialogues and confrontations between the brothers and Kudō increase in number and importance throughout Edo-period drama. The Kudō of *ko-jōruri* plays is openly malicious and evil; the more subtle and complex Kudō of medieval narrative and drama simply could not be presented on the early puppet stage.

172. Summary from "Tsurugi sandan," in Yokoyama, *Ko-jōruri shōhon shū,* 2:355–60.

Ko-jōruri plays abound with minor villains, and they had to be invented for the Soga story. Kajiwara's role was expanded (*Kosode Soga*, act 3, above, is an example), and Kudō's two loyal retainers, Yawata no Saburō and Ōmi no Kotōta, appear in numerous Edo-period plays, beginning with *ko-jōruri*. In *The Tale of the Soga Brothers* they stalk Itō Sukechika, and Yawata shoots and kills Kawazu Saburō, the Soga brothers' father. In all versions of the narrative tale, an uncle sympathetic to the Soga brothers kills both Yawata and Ōmi shortly after the murder of Kawazu, but both of Kudō's henchmen were resurrected in puppet plays to supply the puppet stage with its requisite petty villains.

The plot of the seven-day Soga *ko-jōruri* series is as complete and coherent as the Soga story would ever get, but it leaves out the dramatic "Wada's Banquet" episode. The week-long series compressed a story covering several generations into seven plays, but the events of the "Wada's Banquet" episode take place in a single day. If the episode were included in its entirety, the balance of the seven-day series would have been destroyed. Harima no Jō and other reciters may have felt that to include a truncated version of the episode would deprive it of dramatic effect and leave audiences unsatisfied. Whatever the reason, *ko-jōruri* versions of this episode were always performed as independent plays. The practice was paralleled by Edo-period storybook publishers who published *Wada sakamori* as an independent short story. The episode was one of the most popular and well known in early puppet theater. Three versions of it survive today, and they correspond to three stages in the development of the art.

The first, Satsuma Jōun's *Wada sakamori*, published in 1664, is an almost word-for-word copy of the *kōwakamai* play of the same title. Textually it represents no change from the medieval version of the story.

The second version is *Fūryū Wada sakamori* (Up-to-Date Wada's Banquet), by Edo chanter Tosa no Shōjō (fl. 1670s to 1700?). It is a considerably revised version of the episode and is probably one of Tosa's oldest plays—it was certainly performed prior to 1686.[173] The first act of Tosa's play describes the dispute between Gorō and Kajiwara Kagesue (see p. 90), an incident unconnected to the

173. A part of the play, "Tora gozen matsu yoi no urami," was published in Tosa no Shōjō's *danmono shū* in 1686. Torii Fumiko, ed., *Tosa jōruri shōhon shū* (Kadokawa Shoten, 1975), 600.

traditional "Wada's Banquet" story, ending when Gorō crushes Kajiwara's men with the tree. Tosa wrote an original second act and condensed Jōun's six-act *Wada sakamori* into the last four acts of his own play. To do this Tosa discarded much of the medieval version, but he used the most dramatic sections of the Jōun text almost word for word: the confrontation between Jūrō and Wada at the banquet, Gorō's premonition and arrival at the banquet, and the armor-pulling contest.

Tosa no Shōjō did more than just graft two puppet plays together. He added new scenes and characters to the Soga story, taking some tentative steps toward turning the puppet play into a work of Edo-period drama as opposed to Jōun's *Wada sakamori*, which continued the medieval tradition of the Soga story. The puppet plays of the 1670s usually required a "hero versus villain" plot structure. However, the Jōun/*kōwakamai* version is without real villains. Tora's mother treats Tora unsympathetically and Wada gets angry at Jūrō, but neither fit the role of a puppet villain. Tosa invented a new character, Shinzaemon Tsunemori, and made him the villain of the play. Tsunemori appears for the first time in Tosa's original second act, during which he plans Wada's banquet as a trap for the Soga brothers. At the banquet it is Tsunemori who orders Tora to serve the man she respects most, not her mother or Yoshimori, as in traditional versions. After Tora serves Jūrō, Tsunemori throws himself at Jūrō, hoping to start a fight, but Asahina pulls him away. At the end of the episode, although good relations have been restored with Yoshimori, Tsunemori remains an unrepentant villain.

Tosa's second important addition to the story is a long, lyrical section (*danmono*) in the third act, describing Tora's sufferings while waiting for her beloved. In earlier versions of the episode Jūrō arrives in Tora's brothel at the beginning of the play, but in *Fūryū Wada sakamori* his arrival is delayed, and in a *danmono* we learn of the anxiety and loneliness Tora feels during the long hours spent waiting for Jūrō. The subject receives considerably more attention here than in the Noh play *Hitsukiri Soga*. This increasing concern with the feelings of prostitutes is the beginning of what becomes an obsession in later Edo literature and drama.

Danmono were melodic, poetic passages (*fushigoto*, *fushi* refers to melody) that were entertaining in themselves, but they were also used to change the mood and vary the tempo of a play. In *ko-jōruri*, *danmono* were among the first original compositions added to traditional sources, and chanters published separate collections of their *danmono*.[174] *Danmono* collections show us that the vocal arts in *kojōruri* had reached a new level of maturity. Audiences were going to the theater to hear beautiful songs skillfully sung as well as to witness a dramatic story and to marvel at new special effects. In *Fūryū Wada sakamori* the *danmono* contains the most poetic language of the play, but it is also its most unfocused section. Jūrō's name never appears and Tora's is mentioned only rarely. *Danmono* were in fact intended to be used in several plays; with a change of only one or two words the *danmono* of *Fūryū Wada sakamori* could be used in a different play about a woman whose lover is inattentive.

In all medieval versions of the Soga story the brothers were idealized as paragons of brotherly love, and their relationship is harmonious and cooperative. The traditional relationship is maintained in most of *Fūryū Wada sakamori*, but Tosa added a new scene at the end of act 2 in which the brothers deceive and criticize each other. Gorō catches his brother reading a letter from Tora. Jūrō rebukes Gorō for eavesdropping and tries to cover up, claiming that he is studying. Gorō tells Jūrō that, if he is going to "study Tora," then he would rather not have Jūrō as a brother.[175] Jūrō stops protesting, but when Gorō leaves, Jūrō dresses up like a *kabukimono* and goes off to visit Tora.

Tosa no Shōjō emphasized those aspects of the Soga story that had maintained its popularity for hundreds of years: conflicts between good and evil and the suffering of the virtuous. By creating an original act 2, with a new villain and bickering Soga brothers, Tosa was able to change the mood and the meaning of the traditional confrontation at Wada's banquet. Wada Yoshimori, who had been an ambivalent character—sometimes an ally and sometimes an enemy of the brothers—in medieval versions of the story, emerged as a staunch ally in Tosa's play. A portrayal of the brothers' foibles probably enhanced

174. The first chanter to publish a collection of *danmono* was Inoue Harima no Jō in 1674. Uji Kaganojō published his first *danmono shū* in 1678 (Yokoyama Tadashi, *Jōruri ayatsuri shibai no kenkyū* [Kazama Shoten, 1964], 6). *Danmono* collections (*danmono shū*) were the first widely available *jōruri* publications that included significant musical notation. Early *danmono* passages were all *fushigoto*; melodic passages with poetic lyrics.

175. Tosa no Shōjō, "Fūryū Wada sakamori," in Torii, *Tosa jōruri shōhon shū*, 420.

audience identification: good characters who have moments of weakness are more real and more sympathetic than paragons of virtue. Tosa no Shōjō's apparent inconsistency in the brothers' characters is notable mainly because it contrasts with the consistently idealized portrayals we find in medieval works. Seventy years into Edo-period drama, the solid first steps were being taken in a new approach to classical sources.

TWO PUPPET PARODIES OF THE STORY

Nothing better demonstrates a new attitude toward the Soga tradition than the third of the puppet plays based on the episode "Wada's Banquet," *Dōke Wada sakamori* (Wada's Banquet Farce), performed in Edo, probably in the early 1670s.[176] Set in contemporary Edo, *Dōke Wada sakamori* is a scene-by-scene, and sometimes line-by-line, parody of the *kōwakamai*/Jōun play. The plot follows the traditional story exactly, and though many lines are borrowed directly from the *kōwakamai* and Jōun plays, there are also numerous reworked lines and original inserts written in colloquial Edo-period language, replete with contemporary proverbs and the jargon of tradesmen, criminals, and entertainers. The play uses contemporary dances and songs and describes the objects and fashions of Edo in the 1660s and 1670s: popular foods, restaurants, clothing styles, and the names of gangs of *otokodate*.[177]

Burlesque humor and wit, clever or silly, set the tone of the play. The brothers for the most part are depicted as the daring heroes of the *kōwakamai*/Jōun version, but a few lines later they may suddenly be portrayed as stingy, bickering townsmen. The Soga brothers remain impoverished, as in traditional versions, but in *Dōke Wada sakamori* they try to make ends meet by taking part-time jobs in the

176. Yokoyama, *Ko-jōruri shōhon shū*, 6:523.

177. Ibid., 524. *Otokodate* were dashing townsmen who frequented the pleasure districts. The classic *otokodate* of Kabuki was Sukeroku. See Barbara E. Thornbury, *Sukeroku's Double Identity: The Dramatic Structure of Edo Kabuki*, Michigan Papers in Japanese Studies No. 6 (Ann Arbor: Center for Japanese Studies, The University of Michigan, 1982), 66–68, for a discussion of origins and stage presentations of *otokodate*. Yokoyama assumes that *otokodate* existed in normal life, but Thornbury contends that *otokodate* was a term used only on the stage, although deriving from actual townsmen called *machi-yakko*. I side with Yokoyama and subscribe to the argument that cites the outlandish garb of Date clan samurai as the origin of the term.

city—Gorō, for example, becomes a scrap-metal dealer. Even while performing their traditional heroic deeds the brothers tend to speak the idiom of the merchant and pleasure districts of Edo. The appeal of *Dōke Wada sakamori* derived from a new juxtaposition of a heroic medieval tale and the world in which the audience actually lived, emphasizing the "incongruity that is at the heart of comedy."[178] The juxtapositions are crude, and the play is by no means great literature, but *Dōke Wada sakamori* would have had the same appeal for Edo audiences in the 1670s as, say, *A Funny Thing Happened on the Way to the Forum* or *The Boys of Syracuse* has for contemporary American audiences. The following passage is the parody of the armor-pulling scene translated in chapter three (pp. 74–75). Original lines are in italics, with lines borrowed from the *kōwakamai*/Jōun play in normal script. References to contemporary individuals, shops, and so forth are in boldface script:

> Asahina heard the tinkle *and clank* of metal on the far side of the *shōji*.[179] "*Just as I thought, perhaps the scrap-metal merchant who frequents* **Daimonsuji, Ike no Hata, and Akasaka** *has arrived*.[180] *If it's not him it could be the apprentice from the blacksmith*. Please come in," he said, and opened the *shōji* with a slam. When he looked inside, *what* did he see?[181] It was a six-foot tall, powerfully built man, *with a shaven head and forelock, sporting a* **Tenjin beard**.[182] He wore a pure white breastplate. His great sword, *as big as* **Fujimaki Kashin's** *eight-foot five-inch long* **Ise-maru**[183] was pulled six or seven inches out of the sheath. If he attacked it seemed Gorō

178. Gilbert Highet, *The Anatomy of Satire* (Princeton: Princeton University Press, 1962), 67. The line in my text derives from the following sentence: "Parody springs from the very heart of our sense of comedy, which is the happy perception of incongruity."

179. The "clink" of metal in the *kōwakamai* play was Gorō rapping the hilt of his sword against his sheath. The action had the meaning of *en garde*. The farce version exaggerates the sound of metal because Gorō does part-time work as a scrap-metal dealer.

180. The Edo locations mentioned here would not have existed at the time of the historical Soga brothers.

181. The original text refers to Gorō as "what," not "who," as in older texts.

182. The Tenjin beard leaves the chin bare but protrudes downward at both jaws. In current "Soga *taimen*" Kabuki plays Asahina wears a Tenjin beard: see fig. 29.

183. Fujimaki Kashin was a *kabukimono* and quick-draw artist of the early Edo period. Ise-maru was presumably the name of his sword. The art of the quick draw, *iai nuki*, was made more difficult by the great length of the swords used. The goal of the quick draw was to cut down one's opponent in the same motion used to draw one's own sword.

would get the better of him, *so demonlike though he was, Asahina's knees shook, "wada, wada," and he hoped that someone would come to his aid.*[184]

"Well, Lord Gorō, since Sukenari is already in the hall, why don't you come in and have cup of sake?"

"Hey, Asahina, I'll see you tomorrow. I'm dressed for a fight, not a party."

Asahina thought, "*Gorō boasts that using snakes for ropes he can pull a boulder that usually requires 1,000 men to move it. Even though he said it in fun,* I'd like to test his strength." Saying, "So you really won't join us?" he ran nimbly over to Gorō, grabbed two or three thigh plates, and with a strong grip on Gorō's armor, pulled with an "eiya!" The effort was completely without effect. "He really is strong," thought Asahina. "I am Kobayashi no Asahina, champion among 480 men, including the ninety-three warriors of the Miura house, *fine warriors all, pure gold coins and not a plug nickel among them.*[185] If I can't pull Gorō into the hall it will be a great defeat."

Then fourteen, fifteen, twenty, thirty rippling muscles bulged one after another on Asahina's arms and shoulders, evidence of his great strength. *They looked just like the grilled rice cakes at* **Kebei's shop in Yokomachi**. The rippling muscles that covered his chest seemed like bronze needles arrayed on the surface of a *go* board.[186] The muscles rippled from his body to his forehead and back again. He looked just like a griffin standing on its hind legs or a pine entwined in *nine* wisteria vines.

Gorō watched Asahina, "What a fuss he's making!" I am Gorō, famous in the three manors of Usami, Kusumi, and Kawazu because I can ride wild horses *and eat piles of noodles. I won't let this punk Asahina pull me into the room.* If he pulls really hard, the three plates might break off, *in which case I have a long-beamed scale made by the guild master and I'll buy some scrap metal today.* Or, maybe the floor boards we're standing on will crash to the ground. Or, maybe my kneecaps will break and *I'll become a lame beggar and have to ask the master*

184. This is a pun using Asahina's family name, Wada.

185. This section combines traditional words of praise, "a warrior worth 1,000 men" (*ikki ni sennin*), with a townsman's statement of worth using the metaphor of coins, *kosen majirazu hashiba no zeni.* My translation follows the coinage metaphor.

186. Comparing the "rippling muscles" to both rice cakes and bronze needles seems to make little sense and may be a copying or printing error. In the *kōwakamai*/Jōun version Asahina's chest hair was compared to needles.

> *for alms.* One of these three is sure to happen!" He stood firmly in a powerful posture.
>
> Asahina pulled with an "eiya!" *and something had to give.* The armor broke with a snap; Asahina crashed backward onto the floor *and went unconscious. He lay there in a faint, but Gorō happened to be carrying a bottle of restorative medicine. He ran over to Asahina and poured some liquid down his mouth, whereupon Asahina regained consciousness.*[187]

To understand this seemingly unprecedented use of the Soga theme for a comic play we must turn our attention once again to the Kabuki theater. In most histories of Japanese drama we read that the close connection between the puppet theater and Kabuki, taking the form of direct competition and mutual borrowing of plays and performance techniques, began only after the banning of boys' Kabuki in 1652. In fact, the same comic actors performed for both theater forms throughout the seventeenth century. In the first half of the century they performed comic dances, traditional *kyōgen*, and *kyōgen*-like skits between dance pieces in Kabuki and between plays or between acts in the puppet drama.[188] Sometime in the second half of the century comic actors began to use comic puppets for interludes in *ko-jōruri.*[189] These interludes did not rely on one chanter to vocalize all the roles; instead comic actors spoke and sang their parts while manipulating the puppets.[190] Comic puppets were called *dōke ningyō* and were used to present *Dōke Wada sakamori.* It was performed in the manner of a comic interlude and is the only full-length *dōke ningyō* puppet farce that survives today. According to popular tradition the word *dōke* was first used by a comic actor of Kabuki, Saitō Yogorō (dates uncertain),[191] who also performed at the puppet theater of Toraya Kidayū (dates uncertain), a chanter active from the 1650s to the 1670s, immediately after the ban of boys' Kabuki. Yogorō's *dōke* art was a combination of light-hearted, rhythmic dance (derivative of folk dance) and comic

187. "Dōke Wada Sakamori," in Yokoyama *Ko-jōruri shōhon shū,* 6:422–23.

188. Shinoda and Saitō, *Noroma soroma kyōgen shūsei,* 512, describe two *ko-jōruri* programs, one with thirteen comic interludes, and one with two.

189. Ibid., 516. Throughout the seventeenth century, puppets were used to enact Noh plays, and it is likely that the first comic puppets were used for *kyōgen* plays between puppet Noh plays (ibid., 524).

190. Ibid., 516.

191. Ibid., 515–16.

acting that relied on the mimicry and exaggerated vocalization of traditional *kyōgen*. Erotic appeal had been essential to the popularity of Kabuki in its earliest days, but, after women and attractively coiffed young boys were banned from the stage, Kabuki began to rely more on performers who could do something other than charm audiences with their good looks and their dancing. In the 1650s and 1660s, while new acting techniques and types of play construction were in their formative stages, female impersonation, comic acting, and martial dance helped keep Kabuki alive.

In the 1650s through the 1670s Kabuki did not employ full scripts for most of its plays, so it is very difficult to determine the plots or scenarios presented in *dōke* Kabuki. In *ko-jōruri*, however, the tradition of preserving written texts was already well established, and the texts of many comic interludes remain. Since the same comic actors performed in both Kabuki and *ko-jōruri*, it is likely that the same or similar pieces were presented in Kabuki. The surviving texts include, remarkably, one Soga play. It is called *Takenoshita Mago Hachizaemon* and was probably first performed in the 1670s or 1680s.[192] A summary follows:

> Takenoshita is an entertainer returning home from a big New Year's party at the Hōjō mansion. Jūrō is at home with Oniō. Oniō has made New Year's calls on behalf of Jūrō to several daimyo. He has also visited Tora and has brought back a letter for Jūrō. Jūrō is unhappy because he is so poor this New Year that he cannot send a robe to Tora, and he cannot think of any way to acquire one.
>
> Takenoshita and his followers arrive at Jūrō's house and ask to be let in. Jūrō responds that it is all right for them to enter, but that they should not expect to be served anything to eat or drink. They reply that they ate their fill at the Hōjō mansion, and enter. Takenoshita talks about the various entertainments they saw at the Hōjō mansion, including a *sumo* wrestling match. One wrestler tried to use a special kick throw invented by Jūrō's father, a famed wrestler. Jūrō insists on demonstrating the throw and persuades Takenoshita to strip to the skin even though it is very cold. The whole time that Takenoshita and Jūrō have been conversing Oniō has lain hidden in the *kotatsu* (a brazier beneath the floor), and he reaches out of the *kotatsu* and steals

192. From a conversation with Shinoda Jun'ichi, the leading authority on comic puppet plays, 23 October 1982.

> Takenoshita's clothes just as Jūrō throws him violently, using his father's technique. Oniō and Jūrō escape in the ensuing confusion, and Jūrō shouts at Oniō to take the clothes to Tora.
>
> When Takenoshita gets up he is surprised to find Jūrō gone. He tells his retainers to steal something to wear from Jūrō's clothes chest but all they can find is a sleeveless undershirt. Takenoshita puts it on, and leaves, complaining of the cold. He says he cannot go home in such a sad way and calls for musical accompaniment. Takenoshita and his retainers exit singing and dancing.[193]

The plot of the interlude relies on the traditional *kyōgen* motif of clever trickery, but *Takenoshita Mago Hachizaemon*, like most comic puppet interludes, includes elements that set it apart from traditional *kyōgen*. The light-hearted, danced exit replaces the chase exit typical to *kyōgen* plays of this type. In the vast majority of traditional *kyōgen* plays, the characters have no names or individuality—they are types, such as masters, servants, peasants, swindlers, wives, and so on[194]—but in *Takenoshita Mago Hachizaemon*, Jūrō and Oniō are specific historical personages with whom the audience was well acquainted. Their portrayal here shows a new attitude toward the Soga story. The brothers' sacred mission is never alluded to; instead, Jūrō's only goal is to acquire somehow a New Year's present for his mistress, and with no compunctions he resorts to thievery. In traditional presentations of the Soga story, audiences and listeners sympathized with the brothers because of their poverty, but in *Takenoshita Mago Hachizaemon* their poverty is mocked. Jūrō is a stingy host who has nothing in his house worth stealing. The audience would not, however, have considered Jūrō an unsympathetic character. He is clever, strong, and more than a little gallant, for in his poverty he thinks not of himself but of his lover, Tora. Cleverness and gallantry were among the ideals of the townsman (*chōnin*) class, and although thievery was of course a crime, crimes could be overlooked and were even celebrated

193. The plot summary is taken from a text appearing in Shinoda and Saitō, *Noroma soroma kyōgen shūsei*, 207–12.

194. A notable exception to this rule includes the full-length *kyōgen* play performed between the acts of the Noh play *Youchi Soga*. The play is entitled *Ōtōnai*, and in it Ōtōnai describes the Soga brothers' murder of Kudō. In the *kyōgen* play *Asahina*, Asahina has died and is going to go to Hell, but he soundly thrashes Enma, the king of Hell, and escapes to Heaven.

in literature if the criminal were romantic and dashing, or if he committed his crime not out of greed but for love, or out of sheer exuberance. These kinds of characters appeared with increasing frequency on the Edo stage and are the central characters in many stories by Ihara Saikaku (1642–92), the greatest fiction writer of the Edo period.

In *Dōke Wada sakamori* the setting and the Soga brothers' speech are drawn from contemporary *chōnin* society, but their acts of heroism are exactly the same as in medieval versions of the episode. In *Takenoshita Mago Hachizaemon*, performed a few years later, Soga Jūrō appears in a short, original episode set in the historical past but embodying some of the newly emerging positive values of the *chōnin* patrons of the puppet theater. The "amorous and witty rake" was becoming as attractive a character as the "virtuous samurai embroiled in a romantic entanglement," and portrayals of Soga Jūrō would change accordingly.

SOGA PLAYS IN EARLY KABUKI

It was only after the ban of boy actors in 1652 that Soga plays began to be presented on the Kabuki stage. Unfortunately no texts remain from this early period, and performance records are very incomplete. At best we know the titles of plays, who played the leading roles, and the reception given them. The first play was *Soga juban giri*, presented at the Yamamura Theater in Edo in 1655. It is not clear how closely related the play might have been to *kōwakamai*, Noh, or *ko-jōruri*, each of which include a play called *Jūban giri*. A diary, *Kanbun nikki*, records details about the play: some fourteen or fifteen actors, clad in helmets and armor, presented a fight scene including many *misemono*,[195] in this case, probably acrobatic stunts. *Soga jūban giri* played in Edo at the beginning of the age of *kinpira jōruri*, and actors may have imitated the violence of the puppet stage. The play ran for thirty days, a long run for the time.

The second Soga Kabuki play, *Tsuizen Soga* (The Soga Memorial Service), was performed in Osaka and Sakai (a port city south of Osaka) in 1662. The same title was used for the seventh play of the one-week *ko-jōruri* series, and the Kabuki play probably derived at least loosely from the puppet play. No text or detailed description remain, but we know that the brothers' ghosts appeared in the Ka-

195. Hattori, *Kotobuki kongen Soga*, 1.

buki play, performed by dancers, and that the leading roles were Oniō, Dōsaburō, Tora, and the Soga mother.[196]

In 1663 *Wada sakamori* was performed in Kyoto. This was one year earlier than the publication of Jōun's script, but it is likely that Jōun, and perhaps other chanters, had presented prior to 1663 a puppet version of the banquet episode based closely on the *kōwakamai* play.

In the 1660s Kabuki scripts were haphazard products and were not being recorded, either for future use in the theater or to be read as story books. A passage from *Yakusha rongo* (The Actors' Analects) describes how plays were prepared in the first few decades of men's Kabuki (*yaro* Kabuki; unless the distinction is required, I will refer to *yaro* Kabuki simply as Kabuki): the leading actor decided on a plot or story and its breakdown into scenes, and with the help of an "author" or "authors" he invented speeches for the various actors. At rehearsal time the actors listened to the lines they were supposed to say, writing down at most the opening sentences of their parts. On stage they relied on their memory and imagination to fill out their roles.[197] Sometimes the leading actor handed over a plot summary to an author with the request that he use it to make a new play. The author submitted the completed play to the main actors, who exercised the right to change any lines they saw fit or to reject the play outright.[198] Kabuki actors probably treated *ko-jōruri* scripts in the same off-hand way; it is unlikely that the first Soga Kabuki plays were presented with line-for-line fidelity to the *ko-jōruri* texts upon which they appear to be based.

At the time boys' Kabuki was banned, only comic actors had received real training as actors. As plays with more complex plots and with a greater variety of characters were brought from the puppet to the Kabuki stage, many comic actors changed specialties in mid-career and took on the roles of heroes or villains.[199] The fact that so

196. Ibid. The names of the actors suggest that the roles of the brothers' ghosts were danced rather than acted: Jūrō's ghost was played by Komai Kozaemon, and Gorō's ghost by Hyōshikata Manzaemon. "Komai," literally "small dance," refers to the dance of *kyōgen*, and "Hyōshikata" literally means "rhythm man."

197. Charles J. Dunn and Bunzō Torigoe, *The Actors' Analects* (Tokyo: University of Tokyo Press, 1969), 118.

198. Ibid., 98–99.

199. See Gunji Masakatsu, *Kabuki no katachi,* vol. 2 of *Gunji Masakatsu santei shū* (Hakusuisha, 1990), 119–93, for an excellent study of the relationship between *kyōgen* and Kabuki.

many actors of the latter decades of the seventeenth century had begun their careers as comic actors has had a lasting impact on the interpretation of many roles in Kabuki. Where the title of a seventeenth-century Kabuki play is the same as a *ko-jōruri* play, we cannot assume that the former was equally serious. The titles of the first three Soga Kabuki plays suggest that, during the first decade after the end of boys' Kabuki, men's Kabuki relied heavily on *ko-jōruri* for its dramatic stories. But the Kabuki theater of the 1660s boasted neither the narrative traditions nor the acting skills to present plays in accordance with *ko-jōruri* texts. Because Kabuki did not yet use the *jōruri* chanter and *shamisen* player of puppet theater, much of the narration was omitted, and new dialogue was added. The leading roles must have been reinterpreted to suit performers with experience in dance, comic acting, and female impersonation. Audiences appear not to have minded that Kabuki actors mutilated puppet plays; rather they seem to have enjoyed the new interpretations of old heroes. As *Dōke Wada sakamori* demonstrates, it was not long before *ko-jōruri* was borrowing from Kabuki; *Dōke Wada sakamori* was performed some six to ten years after the Kabuki play *Wada sakamori* and probably drew on Kabuki conventions of comedy, as well as on earlier *ko-jōruri* texts.

In 1665 a three-act play entitled *Soga* was presented in Edo. This play, the first over two acts long in the history of Kabuki,[200] told the story of the brothers' adventures at Hakone, their parting from their mother, and, at the end, their night raid at the base of Mount Fuji. No text survives, but records indicate that the final combat scene received acclaim and that the second act was so moving that the audience wept.[201] Act 2 demonstrated that a decade after the beginning of men's Kabuki, actors of male roles were striving to express tender emotions onstage. *Soga* marked an important milestone in Kabuki because it was the first multi-act dramatic play in which it is certain that there was no pleasure-district scene. It was the closest Kabuki had yet come to a purely historical drama, and the playwright, Kawarazaki Gonnosuke, relied on material that had proven successful in the puppet theater. The play also marked a new turn toward serious drama and away from Kabuki's long-standing tradition as performance meant to exhibit the latest fashions in clothing, dance, and romantic dalli-

200. Ihara Toshirō, *Kabuki nenpyō* (Iwanami Shoten, 1956), 1:93, 95.
201. Ibid., 95.

ance. Once again the familiar Soga story was the thematic material of choice for a playwright making a significant theatrical innovation.

The next recorded Soga Kabuki play, *Kachidoki homare Soga* (The Valiant Soga Battle Cry) was performed in Edo in 1675. In this, the first Kabuki play to tell a significant portion of the story of the Soga brothers, the leading actor, Ichikawa Danjūrō I, took the part of Gorō. Chapter six will describe Danjūrō's impact on the Soga story in Kabuki.

UJI KAGANOJŌ'S CONTRIBUTIONS TO *KO-JŌRURI*

In 1675, the same year Danjūrō presented his first Soga play, a hitherto unknown *jōruri* chanter, Uji Kaganojō (1635–1711), opened a new puppet theater in Kyoto. Kaganojō was the first *jōruri* reciter who had received serious training in other vocal arts, and from the outset of his career he introduced changes to *ko-jōruri*. His innovations paved the way for the emergence of the mature puppet theater of Chikamatsu and Takemoto Gidayū.

Kaganojō began his career in *ko-jōruri* at the relatively late age of forty-one; for more than twenty years prior to 1675 he trained in *utai* (Noh singing), *kyōgen*, *heikyoku*, *kōwakamai*, and *kouta*, devoting himself primarily to *utai*. He had an excellent voice and might have become a professional Noh actor, but, as he sadly wrote in his autobiography, Noh actors taught the secrets of their art only to their sons.[202] He sought to impart to *ko-jōruri* the thematic depth, musical solidity, and sound structural framework of Noh. Although his early plays were mostly revised versions of Harima no Jō's plays, after a few years of experience in puppet theater he began to dramatize aristocratic literature not previously used there; for example, *Genji monogatari*, *Eiga monogatari* (A Tale of Flowering Fortunes), *Tsurezuregusa* (Essays in Idleness), and *yūgen* Noh plays.[203] Maintaining that "*utai* is the parent of *jōruri* singing,"[204] he brought the vocal style of *ko-jōruri* closer to Noh and emphasized the importance of musical composition,

202. Takahashi Hiroshi, "Uji Kaganojō," in *Engekishi kenkyū* (Daiichi Shobō, 1932), 147.

203. See ibid., 148, for Kaganojō's early dependence on Harima no Jō's plays, and 155, for new themes in *ko-jōruri*.

204. Ibid., 151. The quote is from Kaganojō's *Take no ko shū*. For a translation of the preface of that work, see Gerstle, *Circles of Fantasy*, 183–88.

developing a musical notation based on that of Noh.[205] Early in his career, Kaganojō, influenced by Zeami's commentaries on Noh, wrote several treatises on *jōruri* in which he expressed the high ideals of his art and insisted that performers must devote themselves wholeheartedly to their training.[206] He continued to improve the literary and musical quality of *danmono.* His most important *danmono* were *michiyuki* travel scenes, in which he interwove characters, settings, and seasons in ornamental passages that demonstrate the breadth of his knowledge of classical poetry and drama. The *michiyuki* were a standard feature of Kaganojō's plays, and he published an independent collection of them in 1678 in *Michiyuki zoroe* (An Assortment of Michiyuki).[207] His early *michiyuki* retain the nonspecific, interchangeable character of other contemporary *ko-jōruri danmono.*

Among Uji Kaganojō's greatest contributions to the puppet theater were his incorporation of the *jo-ha-kyū* structure into various levels of play crafting and his creation of a substructure of contrasting musical passages.[208] Kaganojō had mastered numerous musical forms, and he realized that musical variety was the surest means to entertain an audience for a play several hours long. It was not a totally new discovery—a glance at the scenes outlined in Harima no Jō's *Kosode koi* (Pleading for the Robe) (see pp. 89–90) show that earlier chanters likely used dramatic changes of musical style to go with changing emotions and types of scenes—but Kaganojō organized his musical segments in an over-arching *jo-ha-kyū* framework at the level of the individual act, and in the play as a whole. He did away with the standard six-act play, using instead five acts organized like the five *dan* of a Zeami play: one *jo* act, three *ha* acts, and a concluding *kyū* act. Kaganojō wrote that each act should be characterized by a distinctive musical style, but that there should be musical variety even within a single act. The variety was achieved by juxtaposing lyric

205. See ibid., 187–88, for Kaganojō's introduction to his musical notation.

206. Takahashi, "Uji Kaganojō," 150–51. Several of Kaganojō's collections and treatises have been published in Yokoyama Shigeru, *Kaganojō danmono shū* (Koten Bunko, 1958).

207. For Kaganojō's *danmono*, see ibid. Included are "Michiyuki zoroe" (1678), "Take no ko shū" (1678), and "Ōtake shū" (1680).

208. See Gerstle, *Circles of Fantasy*, 24–29, for Kaganojō's main contributions to the structure and music of puppet plays. The succeeding paragraph is based on Gerstle's work in this and subsequent sections of his book.

fushigoto interludes in different musical styles with dramatic or emotional *jigoto* scenes that carry the plot of the play forward.

In his autobiography Kaganojō claimed that he had developed his art in accord with the ideals of Noh, but a reading of his plays shows that he wrote and performed very much within the world of post-*kinpira ko-jōruri*. His audience was composed, after all, not of aristocrats and samurai but of Kyoto commoners. He included sufficient *karakuri* to satisfy audiences' delight in exciting puppetry and special effects, and he followed many of the traditions that Harima no Jō had established in his Osaka puppet theater: *giri-ninjō* conflicts and scenes of pathos and flowing tears were particularly popular among Kansai audiences.

Kaganojō performed a prodigious number of plays in his thirty-five-year career; some he wrote himself (often with the aid of disciples), some were commissioned, and still others he used more or less as he found them. His first play, presented in 1675, was a Soga play entitled *Tora tonsei ki* (An Account of Tora's Life as a Nun). No text of the play is extant, but three *danmo-no* survive because they were published in separate collections. Three Soga plays by Kaganojō bear titles identical to Noh and *kōwakamai* plays: *Kosode Soga*, *Genbuku Soga*, and *Youchi Soga*. The texts do not survive, and there is no clue to what extent they resembled Noh and *kō-wakamai*, or in what way Kaganojō may have modified traditional sources. The text of *Konge Soga* (The Origins of the Sogas) does not survive either, but its title suggests that Kaganojō borrowed a Harima no Jō play for his own production.

Although four of Kaganojō's five Soga plays appear to be derivative works, it is clear that he was not content merely to modify existing plays and traditional sources; he sought to present puppet plays that would be more effective dramatically than those of any predecessor or rival. To achieve this, he himself wrote original plays that had a superior literary quality to any previously performed in *ko-jōruri*. That was not all; he commissioned plays for his theater from the two greatest authors of the entire Edo period, Saikaku and Chikamatsu.[209]

209. The next chapter will discuss Chikamatsu's plays. Saikaku wrote *Koyomi* (The Calendar); see Keene, *World Within Walls*, 175–76, and the most important sections of *Kaijin Yashima* (The Foreigner at Yashima), if not the entire play.

UJI KAGANOJŌ AND SAKATA TŌJŪRŌ

In his treatises Kaganojō appears as a traditionalist, exalting the ideals of Noh, traditional vocal arts, and the literary models of the past, but in practice Kabuki exerted just as much influence on his art as Noh. We have already seen that in the 1660s and 1670s ***ko-jōruri*** and Kabuki had developed a symbiotic relationship of financial competition and borrowing of literary material, performers, and performance techniques. This relationship became even more intimate in the last quarter of the century. In the early part of the seventeenth century the audiences for the two arts differed considerably. ***Ko-jōruri*** drew newcomers to the city, presumably because the clarity of presentation and the traditional stories and morality appealed to people from the provinces. Kabuki, however, was frequented by patrons of the pleasure districts and by townsmen who wished they could also belong to that world and follow the latest fads in dance, fashion, jargon, and so on. In the Kansai region during the second half of the seventeenth century, ***ko-jōruri*** audiences became more sophisticated (as we can see by Harima no Jō's modifications of the ***kinpira jōruri***, and the relatively short duration of the ***kinpira jōruri*** craze). At the same time Kabuki in both regions was forced to make radical changes following the ban on boy actors. Beginning in the 1660s in Edo and the Kansai, the same theatergoers were likely to visit both the puppet and the Kabuki theaters, and this led to intense competition between them. Beginning with Okuni, Kabuki had responded to its audience's unrelenting demand for novelty, and in the second half of the seventeenth century ***ko-jōruri*** felt the same pressure. Kaganojō responded partly by broadening the literary basis of his art and by improving the music and structure of ***ko-jōruri***, but he also incorporated into his puppet theater the innovations being made in Kansai Kabuki, and it was the appearance of a new Kabuki acting style that would open up a whole new vista of literary creativity in the puppet drama.

The most important new development in Kabuki in Kyoto and Osaka was the birth of ***wagoto*** acting. ***Wagoto*** means "gentle business,"[210] and its roots go back to the ***keisei kai*** (prostititute purchasing) scenes of women's Kabuki. ***Wagoto*** scenes included brothel scenes, lovers' trysts, and scenes of heightened emotion between family mem-

210. Several American scholars, including Bowers, Ernst, and Keene, have translated the ***koto*** of theater terminology as "business," and I will follow their practise.

bers or lovers. Various terms were used in the late 1600s to describe Kabuki's emotional scenes: *keisei kai*, *nuregoto* ("damp business," referring to love and/or weeping), *kagegoto* ("shadow business," referring to "love in the shadows"), *keiseigoto* ("courtesan business," love scenes involving courtesans), and *kuzetsugoto* ("lovers' quarrel business"). The general term *wagoto* was coined in the 1720s[211] and included all of these scenes as well as the subdued, somewhat effeminate acting style employed by actors who played the roles of young lovers.

Wagoto-like scenes were staged in all puppet plays, with the exception of Edo *kinpira* pieces. Harima no Jō put scenes evoking tender emotions into his later *kinpira* plays,[212] and these kinds of scenes have been part of the Kansai puppet tradition from his time until the present. The first famous Kabuki *keiseigoto* actor was Murayama Hachirōbei (dates uncertain) of Kyoto, whose technique was described as "gentle, realistic, imbued with love."[213] He was followed by Arashi San'emon I (1635–90) who is credited with pioneering the "young lover in disguise" (*yatsushi*) role.[214]

The consummate master of *wagoto* was Sakata Tōjūrō (1647–1709). Tōjūrō was the son of a theater manager and producer (*zamoto*), and he himself became the *zamoto* of the Kyoto Mandayū Theater. Little is known of his youth, but his first major success was in 1678 as Izaemon, the young lover of the famous courtesan Yūgiri, in *Yūgiri nagori no shōgatsu* (Yūgiri's Farewell New Year). Yūgiri was a real person, a courtesan of the Shimabara pleasure district in Kyoto, who came to figure in many plays about her loves. Tōjūrō specialized in leading roles as an amorous young man. He rarely played a strong, martial character, and his dancing was notoriously poor. He was vocally very expressive, and he made acting, not dancing or displays of martial arts, the central part of his Kabuki performance. A few lines from *Nijin shū* (Dust in the Ears) reveal his philosophy of acting: "Whatever role the Kabuki actor performs, his aim must be to reflect reality," and "Gestures should not be contrived; they appear spontaneously from an excess of feeling when one is happy or angry. How can

211. Torigoe Bunzō, *Genroku kabuki kō* (Yagi Shoten, 1991), 321.
212. Takahashi, "Uji Kaganojō," 149.
213. Dōmoto, *Kamigata geinō no kenkyū*, 55.
214. *Yatsushi*, from the verb *yatsuru* (to disguise oneself), commonly referred to wealthy young men who came in disguise to the pleasure district. The term *yatsushi* came to mean the young rakes themselves.

gestures be considered external movement?"[215] Despite this espousal of intuitive acting, Tōjūrō advocated a serious study of the vocabulary, actions, and mannerisms of the character to be portrayed, especially if it was an unfamiliar role. Stories and quotations recorded in *Yakusha rongo* bring to life Tōjūrō's character and approach to the drama. He was a serious actor and a gentleman, a demanding leader who nevertheless understood the needs and limitations of subordinate actors and could elicit their best efforts.[216]

Kaganojō and Tōjūrō were close friends, and much of Kaganojō's success was due to his timely assimilation of new trends in Kabuki. Kaganojō revolutionized *ko-jōruri* by adding to his plays popular dances and songs from Kabuki and by using the language of the pleasure district for *nuregoto* scenes in historical plays. Kabuki style became an important part of his puppet drama.[217] The inspiration that Kaganojō and Tōjūrō drew from each other led to the creation of a new type of puppet and Kabuki play: the domestic-history play, or *sewa-jidai mono*.[218] The characters in these plays were drawn from medieval literature, but their loves and sorrows, not their heroics, formed the core of plays and their presentation. Although ostensibly set in the past, traditional characters spoke classical Japanese flavored with contemporary idiom and usually wore the latest fashions. *Sewa-jidai mono* gave Tōjūrō a broad new range of heroes to play, and the loves and sorrows he portrayed on stage could have a historical importance impossible in a contemporary affair between a rake and a prostitute.

Although Tōjūrō and Kaganojō wrote and presented *sewa-jidai mono*, it is difficult to say who invented the genre because, as we have seen, movement toward the form began with the declining popularity of *kinpira jōruri*. Original source works such as *Soga monogatari* and *Gikeiki* include substantial passages describing the romantic escapades of their heroes, and it was not difficult for creative playwrights to modify and expand these sections. Soga plays were among the earliest *sewa-jidai mono*, and the Soga story underwent its most radical trans-

215. Kawatake Shigetoshi, *Kabuki sakusha no kenkyū* (Tōkyō-dō, 1940), 23. For a translation of "Dust in the Ears," see Dunn and Torigoe, *The Actor's Analects*, 67–121.

216. Ibid., 187, for a list of all the places in *The Actors' Analects* where Tōjūrō is mentioned.

217. Takano Masami, *Chikamatsu to sono dentō geinō*, (Kōdansha, 1965), 136.

218. *Sewa* means "rumors," or "everyday life," or "low life." *Jidai* means "historical period."

formations in plays of this type. The best and most influential Soga *sewa-jidai mono* were written by Chikamatsu Monzaemon, the subject of the next chapter.

Chapter Five: Chikamatsu Rewrites the Soga Story

Let us turn our attention to the Soga story onstage, as it was presented around 1680, a few years before the appearance of Chikamatsu's first plays. The theatergoer might watch the whole dramatic epic unfold before him in the seven-day *ko-jōruri* sequence, or, between the acts of an unrelated play, he might see a clever Jūrō stealing clothes in a twenty-minute farce that bore little relationship to the traditional story. On the Kabuki stage popular episodes from the story were used as vehicles for martial dance or emotional scenes. In *ko-jōruri* plays dramatic scenes of confrontation were juxtaposed with tender expressions of love and the sorrow of parting, following the traditions of the *rufubon*, Noh, and *kōwakamai*, but with ever-increasing intrusions from the Edo-period theater world, including more and nastier villains and the use of contemporary vocabulary, attire, music, dance, and innovative puppetry.

Dōke Wada sakamori stands as evidence of the popularity of the Soga story. Its author assumed that puns based on the words of the traditional *Wada sakamori* would be recognized by his audience. The same play demonstrates that the audience of the 1670s thought of the Soga story as an old, traditional tale and enjoyed the incongruity of hearing an old tale retold in a new idiom and set in a contemporary city. The popularity of the medieval narrative had been due primarily to the fact that it was an exciting and moving story, but medieval reciters also used *The Tale of the Soga Brothers* to teach morality and the power of gods, Buddhas, and virtuous priests. In the 1670s the complete Soga story was being told from beginning to end in a new form, the seven-day *ko-jōruri* series, but the Soga story and its characters were also being used in new ways: to facilitate dance and exciting puppetry and to make people laugh or cry with scenes of parody and pathos. Despite new uses for the Soga story, its plot and characters remained much the same: the brothers were virtuous, heroic, and devoted to their cause; the women were faithful to their men while their men lived and devout Buddhists after the vendetta.

CHIKAMATSU, KAGANOJŌ, AND *YOTSUGI SOGA*

The career of Chikamatsu Monzaemon marks a radical change in the Soga story in Japanese drama. We have seen that, in the early Edo period, playwrights drew inspiration from the Soga narrative and from ***kōwakamai*** and Noh plays; they tried to create effective new plays by modifying these traditional sources. Chikamatsu carried these hesitant steps much farther, transforming the main characters of the Soga story into fully contemporary Edo-period types. Tora and Shōshō became archetypical courtesans of the Edo licensed pleasure district. Chikamatsu was very free in his depiction of the Soga brothers. Depending on the play, they could be dour, Edo-period samurai, devoted singlemindedly to honor and family, or they might be profligate rakes who cared not a whit about avenging their father's death. Instead of writing an occasional original scene for his plays as Tosa no Jō and Harima no Jō had done, Chikamatsu wrote fully original five-act plays with stories that supplemented or even replaced the traditional story of the vendetta. Influenced by Chikamatsu, later playwrights of the puppet and Kabuki theaters exercised remarkable freedom in the plot construction, characterizations, and thematic emphases of their Soga plays.

Chikamatsu's break with the four-hundred-year-old Soga tradition was not achieved in a single play, nor could he have made the innovations he did had he worked for a single ***jōruri*** chanter. His collaboration with three of the outstanding performers of the Edo period stimulated and even required him to completely rework the Soga story in the thirteen Soga plays that he wrote. (See appendix F for a list of the plays and their dates.)

Much has been written about Chikamatsu Monzaemon: his life, his literature, and the theatrical world in which he lived. Little is known about his early career, but two entries in ***kabuki hyōbanki*** (evaluation books) indicate that in his early twenties Chikamatsu worked as a property man, stage designer, and assistant playwright at Kyoto's Mandayū Kabuki theater, and that on at least one occasion he won acclaim for his creation of exciting effects for the stage.[219] Nevertheless, the importance of Chikamatsu's apprenticeship to Kaganojō cannot be overemphasized. One Japanese biographer wrote that the twenty-three-year-old Chikamatsu "ran to Kaganojō's newly opened theater" to work with him.[220] Kaganojō's class and background resembled Chikamatsu's: both were from samurai families, both had studied aristocratic arts (in Kaganojō's case, Noh, and in Chikamatsu's, court poetry), and Chikamatsu may have been disowned by his family as Kaganojō had been.[221] During Chikamatsu's early years of apprenticeship he wrote plays or parts of plays, but all were published under Kaganojō's name. Debates over authorship still continue, and we will probably never know for certain which plays or acts Chikamatsu wrote. There is evidence that he may have written up to fifteen plays published under Kaganojō's name, but Kaganojō probably exercised a strong controlling hand, supplying his student with plot frameworks and requiring *nuregoto, fushigoto,* and special-effects scenes at certain places in these plays.[222] We can assume, however, that the puppet plays whose published texts identify Chikamatsu as the author were Chikamatsu's plays despite the fact that he was still working with and for Kaganojō. Chikamatsu was the first professional playwright in Japan's history. All of the great playwrights who preceeded him were primarily performers, whereas Chikamatsu never performed in a play.

The earliest play that is unquestionably by Chikamatsu is *Yotsugi Soga*, published and performed in 1683. It is a work that embodies an exciting new approach to traditional literature and drama. The play was a tremendous success, and there is no question that Chikamatsu sensed precisely what kinds of stories and scenes his audience craved—innovations that would excite with their novelty yet leave no one baffled or confused. Chikamatsu told a new Soga story in *Yotsugi Soga*, and the play has an innovative opening: instead of the customary "And then" of *kōwakamai* and *ko-jōruri*, Chikamatsu begins with a brief poetic (*fushigoto*) description of Fuji Plain in the fifth month. The passage introduces the time and location of the first action in the play, Yoritomo's interrogation of Gorō the day after the vendetta.

219. Ihara Toshirō, *Kabuki nenpyō* 1. References to Chikamatsu are excerpted from the following *hyōbanki*: "Kokin yakusha daizen" and "Ukagami," pp. 128 and 165.
220. Kawatake Shigetoshi, *Chikamatsu Monzaemon* (Yoshikawa Hiroshi Bunken, 1958), 20.
221. Ibid., 24.
222. Ibid., 25.

The opening passage concludes with a statement praising Yoritomo for bringing peace to the nation. The new opening may derive from the *shidai* or *sashi* passages that begin many Noh plays, but Chikamatsu's passage is in his own style, neither grammatically nor stylistically copied from any opening passage in Noh. The beginning of *Yotsugi Soga* changed forever the convention of opening puppet plays and paved the way for experimentation and development. In time the introductory sections of these plays came to include some of the finest poetry in the genre.

To write a new Soga story was a radical departure from tradition, but Chikamatsu's construction of the first act ensured that his audience would be able to follow the plot of the play and his new approach to the story. Immediately after the unconventional opening, Chikamatsu described the shogun's interrogation of Gorō in a scene very close to the *kōwakamai/ko-jōruri* version with which the audience was familiar. In this scene Chikamatsu introduced the heroes and villains of his play and set forth the heroes' task. Oniō and Dōsaburō, the Soga brothers' two faithful servants, will attempt to kill Inubōmaru (Kudō Suketsune's son, who later uses his adult name, Arai Kotōta) and Shinkai Arashirō, two men who insult Gorō during the course of the interrogation. Oniō and Dōsaburō's mission parallels the Soga brothers' well-known quest. Chikamatsu was the first playwright to use a first act close to traditional sources in order to introduce an original play.

At the beginning of the second act, Oniō and Dōsaburō fall to quarreling over who should carry out the vendetta and who should carry the Soga brothers' keepsakes back to their mother. The quarrel parodies the Soga brothers' harmonious relationship and their sufferings. For example, when the older Oniō threatens to disown Dōsaburō, the punishment that caused Gorō so much anguish, Dōsaburō retorts that he does not care a whit if he is disowned and threatens to disown his elder brother in turn. The two brothers almost come to blows and part in anger.

Tora and Shōshō are the main characters of the second act. For the first time in the puppet theater they are convincingly portrayed as courtesans of a contemporary brothel. They pine for their sweethearts and discuss their love in the idiom of the pleasure district: "He came to me from the time I was a young novice, and we grew more and more intimate. I cut off my little finger for him, gave him locks of my hair, tattooed myself as pledge of my love, and felt no shame if others knew."[223]

The two villains, Kotōta and Arashirō, appear at the brothel and make crude advances to Tora and Shōshō, only to be driven away by Oniō, who is ignorant of their identity. Oniō tells the women of the vendetta, and they lament the deaths of their lovers. Oniō gives the keepsakes to the women to take to Soga village, and they tell him that the two enemies he has been seeking were the very ruffians he just chased away. Oniō hurries off in pursuit.

Tora and Shōshō travel from Ōiso to Soga village with the keepsakes, and their journey is described in a *michiyuki*. A comparison of the *michiyuki* in *Yotsugi Soga* and in Kaganojō's *Tora tonsei ki* shows that Chikamatsu, although still much indebted to his teacher, had already begun to experiment with the form.[224] Both *michiyuki* consist of melancholy remembrances expressed in images of evanescence. The language and the flow of the two passages are much alike, but Chikamatsu's *michiyuki* is more closely tied to the characters in the play. The names of Tora, Shōshō, and the Soga brothers are mentioned. Both *michiyuki* present a succession of poetic images and allusions, but in Chikamatsu's the ladies' horse plays an important part throughout the passage. It is mentioned as Jūrō's last gift to Tora (following the *rufubon*), and it is compared to the horse that the Buddha rode when he left lay life to seek the Way. The puppet horse would have given this *michiyuki* unique staging. Characters in *michiyuki* usually walk, but the women in *Yotsugi Soga* often ride together on the horse. They dismount several times along the way, and their stops emphasize the importance of locations connected with the memory of the Soga brothers. The neigh of the horse is contrasted with the ladies' weeping. In this *michiyuki* Chikamatsu's concern with original staging, occasional references to the actual geography of the ladies' journey, and focus on the feelings of specific characters appear as tentative first steps taken in a process that would culminate with the splendid *michiyuki* of his "domestic plays" (*sewamono*).

After the *michiyuki*, Tora and Shōshō arrive at the mother's home and are greeted by the Soga brothers' sister, who tells them that

223. Chikamatsu Monzaemon, "Yotsugi Soga," *Chikamatsu zenshū*, edited by Fujii Otoo (Asahi Shinbunsha, 1925), 2:21.

224. For the *michiyuki* in "Ōiso Tora tonsei ki," see Yokoyama, *Kaganojō danmono shū*, 17–19. For the "Tora Shōshō michiyuki" in "Yotsugi Soga," see Chikamatsu, *Chikamatsu zenshū*, 2:26–29.

her mother is prostrate with anxiety for her sons. Tora and Shōshō inform the sister that they intend to become nuns, but first they want to give the mother keepsakes of her sons. The sister tells them not to break the tragic news directly, but to put on the brothers' clothes and impersonate them (see fig. 17). The ensuing dance scene derives from the Noh play *Fumisaki Soga*, but in the Noh play the lyrics for the dance describe the splendor of the Fuji hunt, including a *mon-tsukushi* (a poetic list of the samurai crests on the tents in the camp on Fuji Plain),[225] a description of the incident in which Jūrō's horse stumbled when he shot at Kudō, but only one sentence on the night raid and the killing of Kudō Suketsune. In Chikamatsu's *fushigoto* passage Tora and Shōshō describe the consummation of the vendetta and the brothers' fight with ten men, the "Jūban giri" episode. Chikamatsu mixed lines from various traditional sources with original lines so deftly that the "Tora Shōshō jūban giri" stands as a virtuoso account of the brothers' last hours (see pp. 141–42 for an analysis and translation of the opening section of this passage).

In *Yotsugi Soga* the mother collapses in tears when Tora and Shōshō tell her that her sons are dead, but her spirits are somewhat restored when Tora shows her Jūrō's three-year-old son, Sukewaka. Now the mother weeps as her grandchild sits on her lap clapping his hands. It is an image of striking contrasts, youth versus age, and hope versus despair.

The fourth act is again set in the pleasure district where Kotōta and Arashirō return to visit Tora and Shōshō. This time they seize little Sukewaka. The women are astonished and horrified, but their pathetic and desperate pleading does not move the callous villains. Finally Tora and Shōshō decide to use their feminine wiles. They pretend to be attracted to the villains and treat them to a drinking party, while at the same time secretly sending for help. When the villains are drunk, the women tell them that Oniō and Dōsaburō are coming and suggest that the villains hide in two large chests, which they do. Asahina arrives and a *karakuri* scene ensues: Asahina puts a huge boulder on top of each chest, trapping the villains. One smashes his way out but is squashed by a falling boulder, and the other is captured (see fig. 18). Perhaps Chikamatsu's chest scene was inspired by the Noh play *Hitsukiri Soga*, but there is no way to be sure.

225. The *tsukushi* or "literary list" has its origins in the pillow words of Japanese court poetry. Lists of items were an important part of Sei Shonagon's *Makura no sōshi* (Pillow Book, ca. A.D. 1000).

Fig. 17. Above: Tora and Shōshō don the Soga brothers' robes and dance before the brothers' mother and sister. Below: the Tora, Shōshō *michiyuki*. From Chikamatsu's *Yotsugi Soga*, 1684. Courtesy of the Tokyo Geijutsu Daigaku Collection.

Fig. 18. Above: Asahina crushes villains with boulders as Tora and Shōshō look on, holding the Soga heir. From Chikamatsu's *Yotsugi Soga*, 1684. Courtesy of the Tokyo Geijutsu Daigaku Collection.

In the first scene of the fifth act Tora appears before Yoritomo and asks that he pardon the surviving villain. Her compassion stands in contrast to the fury of Asahina in the previous scene. The play concludes with a celebratory and decorative *fūryū* dance performed by Tora and Shōshō for Yoritomo. The lyrics of this scene describe the four seasons in the pleasure district and the feelings of courtesans while waiting for the men they love. The play ends with a new sense of worldly success and felicity: the brothers' fame will live forever, and so will the Soga family, thanks to Tora and the Soga heir, Sukewaka.

The innovations that Chikamatsu made in *Yotsugi Soga* had a lasting impact on popular perceptions of the Soga story, and on the art of *jōruri* play writing as well. Lyrical opening passages and topical *michiyuki* became standard features of puppet plays. A Soga heir figures in many later plays, and "hiding in chest" scenes became so numerous as to seem trite. All literary historians agree that the conversion of Tora and Shōshō into contemporary courtesans was a significant breakthrough in the development of Edo-period dramatic literature. Earlier *ko-jōruri* had given the heroines of medieval and classical literature the superficial traits of contemporary courtesans. In *Dōke Wada sakamori*, for example, Tora's speech includes the jargon of the pleasure district, but her actions follow the traditional story. In *Yotsugi Soga* Tora and Shōshō live in the pleasure quarter, speak the language, and express the thoughts and feelings of professional courtesans. Tora and Shōshō do not become nuns as they had in every previous narrative and dramatic account; instead, at the end of the play they become matrons of a wealthy brothel. Although they mention in act 3 that they plan to become nuns, their lives as entertainers are so important that the ladies never actually take the tonsure.

Tora and Shōshō are professional entertainers, and in four scenes the Tora and Shōshō puppets danced and "sang" in contemporary styles, putting the audience in the position of surreptitious pleasure-district clients outside the theater's "fourth wall." The four scenes are the *michiyuki*, the "Tora Shōshō jūban giri" dance, the drinking party for the villains, and the *fūryū* dance for Yoritomo. The last three were typical entertainment scenes used in Kabuki, and their inclusion attests to the popularity of Kabuki, as well as to audience interest in puppet imitation of popular dances. Despite a significant change in the portrayal of Tora and Shōshō, they are just as virtuous in *Yotsugi Soga* as in the traditional versions of the Soga story. In the women of *Yotsugi Soga* we see, for the first time in the Soga story, feminine virtue completely detached from religious devotion. Tora and Shōshō are the first of many virtuous and strong courtesans that Chikamatsu would create for his plays. These women are completely faithful to the men they love, even if that fidelity sometimes requires them to sacrifice their own lives. They are beautiful and talented entertainers, but they are also intelligent, resourceful, and compassionate. Thanks in part to Chikamatsu, onstage, courtesans in love became the new secular model of feminine virtue for the commoner class.

Many elements of *Yotsugi Soga* are clearly the result of Kaganojō's instruction: (1) the use of sources from various traditions—court poetry, Noh, popular dance, Kabuki, *kōwakamai*; (2) an important *karakuri* scene; and (3) the use of a *michiyuki* as the central poetic passage. But Chikamatsu's play surpassed his teacher's previous efforts in its effective interweaving of historical characters and contemporary settings in an original plot.

Chikamatsu crafted *Yotsugi Soga* to suit Kaganojō's pattern of varying musical styles in an overall play structure based on *jo ha kyū*. In this play we clearly see what C. Andrew Gerstle calls the "cyclical construction," which would characterize Chikamatsu's later history plays.[226] History plays usually open on an exalted plane, in the court of a nobleman or daimyo, with images of beauty and harmony. The harmony is threatened or destroyed during the first act. In the second act the action descends into the world of commoners, and outright conflict is almost certain to occur. The lowest point is reached in the third act, in which occurs the most painful suffering and the most tragic events of the play. In the fourth act the suffering and tension are relieved, usually by a decorative *fushigoto* scene or by the lighthearted physical action of a *karakuri* scene. In the fifth act the action returns to the exalted plane of the first act, the outstanding problems are resolved, and harmony is restored.

The concept of human events and history as being cyclical in nature derives from Buddhist thought, and a cyclical structure was used in numerous works of traditional literature.[227] *The Tale of the Soga Brothers* itself, both in *manabon* and *kanabon* versions, corresponds

226. Gerstle, *Circles of Fantasy*, 68–111, examines the cyclical structure of four history plays by Chikamatsu (including *Yotsugi Soga*). Musical and compositional charts of *Yotsugi Soga* can be found on pages 76–77.

227. Gerstle (ibid., 64–68) discusses the Buddhist origins of the cyclical patterns that organize many works of traditional Japanese literature. He concentrates his focus on the cyclical structure of *Heike monogatari*.

almost exactly to Chikamatsu's cyclical structure for history plays. It begins with the creation of Japan and a description of a unified noble family and then descends into warfare and internecine strife that reduces the Soga boys to penury and orphanhood. A little more than halfway through the tale the brothers die tragically. At this point the movement begins to ascend to a higher social and moral plane. The shogun recognizes the brothers' heroism, they are deified, and the heroines live and teach as paragons of Buddhist compassion and virtue. The seven-play, *ko-jōruri* Soga tale had, as a matter of course, retained the source story's cyclical nature. Chikamatsu recognized that story and structure could be considered separately, for in *Yotsugi Soga* he wrote a new story, structuring it in a traditional way that was for his audience both convincing and satisfying. *Yotsugi Soga* was a model *sewa-jidaimono.* Chikamatsu and Kaganojō used scenes and motifs from this play again and again, and Chikamatsu rewrote it as a Kabuki play for Tōjūrō to perform. It was a popular sensation, and it launched Chikamatsu's brilliant career.

The next Soga play that Kaganojō presented he wrote himself: *Yoritomo hamaide* (*Yoritomo on the Beach*).[228] Kaganojō's only original contribution to the Soga story occurs in the second act, when Kudō's retainers seize the Soga brothers' house by force from their mother and her retainers. In the rest of the play Kaganojō follows the traditional story, changing it only to dramatize scenes of suffering even more strongly than they appear in earlier works. In this play Tora and Shōshō become nuns.

Yoritomo hamaide demonstrates that despite the popularity of Chikamatsu's *Yotsugi Soga*, the composition of Soga puppet plays would not be changed overnight. Kaganojō used the cyclical plot structure described above. But unlike *Yotsugi Soga*, *Yoritomo hamaide* was not particularly successful.[229] The structure of the two plays is the same, and we can assume that Kaganojō's musical composition and vocalization was equally competent for both plays. There is no reason to assume that the manipulation of puppets was more or less skillful for either play. The major difference in the two plays is the literary text. Judged in comparison with Chikamatsu's later plays, *Yotsugi Soga* is no masterpiece, but it was much more innovative than *Yoritomo*

228. Takano Masami, "Chikamatsu Sogamono kō," *Kokugo to kokubungaku* 10.4 (1933): 150. Some sources attribute the play to Chikamatsu, but analysis of the play's literary style supports Takano's conclusion.

229. Conversation with Shinoda Jun'ichi, 23 November 1982.

hamaide. Its characters are more up-to-date, and it abounds with new scenes and events. What attracted Chikamatsu to the puppet theater must have been the fact that given the soundness of Kaganojō's ideas on musical structure, and the quality of his presentational style, the ingenuity of literary texts could determine theatrical success.

In *Ōiso Tora osana monogatari* (The Story of Tora's Childhood), presented in 1694,[230] Chikamatsu added another original chapter to the traditional Soga story. The play tells the story of Tora's girlhood, interweaving material from the Yoshitsune and Soga traditions.[231] Shizuka Gozen, Yoshitsune's mistress, is a leading character. The plot framework is a vendetta story in which Tora and her brother strive to kill Kajiwara Kagehisa, their father's murderer. With Jūrō's help they succeed in their vendetta, killing Kagehisa at the Fuji hunt. Jūrō and Gorō are relatively unimportant characters.

In both of Chikamatsu's early Soga plays the Soga brothers are peripheral figures. Where they do appear they retain the personalities and motivations of the traditional story. Scenes including both the brothers and their mistresses are rare, and the few Chikamatsu wrote describe a conflict or confrontation with a third character. In early Genroku-period Kabuki plays, courtesans' lovers were invariably meek and dissipated young men, so Chikamatsu probably found it difficult to change the brothers characters to fit the "young lover" role necessary for romantic scenes in the pleasure district.[232] There was no precedent for an erotic or romantic scene between a historical, martial hero and an Edo-period courtesan. The presentational demands

230. The *jōruri* performance dates I use are based on the Gidayū Nenpyō Kinsei Hen Kankōkai, ed., *Gidayū nenpyō: kinsei hen,* 6 vols. (Yagi Shoten, 1979). It is now regarded as the most authoritative source. The entry for *Ōiso Tora tonsei monogatari* in volume 2, page 12, of this work gives 1694 as the date of the first known performance but states that there may have been earlier performances. Noda Yukio, "*Soga monogatari* to Chikamatsu," *Koten kenkyū* 6.10 (1941): 36, cites 1702 as the first performance date. Yokoyama Tadashi, "Chikamatsu no Soga jōruri," *Kokugo to kokubungaku* 25.6 (1956): 14, and Takano, *Chikamatsu to sono dentō geinō,* 133, guess that the play may have been performed as early as 1687.

In general I am going to refrain from participating in disputes over publication and performance dates.

231. In Kabuki the practice of interweaving characters from different fictional "worlds" is called *naimaze.* Thornbury, *Sukeroku's Double Identity,* 28, discusses *naimaze* in Soga Kabuki. Although the term was coined in the eighteenth century, the practice began much earlier.

232. Kitano Beni, "Chikamatsu Soga jōruri: seikaku byōsha o chūshin to shite," *Jissen bungaku* 16 (1962): 35.

of the puppet theater, the choice of puppet heads, and conventions of manipulation reinforced the conservatism of *jōruri* play crafting. As Takano Masami puts it, "in Chikamatsu's early plays we find *nuregoto* and *fushigoto* scenes in which the women talk about love or suffer because of love, but no *keiseigoto*" (actual love scenes with courtesans).[233] *Keiseigoto* love scenes were introduced to *sewa-jidaimono* puppet plays a few years after *Yotsugi Soga*,[234] but the contradiction between the traditional Soga brothers and the "young lover" role was too great for them to appear immediately in love scenes with the contemporary courtesans that Tora and Shōshō had become.[235]

CHIKAMATSU'S SOGA KABUKI PLAYS

After his apprenticeship to Kaganojō, Chikamatsu became a professional, nonperforming playwright, the first in Edo theater, and although he wrote plays for both Kaganojō and Takemoto Gidayū, Kaganojō's brilliant student of chant, the next artist to profoundly influence Chikamatsu was Sakata Tōjūrō. Chikamatsu wrote thirty-one Kabuki plays between 1685 and 1703, and in more than half Tōjūrō played the leading role. Some of Tōjūrō's greatest successes were achieved acting in Chikamatsu's plays. During most of his career as a Kabuki playwright Chikamatsu served as one of two staff playwrights at the Mandayū Theater in Kyoto. The other playwright was Kaneko Ikkō (d. 1728) (also called Kaneko Kichizaemon) who also worked onstage as the leading comic actor in the Mandayū Theater company. Entries in Ikkō's recently discovered 1698 diary indicate that plays previously thought to be solely by Chikamatsu were in fact collaborations for which Ikkō often did most of the work. Printed, illustrated versions of the plays, called *e-iri kyōgen bon*, were published after the plays' stage runs, and they were all signed by Chikamatsu, with no reference to Ikkō. Thanks to Kaganojō, Chikamatsu had already developed a relationship with Kyoto publishers,[236] and he modified the stage scripts for publication. It is likely that Ikkō allowed

233. Takano, *Chikamatsu to sono dentō geinō*, 137.

234. The first *keiseigoto* as part of a *jōruri* play appeared in Saikaku's *Koyomi* (The Calendar). He wrote it for Kaganojō, who performed the play in 1685 (Kitano, "Chikamatsu Soga jōruri," 35).

235. Ibid., and Takano, "Chikamatsu Sogamono kō," 130.

236. Suwa Haruo, "'Kaneko Ikkō nikki' ni miru Chikamatsu to Kaneko Kichizaemon no kankei," *Kabuki kenkyū to hihyō* 11 (1993): 43.

Chikamatsu to take sole credit for published versions of their collaborative work because Chikamatsu needed the income more than Ikkō did.[237] As a leading actor, Ikkō's salary at the Mandayū Theater was much higher than that of a mere playwright.

Only twenty of Chikamatsu's Kabuki texts survive as *e-iri kyōgen bon,* and they vary greatly, ranging from novelizations and summaries of plays to more thorough reproductions of onstage dialogue and narration. Unfortunately many Chikamatsu-Ikkō Kabuki texts were lost before publication, having been cremated with Tōjūrō in 1709.[238]

In 1695 Tōjūrō played Jūrō in Chikamatsu's first Soga Kabuki collaboration, *Soga tayū zome* (The Soga Infatuation with Courtesans), performed as part of a Kansai Kabuki custom of presenting Soga plays in the *bon* season "in a spirit of reverence for the Soga brothers."[239] The seventh month *bon* festival is a celebration of the return of the spirits of dead ancestors, but, given the spirit of the *bon* holiday, the reader will be surprised to find a very irreverent treatment of the Soga brothers in Chikamatsu's *bon* plays. Chikamatsu's Soga Kabuki plays clearly owe as much to earlier, satirical Kabuki plays as they do to *Yotsugi Soga* and *Ōiso Tora osana monogatari.*

We know that Jūrō was portrayed as a *wagoto* character in at least two Kabuki plays before 1695,[240] but just one text survives for a pre-Chikamatsu Soga Kabuki play. *Wakoku fūryū kyōdai kagami* (The Japanese Mirror of Stylish Brothers), of unknown authorship, was performed in Osaka in 1694. In this play Jūrō and Gorō are the main characters, but the plot of the play is considerably different from the traditional story. Several traditional motifs are presented in a new sequence and in the form of absurdly improbable *shukō.* The pardon of Gorō is an example: Gorō and his mother meet by chance at a mountain pass barrier gate, where Gorō begs her to pardon him. She adamantly refuses, even when he threatens to kill himself, and she slips through the barrier gate just before it closes for the night. Gorō then smashes down the gate, and the barrier guard thus prepares to shoot

237. Ibid., 43–44.

238. Gunji Masakatsu, *Kabuki no hassō* (Kōbundō, 1959), 192.

239. Gunji Masakatsu, *Kabuki ronsō* (Kyoto: Shibungaku Shuppan, 1979), 282. The reference he cites is the *hyōbanki* (actor evaluation book) *Yakusha mannenreki,* 1700.

240. The Edo play was *Kamakura kōshoku gonin onna* (Five Women of Kamakura Who Loved Love), and the Osaka play was *Soga nage Shimada* (The Soga Shimada Hairdo).

him down (see fig. 19). At this point Gorō's mother runs back to Gorō, and, revealing her true feelings, she throws herself in front of her son to shield him from hostile arrows. She pardons Gorō on the spot. The guard hurls down his weapons and shouts congratulations—he has orchestrated the entire pardon scenario at the command of feudal lords who support the Soga brothers.

The author of the play invented several more scenes of the same sort. In one, possibly deriving from *kyōgen*,[241] the villain Yawata impersonates the ghost of Itō Sukechika in an attempt to trick Gorō into making a hopeless attack on the shogun Yoritomo. In the concluding scene, Kudō attends a grand banquet at a brothel in the pleasure district. Jūrō and Gorō impersonate comic performers and assassinate their enemy during the *kyōgen* performance.

One scholar calls the play "exasperatingly nonsensical" and suggests that Tōjūrō wanted better Soga plays to perform in.[242] Nevertheless, the single example of *Wakoku fūryū kyōdai kagami* suggests that Chikamatsu and Ikkō's use of disguises and scenes from comic plays probably derives from earlier Kabuki plays presented in the Kansai. The one martial scene in *Soga tayū zome* displays elements of Edo *aragoto* acting, probably inspired by Ichikawa Danjūrō's *aragoto* art. The play was written just one year after Danjūrō had spent a full season performing in Kyoto, and we know from the Ikkō diary that both Chikamatsu and Ikkō worked hard to build on the success of actors in other troupes as well as the work of rival playwrights (see the following chapter for a detailed discussion of the impact of Danjūrō's *aragoto* acting on Edo Soga Kabuki plays).

Chikamatsu's *e-iri kyōgen bon* version of *Soga tayū zome* is the first surviving Soga play certain to have been a *bon* play, and it represents another major break from the traditional Soga story. Tōjūrō had probably played Jūrō before, and Chikamatsu made Jūrō the leading character in his play. The Soga brothers reentered Chikamatsu's Soga world as protagonists, but Jūrō's character was redesigned to fit Tōjūrō's "young lover" acting specialization. The women of the story were made more erotic by their male disguises: male actors of course played Tora and Shōshō, and it was a special challenge for them to appear feminine even when dressed in male garb. The following plot

241. In the *kyōgen* play *Buaku* the hero impersonates his own ghost to convince an enemy that he is already dead.
242. Takano, "Chikamatsu Sogamono kō," 134.

Fig. 19. Gorō smashes the barrier gate as his mother looks on. From the *e-iri kyōgen bon* of *Wakoku fūryū kyōdai kagami*, ca. 1694. Courtesy of the Tokyo Geijutsu Daigaku Collection.

summary illustrates that this play marks a major turning point in playwrights' approaches to the traditional Soga story:

> Act 1. A Shrine in Hakone: The play opens with a *shidai* passage exactly like the opening of a Noh play.[243]
>
> Oniō and Dōsaburō pray for the success of the Soga brothers' vendetta. Two daughters of Wada Yoshimori appear and ask Oniō and Dōsaburō to arrange marriages for them with the Soga brothers. The girls' conversation is flirtatious and bantering in a way completely unbecoming the daughters of a samurai, the first instance of such dialogue in Chikamatsu's Soga plays. The retainers explain that the brothers are infatuated with their courtesan mistresses and are uninterested in marrying anyone else. Tora has borne Jūrō a son, and Jūrō is so attached to her and the child that he has lost interest in the vendetta. The retainers reveal that they have kidnapped the baby in hopes of breaking Tora's hold on Jūrō.
>
> Kudō Suketsune and his men arrive and recognize Oniō and Dōsaburō. Kudō, a fierce Kabuki villain, glares malevolently at Oniō and Dōsaburō. An argument ensues and Oniō and Dōsaburō beat two of Kudō's henchmen, Ōmi and Yawata, with sticks. Just as it appears an unequal fight will begin, Zenjibō rides up and chases away Kudō and his retainers. Zenjibō is the only martial hero of the play, but he appears only in this brief scene. Oniō and Dōsaburō lose the Soga baby in the confusion of the fight.
>
> Act 2. A Roadside Teahouse: Tora and Jūrō have put on disguises to go in search of their child. She impersonates a young boy and Jūrō pretends to be her servant. The two meet Gorō and Shōshō, also in disguise, at a roadside teahouse. Gorō is disguised so that he can approach his mother (she has disowned him and driven him from home), and Shōshō is disguised as a young dandy. The ladies finally discover the true identities of everybody and bring the brothers together for the first time "since they were five and three years old."[244] In this scene Tora finds her baby, only to have it immediately snatched away by the villain Ōmi. The Soga brothers

243. Tōjūrō used elements of Noh and *kyōgen* in his presentations, and in this play Chikamatsu incorporated scenes and techniques from both. See Gunji, *Kabuki no hassō*, 157–60, for uses of Noh and *kyōgen* in Genroku Kabuki.

244. Chikamatsu Monzaemon, "Soga tayū zome," in *Chikamatsu kabuki kyōgen shū*, edited by Takano Tatsuyuki (Rinsen Shoten, 1926), 2:501. Chikamatsu dramatized the reunion by saying that the brothers have been parted for many more years than was the case in any traditional source.

immediately pursue the villain and cut off his head, killing the man who "actually shot their father."[245]

Act 3, scene 1. Tora's Brothel in the Pleasure District: Tora's matron is a greedy and heartless woman who wants to make a handsome profit by selling Tora to Kudō. Tora has a stupid and ugly sister in the brothel whom she easily and coldly manipulates. Tora wants to delay Kudō by sending him the tip of her little finger as a pledge of love, but she has already cut hers off (presumably both hands) and sent them to Jūrō. So Tora tricks her sister, cuts off her sister's finger with a kitchen knife, and sends it to Kudō. The pledge notwithstanding, Kudō's retainer Yawata insists on taking Tora to Kudō's mansion right away. Tora puts on a Noh costume to impersonate an old woman, but, after initial bewilderment, Yawata recognizes Tora and drags her away.

Act 3, scene 2. Just outside the Pleasure District: Jūrō has a second courtesan mistress, Kamegiku. The brothel owner is angry with her for squandering her attention on the penniless Jūrō, so he takes her out of the pleasure district, ties her to a tree, and beats her mercilessly. The Soga brothers look on but are too cowardly to intervene. They untie Kamegiku after the owner leaves. Kamegiku slanders Tora, saying that Tora has gone to Kudō of her own free will. Jūrō believes the story and pledges his love to Kamegiku. Wada Yoshimori and Kudō appear, on their way to a big party in the pleasure district. Yoshimori invites the brothers to join him at the party.

Act 3, scene 3. Tora's Brothel, at Kudō's Party: The brothers are called upon to enact the ***kyōgen*** play ***Hanago.*** Unknown to the brothers, Tora has been given the third part in the play. Chikamatsu skillfully interweaves the plot of the ***kyōgen*** play with the confused relationship between Jūrō and Tora. While performing the play, Jūrō and Tora confront each other unexpectedly and are unable to continue. Instead they break character and shout at one another, each accusing the other of infidelity. Their fighting spoils Kudō's fun, so he drags Tora off with him to another room. When Tora prepares for bed she persuades her sister to take her place with Kudō. Tora then leads the brothers into Kudō's room so they can kill him. After the vendetta the brothers place themselves in the custody of Wada Yoshimori. Wada pretends to

245. Ibid., 2:502. Note that this does not correspond to the ***rufubon,*** which states that Ōmi missed with his arrow and that Yawata actually killed the brothers' father.

fight the brothers, but he purposely lets them escape, and the play ends on this felicitous note.

Soga tayū zome represents the most definitive thematic change of course in the Soga tradition since its birth as an oral tale. In this Kabuki play the Soga brothers have changed from virtuous heroes to erotically attractive but cowardly opportunists. The plot of the play relies on the romantic escapades that were the staple of Tōjūrō's art, and Tōjūrō's plays gave center stage to young philanderers. Gorō retains his short temper, but he shows no bravery or intelligence. Only once do the brothers show personal initiative—when they pursue and kill a villain. In the rest of the play the retainers, Tora, and Wada Yoshimori lead the brothers to accomplish a revenge they could clearly never manage on their own. Tōjūrō's Jūrō was emotional and romantic but a weak character—a typical "young lover." Strong, martial characters are unimportant.

In the play the Soga story lost its tragic character entirely, emerging as a sort of comic melodrama. The play's structure resembles certain European comedies that begin with a situation of confusion and concealed identity: in *Soga tayū zome* the brothers and their mistresses do not recognize each other because of their disguises, Tora's baby is lost, and the brothers have no intention of avenging their father. The confusion continues until after the *kyōgen* play in act 3, scene 3, when Tora and Jūrō are reconciled. The play ends with an understanding between the "good" characters: the brothers, Tora, and Wada Yoshimori. For the first time in the Soga tradition, it is explicitly stated that the brothers do not die as a result of the vendetta, but get off scot-free.

Chikamatsu's use of *Hanago*, the famous *kyōgen* play about concealed identity and infidelity, stands out because it mirrored the love triangle already established in *Soga tayū zome*. The "play within a play" device followed naturally from the use of other semi-independent scenes, such as *michiyuki* and *danmono*. The Soga brothers perform a *kyōgen* play in the last act of *Wakoku fūryū kyōdai kagami*, and Saikaku expanded on the *Hanago* plot when he wrote *Kaijin Yashima* (The Foreigner at Yashima), presented by Kaganojō in 1685,[246] but *Hanago*

246. The *Ayatsuri nendai ki* (1727) credits Saikaku with writing the play. In Kaganojō's "Kotake shū" (see Yokoyama, *Kaganojō danmono shū*), Kaganojō states that Saikaku wrote the important sections of the play: the *michiyuki*, an adaptation from the Noh play *Ataka*, and the section based on the *kyōgen* play *Hanago*.

was not performed as an autonomous play within Saikaku's work. The use of plays within plays became a recurrent structural device in Chikamatsu's dramaturgy.

Two years after *Soga tayū zome*, Tōjūrō took the leading role in Chikamatsu's second Soga Kabuki play, *Daimyō Soga* (A Soga Play for the Feudal Lord). It was a rewritten version of *Yotsugi Soga* and was presented as a *bon* play. A comparison of the puppet and Kabuki plays is an extremely valuable exercise, clearly demonstrating Chikamatsu's approaches to the different requirements of the two arts in the middle of the Genroku period. Some of the more important points include:

> 1. The Kabuki version begins as a "play within a play." In the first act a daimyo and his retainers decide to stage a Soga play. The conflicts among the members of the daimyo retinue are interwoven with the plot of *Yotsugi Soga*. Disguises and confused identities were essential to late seventeenth-century Kabuki, and playwrights experimented with the "play within a play" artifice for the purpose of creating multiple identities for characters. Chikamatsu later used a "play within a play" framework in the opening scene of perhaps his best Kabuki play, *Keisei Mibu dainenbutsu* (The Courtesan and the Great Buddhist Service at Mibu Temple).[247]
>
> 2. The Kabuki play reflects audience interest in such aspects of the theater world as Tōjūrō's career and personality, how plays are selected and cast, and quarrels and intrigues among actors.
>
> 3. The Kabuki version consists of approximately ninety-five percent dialogue, whereas the puppet play is predominantly narration. There are almost no lines in common between the two plays.
>
> 4. The Kabuki play is even less serious than the puppet play. Most of the dialogue is in a bantering tone—for example, the ill-will between Oniō and Dōsaburō in *Yotsugi Soga* becomes in *Daimyō Soga* light-hearted trickery and competition over women. *Daimyō Soga* contains no sections that might create a feeling of pathos.
>
> 5. For the Kabuki play Chikamatsu added scenes that exploited actors' individual talents and concealed their weaknesses. The competition between Oniō and Dōsaburō over which man will get a pretty wife and which an ugly one

247. See Keene, *World Within Walls*, 251–52, and Laurence Kominz, *Three Pioneer Kabuki Actors and Their Legacy Today* (Tokyo: Kodansha International, 1995), for plot summaries and analyses of this play.

> suited Tōjūrō's specialty in gay, romantic scenes. Tōjūrō was a notoriously poor dancer, and although dance was an important part of Kabuki, Chikamatsu deleted several dance scenes in *Yotsugi Soga* from *Daimyō Soga*. Chikamatsu added to *Daimyō Soga* several *aragoto* scenes featuring Asahina, a conflict in the dark (*danmari*), and a new ending in which Gorō's little son kills the chief villains. *Aragoto* acting, pantomime scenes, and important roles for child actors have been "crowd pleasers" in Kabuki from the Genroku period until today.

If *Yotsugi Soga* is in many ways a parody of the traditional Soga story, *Daimyō Soga* is a parody of a parody. The prevailing tone of the work is playful. In the three oldest surviving Soga Kabuki plays, the influence of comic acting remains very strong although it was forty years since Kabuki's only real actors were *kyōgen* actors and the main appeal of the art was dance and the eroticism of its performers. *Daimyō Soga*'s "play within a play," its interweaving of the theater world and the world of samurai, and its improbable interplay of "real" and fictional conflicts demonstrate Chikamatsu's imagination and wit, and a playful, irreverent attitude toward the Soga story.

KABUKI DRAMATURGY AND THE PUPPET STAGE

Chikamatsu did not write any more Soga Kabuki plays, but his next puppet play shows that the literary style he learned in writing Kabuki had a strong influence on his approach to writing for puppet drama. It is in *Soga nanatsu i ro ha* (The Seven Soga ABCs), presented by Kaganojō in 1698, that the milieu and values of the pleasure district most deeply penetrate Chikamatsu's Soga story.

In the first act, when Tora is still a novice courtesan (*kamuro*), she saves Jūrō's life in a confrontation with Kudō. In the second act she becomes a full-fledged courtesan. Chikamatsu describes in detail her investiture activities and her first round of calls at pleasure district tea houses. Jūrō returns to Ōiso to thank the girl who rescued him, only to find that she has become a courtesan. The two fall in love, and Tora pledges to be faithful to Jūrō, assuring him that his poverty will not affect her deep love. Later the villains, Kudō, Kajiwara, and Ōtōnai (an ugly, comic villain) go to the pleasure district to amuse themselves by teasing the novice who rescued Jūrō.

Kudō recognizes Tora as Jūrō's rescuer and threatens to ransom her for three days, during which time he will put her at the mercy of all of his men who will "have her standing and lying."[248] Kudō boasts of his riches, which make this possible, and orders Ōtōnai to rape Tora on the spot. Tora runs from the room in tears, and even though the proprietress orders her to return to the important guests, Tora adamantly refuses. The angry proprietress demotes Tora, beats her, and drives her away clothed only in rags.

When the brothers learn what has happened to Tora they are angry and sad, but they can do nothing. Gorō wants to punish the proprietress, but Jūrō restrains him, saying, "Courtesans' lives are, after all, governed by money. We would be in the wrong."

Gorō replies, "If only I had 5,000 *ryō*, I'd make that proprietress crawl!"[249] This scene reflects the era of the "big spender" patrons of the top courtesans. In the pleasure district money was power, and samurai virtues counted for nothing at all.

The third act opens with a scene set at the shabby home of the Soga brothers. The poverty of the pathetic Soga family is emphasized and presents a stark contrast to the opulence of the pleasure district scene in the previous act. Jūrō's mother gives Jūrō her last ten *ryō* to present to Tora as an expression of thanks for saving Jūrō's life. The mother delivers a short monologue in which she expresses sympathy for prostitutes and extols their fidelity despite their many sufferings and humiliations. It is an explicit statement of attitudes Chikamatsu must have held himself, if we can judge by his always sympathetic rendering of prostitutes in his post-Kabuki Soga plays and in his domestic tragedies. Jūrō discovers Tora in a wretched hut, clothed in rags, and weeping. People around the hut are taunting her. Jūrō cannot approach because he is afraid to be recognized, and he is forced helplessly to observe her suffering.

The fourth act takes place during the *bon* holiday. The whole Soga family makes a pilgrimage to Kawazu's grave at Hakone, but Gorō must go separately and in disguise because he is still disowned. The journey of Tora and Shōshō to the grave is the *michiyuki*, a beautiful passage interweaving imagery of early autumn, *bon* festivities,

248. Chikamatsu, "Soga nanatsu i ro ha," *Chikamatsu zenshū*, 5:21.

249. Ibid., 25. Five thousand *ryō* would have been worth about a half million dollars in Genroku Japan.

and the Buddhist hells. At Hakone Temple it is an auspicious day. Kudō's son, Inubōmaru, has entered the priesthood and thus is being treated lavishly, as befits the son of a close retainer of the shogun. Gorō observes the ceremony and is outraged that Inubōmaru, an ignorant lout, has been given a seat of honor far above his station as the least experienced acolyte. Gorō interrupts the ceremony and demands that proper decorum be restored. He argues with Kudō's retainer, Ōmi, and says that Inubōmaru does not even know his "*i ro ha*" (ABCs). Gorō proceeds to give a lecture on the relationship between calligraphy and Buddhist symbolism. Inubōmaru is humiliated, and a fight breaks out. Gorō kills both Inubōmaru and Ōmi, lifts up the two corpses, and effortlessly throws them into an open grave at the temple.

At Kawazu's grave, a ghostly figure appears over Lake Hakone and approaches Jūrō and his mother; it is Kawazu's spirit, and it speaks in the manner of the spirits in Noh plays. Jūrō's mother laments that her prayers have not released her husband's spirit from torment. The spirit replies that only one hindrance remains to his salvation—her unkind treatment of Gorō. Gorō emerges from his hiding place, and the family is happily reunited.

The conclusion of the play is a *karakuri* fight scene in the form of a chase on horseback. Gorō pursues Kajiwara and Kudō, jumping from horse to horse, and at one point three puppets are riding together on a single puppet horse. Kudō escapes but Gorō kills Kajiwara. Gorō's mother is aghast that her son killed a man on a religious holiday, but Kawazu's spirit is pleased and announces sonorously that it can now go to paradise. The play ends with rejoicing: the brothers martial and filial virtues are extolled as their father ascends to Heaven.

The impact of Kabuki on *Soga nanatsu i ro ha* is obvious from the plot summary. The pleasure district scenes, the tender love scenes, and Jūrō's sensitive but cringing character derive from Tōjūrō's portrayal of Jūrō as a "young lover." The values of the the pleasure quarters constantly subvert the heroic ideals of the traditional Soga story, as we see when rules of custom and money prevent the brothers from performing virtuous and heroic acts. The *bon* setting in the fourth and fifth acts follows the practice of staging Soga Kabuki plays during the *bon* season.

Soga nanatsu i ro ha reads more like a Kabuki play than Chikamatsu's earlier puppet plays because it contains much more dialogue and less narration. Chikamatsu returned to Kaganojō's cyclical structure for puppet plays, beginning and ending *Soga nanatsu i ro ha* with felicitous scenes and placing his pathos scene in the third act. But there are no exalted settings in this play; it opens in the pleasure district and concludes in a graveyard. The settings are in contrast to, not in harmony with, the felicitous moods in the first and last scenes.

Chikamatsu wrote his next play, *Soga gonin kyōdai* (The Five Soga Siblings) for Takemoto Gidayū, who presented it in 1699. By this time Gidayū had been independent for over a decade and had developed his own singing style and presentational technique. Kaganojō's Soga plays invariably included one or two *karakuri* scenes. In contrast, Chikamatsu's Soga plays for Gidayū contained unique twists of plot (*shukō*) and decorative *fushigoto,* and special stage effects were less prominent. This is because Gidayū's singing style was considerably more dynamic than his teacher's—in fact, Kaganojō was fast losing to Gidayū in the competition for the Kansai puppet theater audience.

Soga gonin kyōdai marks the beginning of yet another change in the characterizations of the brothers. In this play Jūrō, a dissipated weakling in the previous two plays, is endowed with wit, tact, and emotional stability; in the words of one critic, he is a "breathing Jūrō, with a soul."[250] In the first act, for example, Jūrō's cleverness enables him to frustrate an attempt by Kudō to disgrace the Soga family. Jūrō's relationship with Tora is stable compared with *Soga tayū zome* and *Soga nanatsu i ro ha*, and Tora more resembles the fiancée of an arranged marriage than a passionate courtesan.

Soga gonin kyōdai contains two *shukō,* which involve transforming traditional episodes into erotic scenes. One is the coming-of-age ceremony. Shōshō is a woman barber, and she cuts off Hakoō's hair to help him escape detection by Kudo and his men. She seduces him as she cuts and dresses his hair. The cutting of his childish locks transforms Hakoō, a boy, into Gorō, a man. Gorō, convinced he must become Shōshō's lover if he is to remain in hiding, responds to her affection, but soon she is summoned to entertain Wada Yoshimori and Hōjō Tokimasa at a banquet. A new version of the armor-pulling scene follows. Shōshō, like Tora in the traditional story, refuses to go to the banquet, so Gorō reverts to his role as strong man, puts on Shōshō's kimono, and goes to the banquet in her stead. Gorō's female impersonation allows for new erotic and comic elements in the traditional scene. Asahina tugs on "Shōshō's" sash, not on samurai armor. What

250. Kitano, "Chikamatsu Soga jōruri," 37.

starts as an intended seduction turns into a test of strength between Asahina and the "amazon" Shōshō.

In the fourth act of *Soga gonin kyōdai* the Soga brothers' mother is adamant and inflexible in her refusal to pardon Gorō. She transfers her affection to Zenjibō, her third son. The principal characters in the play travel to hear Zenjibō's first public sermon as a full-fledged priest. But when Zenjibō spies Tora in the audience, "his eyes narrow in lust"[251] and he falls madly in love with her. His sermon degenerates into a description of Tora's beauty and culminates when he falls at her feet and begs her to love him. Tora is embarassed and confused, the crowd mocks Zenjibō, and his mother is in an agony of shame and disappointment. She rebukes Zenjibō and tells him that Tora is Jūrō's fiancée, but Zenjibō, cringing before his mother, continues to beg for Tora's love. Unlike the depraved Zenjibō, Gorō seems strong and honorable; the mother therefore summons and pardons him. At this point, as we might have expected, Zenjibō reveals that he does not really desire Tora, but only pretended to, thus sacrificing his career and reputation so that his mother might pardon Gorō. The fourth act depends for its success on the erotic appeal of Zenjibō's apparent fall from enlightenment into lust, a theme that entertained Edo-period audiences in many plays.[252]

Kaganojō presented his last Chikamatsu Soga play, *Uchiwa Soga* (The Soga Fans), sometime between 1698 and 1700. At about the same time, Gidayū presented an almost identical play, using the title *Hyakunichi Soga* (The Sogas' Hundred Days). Chikamatsu probably wrote one of the two plays by 1693, to celebrate the half-millenium anniversary of the Soga brothers' night raid,[253] but the five-year delay between composition and performance remains a mystery. The choice of characters and their portrayal suggest Chikamatsu's pre-Kabuki puppet plays, supporting the 1693 composition date. The brothers are relatively unimportant characters, but where they do appear they are the brave, dedicated heroes of the traditional legend. Chikamatsu combined the worlds of Yoshitsune and the Soga brothers in this play, much as he did in *Ōiso Tora osana monogatari,* which

251. Chikamatsu, "Soga gonin kyōdai," *Chikamatsu zenshū,* 6:223.

252. *Narukami* by Ichikawa Danjūrō I and *Sakurahime azuma bunsho* (The Scarlet Princess of Edo) by Tsuruya Nanboku II are two popular Kabuki plays whose plots center on the fall of a priest from enlightenment into lust.

253. Yamane Tameo, "*Uchiwa Soga* to *Hyakunichi Soga* shiron," *Geinōshi kenkyū* 78 (1982): 1–17.

he wrote at about the same time. Scholars still debate the question of which chanter received a Chikamatsu script first, or whether Kaganojō obtained a text of *Hyakunichi Soga* and copied and renamed it, leaving Chikamatsu the credit for authorship.[254] The only difference between the two plays is that a *karakuri* scene in the fifth act of Kaganojō's play takes the place of a *fushigoto* scene in Gidayū's version.[255] This difference highlights the contrast between Gidayū's preference for musical and poetic scenes, and verbal conflict, and Kaganojō's reliance on puppet dance and special effects.

EXPERIMENTS WITH PLOT, CHARACTER, AND PARODY

Chikamatsu's last six Soga plays are the work of an author who enjoyed a stable and harmonious relationship with his chanter, and who was completely confident in his craft. From 1706 until his death Chikamatsu served as staff playwright at Gidayū's Takemoto Theater in Osaka. With *Sonezaki shinjū* (The Love Suicides at Sonezaki) in 1703, Chikamatsu introduced the "domestic play" (*sewamono*) to puppet theater. Today his domestic plays are considered his finest works, and he used some of the elements of his domestic plays in his later domestic-history plays (*sewa-jidai mono*) and history plays (*jidaimono*). In his last six Soga plays there is a new attitude toward the prose sections (*jigoto*): more attention to the development of character and more serious, less exaggerated portrayals of human suffering. But Chikamatsu's Soga plays never approached the sustained emotion and tightly structured, unidirectional flow of his domestic plays. This was primarily due to the length of Chikamatsu's history and domestic-history plays—three times as long as domestic plays. Chikamatsu and Gidayū believed, as Kaganojō had, that dramatic changes in mood and music were essential to keep an audience attentive for the long history plays.

254. Ibid., 16. *Hyakunichi Soga* enjoyed greater theatrical success.

255. The fifth act of *Uchiwa Soga* includes a *karakuri* scene in which a demon attacks Tora and Shōshō while they are doing a dance as an offering to the brothers' spirits. A white arrow shot from the sky kills the demon, and the brothers' ghosts appear. The ghosts become *arahitogami* and ascend to Heaven. In *Hyakunichi Soga* Zenjibō has a confrontation and then reconciliation with a representative of the Kamakura government. Yoritomo rewards the Soga relatives and explains thirty-six poems by great poets in a poem *tsukushi fushigoto* scene "borrowed from Harima no Jō." Ibid., 14.

The building blocks of a Chikamatsu-Gidayū Soga play were juxtaposed prose (*jigoto*) and poetic-melodic passages (*fushigoto*) of contrasting moods and musical styles, arranged within plots made interesting by numerous new *shukō* in each play. The prose sections challenged Chikamatsu's ability in characterization, the *fushigoto* challenged his wit and poetic skills, and the *shukō* challenged his imagination.

In *Honryō Soga* (The Soga Domain) we see for the first time in Chikamatsu's Soga plays a love affair between two strong, persistent, and clever people. In this play Chikamatsu interweaves the characters and several motifs from the Noh play *Yuya* with an original story about Kawazu Saburō and the youth of the retainers Oniō and Dōsaburō. In *Honryō Soga* the Soga brothers are still children. In the "Kirikane" scene, the near execution of the Soga boys at the order of Yoritomo, Chikamatsu portrays the boys as heroic, but much more believable than they had been in earlier dramatic literature:

> (Kudō is speaking, as the official in charge of the execution): "From sunrise this morning the taking of life is forbidden. The night draws on. Cut off their heads and throw them away—the sooner the better!" Yajirō gave Sukenobu the sword, and Sukenobu (the boys' foster father) pulled his right arm out of his robe[256] and went around behind the children, "All right, this is the end."
>
> Ichiman spoke to his younger brother, "Hakoō, don't forget what mother told you."
>
> Hakoō replied, "Do you mean the message she told us to give father when we see him? She said it would be after our heads were cut off, when we are in the next world."
>
> "No, it's not that. What did she tell you to be sure to do in your last moments?'
>
> "Oh, I remember that very well." The boys looked into each other's eyes. Then they took out paper handkerchiefs, tied up the hair hanging over the back of their heads, and wiped the backs of their necks. Arranging the collars of their robes, they bowed their heads and waited. As might be expected, Sukenobu was overwhelmed.
>
> "Look at that, everyone. Even though it's an order from the shogun, how can I raise my sword against them? I, Sukenobu, faced tens of thousands of enemies in battles in

256. A warrior about to engage in combat pulled his right arm out of the sleeve of his robe in order to increase his freedom of movement.

> Shikoku and the West Country[257] and never lost a fight, but now my hand is shaking and my knees cannot support me. If you want to laugh at me as a coward or a weakling, go ahead and laugh."[258]

Chikamatsu eliminated the exaggeratedly heroic pleas by the children to be executed quickly, which had appeared in both the *kōwakamai* and *ko-jōruri* versions of the scene; the children's calm preparation for death in *Honryō Soga* is much more moving. In the *kōwakamai* and *ko-jōruri* versions Sukenobu collapses all of a sudden, but Chikamatsu's Sukenobu addresses the witnesses of the execution, explaining why he cannot kill the children. This is done convincingly—a strong warrior reluctantly but inexorably giving in to his emotions.

At the same time Chikamatsu was creating more believable characters for his Soga plays, he was putting those characters in more dramatic situations. The passage above is an example. In all previous versions of the "Kirikane" scene Kudō had remained in the background with Yoritomo, encouraging Yoritomo to stick to his decision to execute the Soga boys. Chikamatsu puts him on the beach at Yuigahama in charge of the execution. This makes it possible for the scene to end with a direct conflict between arch-villain and hero (the hero is Hatakeyama Shigetada, who arrives in the nick of time with the shogun's order to rescind the execution).

In his later Soga plays Chikamatsu's protagonists become more serious and morally upright. The brothers are no longer the playful profligates of Kabuki. Instead, they are paragons of filial piety and samurai duty. They pursue the vendetta to serve their father but obey their mother to the extent possible, given the contradictory demands of loyalty to their two parents. They become brave and invincible warriors. They are never bested in combat but allow themselves to lose so that they may spare the lives of samurai to whom they are indebted.

Tora and Shōshō undergo a significant change in status, becoming more like ideal samurai wives than courtesans. In *Soga Kaikeizan* (The Sogas' Mount Kuai-ji) they actually marry Jūrō and Gorō the day before the vendetta. In Chikamatsu's later plays the two

257. This refers to the battles during the last two years of the Genpei War. They took place in Shikoku (Yashima) and in western Honshu (Uji/Seta, Ichi no Tani, Fujito, and Dan no Ura).

258. Chikamatsu, "Honryō Soga," *Chikamatsu zenshū*, 7:533–34.

women share the brothers' hatred of Kudō and Yoritomo and help the brothers carry out their vendetta even though the women know that they are hastening the death of their lovers. In these plays Yoritomo treats Tora and Shōshō as wives of the Soga brothers. In addition, Jūrō and Gorō's mother accepts Tora and Shōshō as daughters-in-law, and they get along much better than mothers-in-law and daughters-in-law usually do in the stereotyped relationships described in traditional literature and folklore. Because Tora and Shōshō are so much like wives, they feel that the brothers' quest for vengeance is their own quest, and thus they follow their men to the Fuji hunt. In *Soga Tora ga ishiusu* (The Sogas, Tora, and the Stone Mortar) they beg to be allowed to fight to the death alongside the brothers. Such scenes, in which beautiful, strong-willed women insist on accompanying their men into physical danger, are still an important feature of romantic plays and films. In none of the plays do the women actually fight or die with the brothers, but in the last two plays their fervant prayers are crucial to the success of the night raid.

In the later plays the brothers' mother is depicted as a woman of very strong love and keen intelligence. In the last three plays her pardon of Gorō is the emotional climax of the work. In *Soga Kaikeizan* Chikamatsu transforms the mother from a suffering bystander into the prime mover of the vendetta. Every action she takes is to further the chances for her sons' success in their attack on Kudō.

Chikamatsu's creation of more serious characters in his later Soga plays was due in part to Takemoto Gidayū's skill at vocalizing emotional dialogue, but it was also related to changing popular attitudes, nationwide, toward revenge and vendettas. Before the Edo period, samurai combat and acts of heroic self-sacrifice were most frequently part of a general conflict rather than a private vendetta. By the mid-Genroku period (the late 1690s) Japan had experienced eighty years of peace. Real images of warfare had faded, replaced by exaggerated and romantic narrative and dramatic accounts. In Genroku Japan a warrior's supreme sacrifice could only come as the result of a private vendetta. In 1687 and 1688 Saikaku published two collections of tales about samurai loyalty, *Budō denraiki* (Transmission of the Martial Arts) and *Buke giri monogatari* (Tales of Samurai Duty). All of the stories in the first collection describe vendettas, as do about one-quarter of the stories in the second. The appeal of the different stories is varied, however. Some were clearly included because of the bizarre events they describe, but several of the stories in *Buke giri monogatari* show the sufferings and dedication of samurai whose ethical code required them to spend years in exile hunting for enemies they never knew.[259]

Several important historical vendettas took place in the Genroku period, the chief of which was carried out by the forty-seven *ronin* (masterless samurai) of the Ako domain. In 1703 they killed Kira no Yoshinaka, whom they held responsible for their master's death two years before. This vendetta was soon presented on stage, and it became, with the Soga story, an archetypical revenge.[260] The story of the forty-seven *ronin* achieved popularity largely because of its dramatic and romantic elements, but the suffering and dedication of the leader, Ōishi Kuranosuke, was emphasized in all accounts. In the Edo period, vendettas were serious business and played an important role in samurai values.[261] The public at large could read about vendettas in narrative or play form. In the Genroku period the reading population and the number of books increased dramatically, and, beginning with the late Genroku period, Chikamatsu may have been writing almost as much for the reading public as for Gidayū and his audiences.[262] Both the reading and theater publics were broadening into multi-class groups, including townsmen and samurai at all levels.[263] Given this situation it is only natural that Chikamatsu's later Soga plays exerted wider appeal than had his Kabuki-style Soga plays. For many of his readers revenge was a topic for serious thought.

259. *Buke giri monogatari* has been translated into English as *Tales of Samurai Honor*; see Ihara Saikaku, *Tales of Samurai Honor*, translated by Caryl Ann Callahan (Tokyo: Monumenta Nipponica, 1981).

260. The most in-depth investigation in English of the early stage versions of the vendetta is Donald Shively, "Tokugawa Plays on Forbidden Topics," in *Chūshingura: Studies in Kabuki and the Puppet Theater*, edited by James Brandon (Honolulu: University of Hawaii Press, 1982), 33–44. See also Donald Keene, "Introduction," in Takeda Izumo II, Miyoshi Shōraku, and Namiki Senryū, *Chūshingura (The Treasury of Loyal Retainers): A Puppet Play*, translated by Donald Keene, foreword by Wm. Theodore de Bary (New York: Columbia University Press, 1971), 1–7.

261. See Mills, "Kataki-uchi," for the laws concerning samurai revenge and several case studies of actual vendettas. Ogyū Sorai, the leading philosopher of the day, wrote a memorial to the shogun defending the forty-seven *ronin*. See Keene, "Introduction."

262. Yokoyama, "Chikamatsu no Soga jōruri," 23. Illustrated *kabuki e-iri kyōgen bon* were also read as story books.

263. Ibid., 22–23.

We have seen how Gidayū's skill at vocalizing characters' emotional sentiments facilitated Chikamatsu's move in the direction of serious characters and emotions, but Chikamatsu often had to take other performers into account when he wrote his plays. He wrote *Soga Tora ga ishiusu* (1716) for the master puppeteer Tatsumatsu Hachirōbei (d. 1734), a specialist in women's roles. In this play Chikamatsu rewrote the Soga story with the brothers as subordinate characters and with the women as more fully developed characters than in any other play. He used a three-act structure, roughly following the structural requirements of a domestic play. Hachirōbei manipulated puppets representing Tora in the first and third acts and the Soga mother in the second act.

Chikamatsu's *fushigoto* scenes are very different from his prose scenes. In his Soga plays the purpose of *fushigoto* scenes is not to define character or to move plots along, but to entertain the audience with poetry, wit, song, and dance. Most *fushigoto* scenes fall into two categories, parodies and travel dances (*michiyuki*). *Michiyuki* in Soga plays tend to be peripheral to the main story, usually depicting one or both of the ladies, either traveling to meet their lovers or traveling after the brothers' deaths. The role of *michiyuki* in his early Soga plays had been to lessen the tension created by a pathos scene occurring just before the *michiyuki*. In *Soga Tora ga ishiusu* the *michiyuki* is one of the relatively rare examples in Soga plays of the combination of *fushigoto* and serious emotion. In it Tora and Shōshō follow Jūrō and Gorō to the Mount Fuji hunt but fall farther and farther behind, finally losing their way. Later they wander around the hunting grounds in search of their lovers, and they also shout or pray to save animals that are in immediate danger of being shot during the hunt. This humane but anti-social activity leads them into a confrontation with the villains. Chikamatsu may have used a serious *michiyuki* in *Soga Tora ga ishiusu* because it is a hybrid work: its short, three-act structure and the preeminence of the women characters make it like a domestic play, but its historical setting and characters are from the tradition of history plays.

In his domestic plays Chikamatsu often placed his *michiyuki* at the end. It was a travel to death and created a sense of epiphany for weak characters enmeshed in tragic circumstances. When *michiyuki* in domestic plays do not come at the end of the piece, they nevertheless create moods of tension and foreboding that presage conclusions of death or capture. In the rare case of a "serious" *michiyuki* in his Soga plays, Chikamatsu immediately lightened the mood with a parody scene.

Having established the pattern of "serious *jigoto*"/"light *fushigoto*," Chikamatsu found it effective to sometimes break the pattern. Like an imaginative *shukō*, this break would seem new and exciting to an audience of afficionados. An excellent example is found in the play *Soga ōgi hakkei* (Eight Soga Scenes Painted on Fans). The *michiyuki* is the most moving in a Chikamatsu Soga play, for in it the brothers are traveling to their deaths. It reads much like Chikamatsu's best domestic play *michiyuki*. Following immediately after this serious *fushigoto* scene is a *jigoto* parody scene, the parting of the brothers and their horses. It makes fun of the emotional last parting from Oniō and Dōsaburō, which is described in *The Tale of the Soga Brothers* (all versions), the Noh play *Youchi Soga*, the *kōwakamai* play *Youchi Soga*, and the *ko-jōruri* play *Jūban giri* (from the seven-day series). In Chikamatsu's *Soga ōgi hakkei* the Soga brothers want to send keepsakes home to their mother, but Oniō and Dōsaburō have gone ahead to set up camp at the hunting ground. Since the brothers are certain that their horses know the way back to Soga village, they decide to send the keepsakes with the horses. The horses, like Oniō and Dōsaburō in traditional versions, wish to accompany the brothers on the night raid: "even if wounded, the horses would carry the brothers all the way to Hades on their final journey."[264] Jūrō and Gorō attach the traditional keepsakes to the horses and pray solemnly for the horses' rebirth as men, telling them that they may be masters and servants again in a later life. The horses cannot reply, but seem to "reprove the brothers and appear to be full of sorrow, even more than men who are able to lament out loud."[265]

Almost all of Chikamatsu's parody scenes were *fushigoto*, and some of his best were rewrites of the "Jūban giri" scene in which the Soga brothers run amok after killing Kudō Suketsune. Chikamatsu based his "Jūban giri" parodies on a "straight" version he wrote for his first play, *Yotsugi Soga*. It was used to accompany Tora and Shōshō's dance after they put on the brothers' hats and robes. The dance described the brothers' final hours for their mother. (In the following text the sections indicated by underlining are word-for-word borrowings from the *ko-jōruri Jūban giri*; italicized lines are taken verbatim

264. Chikamatsu Monzaemon, "Soga ōgi hakkei," *Chikamatsu zenshū*, 8:64.
265. Ibid., 65.

from the *rufubon* version of the narrative; and lines that are both underlined and italicized are identical in the *ko-jōruri* and *rufubon*.)

> At this time *Tairaku no Heimasuke* of Musashi Province called out his name. "You Soga brothers are upstarts! I'll get you!" He came forth, brandishing a great sword more than four feet long.
>
> Jūrō cried, "Here I am!" and jumped out from behind the fence, slashing at Heima with a long horizontal stroke. *Heimasuke trembled in fear and fled* in a manner ill suiting his brave words. "Lord Heima, I'm disappointed in you. You know you can't escape me!" Jūrō struck with his sword, cutting the armor plate on Heima's back and slicing into the shoulder blade. Heima beat a wobbly retreat.
>
> *Now Heima's brother-in-law, Aikyō no Saburō, announced himself and came forward.* Gorō greeted him with a smile, *"Birds sport among the willow branches, and white herons play in the shadows of the knotweed flowers."*[266] Laughing, he struck with his sword. *Saburō's right arm was chopped off, and he fled without looking back.*"[267]

Now let us turn to Chikamatsu's parodies of this scene. The first is the *fushigoto* dance scene "Onna jūban giri" (The Women Fight Ten Men), which appears in *Kasō Soga* (Soga Additions), act 4. It is part of a comic puppet tradition known as *sakana jōruri* ("fish *jōruri*"), probably deriving from *kyōgen*.[268] In *sakana jōruri* puns using names of fish are interwoven in a story unrelated to fish. The setting of Chikamatsu's parody is the pleasure district. Kudō leads a group of samurai to the establishment of Tora and Shōshō to attack the Soga brothers. The tone of "Onna jūban giri" is lighter and more ornamental than that of the passage from *Yotsugi Soga*. A translation of the

266. Ichiko and Ōshima, *Soga monogatari*, 356. Chikamatsu did not complete Gorō's derisive challenge to Aikyō no Saburō; it is as follows: "You would be better off joining those birds. You are all pretty worthless opponents, but I can't choose my enemies. Take a look at how I can fight!" Chikamatsu probably assumed his audience knew these lines by heart and felt free to omit them.

267. Chikamatsu, "Yotsugi Soga," *Chikamatsu zenshū*, 2:33–34. The *rufubon* version is available in Ichiko and Ōshima, *Soga monogatari*, 355–59. The *ko-jōruri* version is found in Yokoyama, *Ko-jōruri shōhon shū*, 2:382–83.

268. The protagonist of the *kyōgen* play *Uo zekkyō* (Fish Sutras) is a charlatan priest whose sutras consist of silly and entertaining strings of fish puns. In the *kyōgen* play *Tako* (Octopus) the prayer *namu amida butsu* ("Hail Amida Buddha!") is replaced with *nama dako, nama dako* ("raw octopus, raw octopus!").

first fight follows. The puns, of course, do not translate into English, so commentary is provided in the right hand column:

Text	Commentary
Tairaku no Hemanosuke attacked, shouting, "I won't let you escape me!"	
When he came forward to attack, Jūrō shouted, "Hey there, Tairaku! If you were a sea bream, you'd be swimming against the tidal bore of the Naruto Strait. Here, take a taste of my steel!" Jūrō raised his sword, and "swoosh, swoosh, swoosh!" filleted him in two slices from his dorsal fin to his rump. Jūrō sported with Tairaku like a mountain blast with a cherry bream.[269]	"Hey there" is ***ika ni; ika*** also means "squid." The ***tai*** of "Tairaku" sounds like "sea bream" (***tai***). Naruto Strait is dangerous, as is Tairaku's position now. *Aji* means both "taste" and "horse mackeral." "Swoosh" (***hira***) is also a fish name (***aliohaelangata***). The ***sakura tai*** is a bream caught in April when the cherries bloom. Just as the blossoms fall before the mountain blast, so Tairaku falls to Jūrō.

Chikamatsu squeezed six fish puns into this brief passage.

Chikamatsu's last version of the episode is "Keisei jūban giri" (The Courtesans Fight Ten Men) in *Soga Tora ga ishiusu.* As in the *fushigoto* parody above, Kudō and his men go to the pleasure district to kill Jūrō. In *Soga Tora ga ishiusu*, Tora and Shōshō tell Jūrō to flee before the pursuers arrive; they assure Jūrō that they can cope with Kudō's men. The women are, as we have seen, the central characters of the play, and Tora and Shōshō drive off the first eight men with sharp words or with deft slaps. The ninth and last opponent is Shinkai Arashirō, whom they inundate with ashes from the brazier, and he runs away in humiliation. Chikamatsu uses puns on different themes for each fight, and the dialogue is laced with expressions and objects of the pleasure district.

269. Chikamatsu, "Kazō Soga," *Chikamatsu zenshū*, 7:620.

Text	Commentary
The first was Tairaku no Heima no Jō. "You presumptuous common prostitute! Let me be the one to begin our secret attack." As he untied his purse strings to take out some change, Tora leaped out from behind the door curtain.	The word "presumptuous" is borrowed from *Yotsugi Soga*. Tora uses the door curtain (*noren*) in the way the brothers used a fence in the narrative, to gain tactical advantage.
"Hey, mister, rather than buy a courtesan you've never seen and who doesn't suit you, better go buy some shellfish! Take this for your foolish pretensions, and stuff your stupid jaw full of puns!" She hit him slap, slap, slap with the palm of her hand.	This pun uses *kai*, meaning "to buy" and also "shellfish." The wordplay uses *otogai* (chin or jaw), *utsukegai* (empty shell), and *utsuke* (foolish).
"I can't take this," he said, and crept away in retreat, a fool with stinging cheeks.	This pun uses *aho* (fool) and *ho* (cheek).
"Do you know who's coming next? I'm a gentleman who will give you deep love and respect. My name of course is Aikyō no Saburō." Piling on the honeyed words, he snuggled up to Shōshō.	Aikyō is the man's name; a homonym means "love and respect."
"How nasty, how disgusting! You can't even buy a prostitute for a quick job, and now you're trying to build a bridge to an unreachable cloud. Even if you go around to the bridge whores, they'll take that thick hide on your face, stretch it on a stick-drum, and make the world's greatest 'fool-drum'—don, don don! Enough of your boorish behavior!" Leisurely puffing on her pipe, she knocked him down. Aikyō fell and grazed his shin on a gutter stone. Though it was a wound no bigger than a flea bite, he wobbled away in retreat.[270]	The wordplay brings together "the bridge over the clouds," which spans the Milky Way to unite the Weaver Girl Star and the Herd Boy Star, and the cheapest prostitutes who wait under bridges (*kumo ni kakihashi geisei*). *Don* is the sound a drum makes when it is struck. *Don-kusai* means "rustic" or "boorish."

The audience would not have considered a scene such as the one above to undermine the serious, virtuous characters Chikamatsu built for Tora and Shōshō in the prose sections of the play. Puppet

270. Chikamatsu, "Soga Tora ga ishiusu," *Chikamatsu zenshū*, 9:28–29.

theater audiences expected very different sorts of entertainment from the *jigoto* and *fushigoto* sections of history plays. Judging from the kinds of plays presented in Kabuki and puppet theater, audiences could not be expected to sit through more than three hours of sustained, serious drama—the duration of Chikamatsu's domestic plays. *Fushigoto* parody scenes were breaks in the serious action of a long history play, replacing the comic puppet interludes that had been discontinued at about the turn of the eighteenth century. The comic puppet interludes had been independent, *kyōgen*-like skits (*Takenoshita Mago Hachizaemon* is an example) unrelated to the plots of the multi-act plays they interrupted. Audience preference for plot-related comic relief represents a change in the direction of melodrama, which demands integration of serious and comic action within the framework of a single play.

In his invention of *shukō* Chikamatsu was even freer of performance constraints than he was when devising *jigoto* and *fushigoto* scenes. In *Honryō Soga* he worked the Noh play *Yuya* into the Soga story, and in *Kasō Soga* he intrigued his Osaka audience with unfamiliar details of the latest trends in Edo Kabuki and the life of the Edo pleasure quarters. In this play Gorō is portrayed in Edo *aragoto* (wild acting) style, and several plot twists are based on Ichikawa Danjūrō's hit play, *Tsuwamono kongen Soga* (The Origins of the Soga Warrior) (see pp. 166–75 for analysis of this play).[271]

In his last four Soga plays Chikamatsu changed the plot of the Soga story by rewriting the hunt and vendetta scenes. In each play the women become involved in the brothers' last hours. Perhaps Chikamatsu's most imaginitive rewriting of these scenes occurred in his last Soga play, *Soga Kaikeizan* (1718).[272] In this play the Soga brothers'

271. Chikamatsu, *Chikamatsu zenshū*, 7:556. The puppet portraying Gorō performed a *roppō* dance. The *roppō* is a swaggering, energetic dance currently performed on the *hanamichi* bridgeway as part of an entrance or exit. It was introduced to Kabuki by Arashi San'emon (1635–90) of Osaka (Dunn and Torigoe, *The Actors' Analects*, 175). A modified "Edo *roppō*" became a standard feature of Edo *aragoto* acting.

272. The title derives from a famous Chinese revenge story in *Shiji* (The Records of the Historian), which is recounted at length in *Soga monogatari*, book 5. It concerns the wars between Wu and Yue, two warring states. Mount Kuaiji was the site where Goujian, the king of Yue, resolved to avenge his humiliating defeat at the hands of the king of Wu. See Burton Watson, trans., *Records of the Grand Historian of China* (New York: Columbia University Press, 1961), 1:513, 2:479–81, for oblique references to the story. Watson omitted the biography of Wu Zixu, advisor to the king of Wu, from his translation, and it tells the story in its most complete form.

mother is the major female character. She is an idealized samurai woman. The appeal of the play lies in its novel plot and in its serious portrayal of the feelings of Jūrō, Gorō, and their mother as they attempt to carry out the revenge. *Shukō* include the brothers' return home during the hunt to marry Tora and Shōshō in a graveyard, a spy in the Soga household who is thwarted by the Soga mother, and Tora and Shōshō praying successfully for rain to delay Yoritomo's departure for Kamakura, making it possible for the brothers to attack Kudō a day later than the traditional date for the vendetta.

Gidayū died in 1714, and the play was presented by his successor, Takemoto Masadayū (1691–1744), who was famous for his sympathetic and moving presentations of human emotions.[273] Masadayū was younger than Chikamatsu, and thus his directions and performance requirements had less influence on Chikamatsu than did those of Chikamatsu's three previous collaborating performers, who were older than the playwright.[274] As a result, *Soga Kaikeizan* may be the closest example of a "pure" Chikamatsu Soga play, that is, a play little influenced by the personal directions of a major performing artist.

Chikamatsu's last Soga plays are superior to his early puppet and Kabuki plays, but, with the possible exception of *Soga Kaikeizan*, none rank among his best. The scholar Kitano Beni, rating *Soga Kaikeizan* as one of Chikamatsu's three best plays, values it because it "represents a final break from Soga Kabuki."[275]

DISHARMONY: THE ESSENCE OF CHIKAMATSU'S SOGA STORY

The structure of Chikamatsu's Soga plays was dictated by the cyclical pattern he used to fashion his history plays. As we have seen, the Soga story fit this pattern from its earliest incarnation as an oral tale. Chikamatsu inherited a traditional tale that was easy to adapt to the Edo-period stage because in every form it appeared the Soga tale was the story of a quest, a simple and readily expandable plot that can accommodate many new subplots and characters. What Chikamatsu added to the tradition were startling contrasts of character and mood. His literary contrasts were to some extent dictated by the musical requirements of Kaganojō and, later, Gidayū. Musical variety was es-

273. Utsumi Shigetarō, *Ningyō jōruri to bunraku,* (Hakusuisha, 1958), 56.
274. Kitano, "Chikamatsu Soga jōruri," 44. Matsuzaki Hitoshi, *Chikamatsu shinpojiumu Nihon bungaku* (Gakuseisha, 1976), 7:264.
275. Kitano, "Chikamatsu Soga jōruri," 44.

sential to the success of history plays, but Chikamatsu took the aesthetic of disharmony and variety beyond the musical level and used it to create his literary style for history plays.

His delight in contrast is at every level of his play crafting. A central thematic contrast in all of the Kabuki and post-Kabuki Soga plays is "the real versus the unreal," and "genuineness versus sham." This conflict takes many forms: disguises of identity and intention, the hiding of true feelings, and the juxtaposition of dream, fantasy, or "play acting" within the "reality" of the plot of a given play.

Social values are usually in disharmony. The conflicting pulls of *giri* and *ninjō* provide the central problem in almost every Chikamatsu play and are certainly at the crux of many Soga plays, but conflicting loci of duty (*giri*)—contradictory "good" values—continued to be part of Chikamatsu's Soga story. Yoritomo is depicted as a misguided but essentially just ruler, and the shogun's law and order are celebrated in the opening passages of several Soga plays. Conflicting levels of *giri* and "*giri* versus *ninjō*" were central to the Soga story from its inception, but Chikamatsu added new, contemporary value conflicts to the story: "wealth versus honor" and "perseverence versus dissipation."

Chikamatsu strove to create contrasts between consecutive scenes of Soga plays so that scenes with similar tones never follow each other. Instead, an alternation of ceremonial, martial, emotional, and comic scenes carried his audiences from crest to trough in a tossing sea of laughter and tears. Startling disharmonies are apparent even in the internal construction of scenes. In traditional aristocratic literature, action and setting are harmonized, but in Chikamatsu's Soga plays they are often in sharp opposition. For example, he set many acts of brutal violence in the gaily decorated pleasure district, and in *Soga Kaikeizan* the Soga brothers marry their brides in a graveyard.

Parody and humor were also ever-present in his Soga plays. He created humor by setting his comic scenes against traditional Soga literature, with its serious, moralistic tone. Chikamatsu and his audiences were very familiar with the traditional literature, and thus when he wrote a parody scene such as "The Courtesans Fight Ten Men," he would have been confident that, even if his audience could not follow his satiric take-off on the original text, it certainly knew that the traditional episode described a heroic, and in the end tragic, event. His fine dramatic sense told him that heroism and tragedy are only a few brush strokes removed from satire and comedy. Many of the scenes and characterizations in the traditional story are so exaggerated that they verge on the ridiculous, and Chikamatsu sometimes rewrote these scenes carrying them into the realm of the absurd. One basis of his parody, like the parody of *Dōke Wada sakamori,* was a sense of different historic ages, an awareness of changing social values with attendant changes in literary language and daily speech. The medieval world and the world of the Edo period were so different that the mere juxtaposition of a line from the *rufubon* with a line of jargon from the pleasure district would have an amusing effect. *Dōke Wada sakamori* relied solely on such crude juxtapositions. Chikamatsu used Edo-period Japanese and the language of traditional drama and poetry to create a new and dynamic idiom for *jōruri.* Contrasts between contemporary and traditional imagery and vocabulary were central to his idiom.

His parody involved more than new language. He often recast traditional scenes and motifs with new characters. We have seen that replacing lofty or strong characters with humble or weak ones is a classic form of parody.[276] In *Yotsugi Soga* Chikamatsu used the servants Oniō and Dōsaburō to parody the Soga brothers, and they became in many later plays standard comic characters standing in opposition to the heroic Jūrō and Gorō. In *Soga ōgi hakkei* he parodied Oniō and Dōsaburō by replacing them with horses. In some parody scenes he replaced men with women: "The Courtesans Fight Ten Men" is typical of this type of parody. In the *rufubon*'s "straight" version of the brothers' last fight, Jūrō and Gorō are heroes, and their words are learned and defiant. It is a typical martial scene in which a hero kills a multitude of enemies. Chikamatsu's parody demonstrates the ridiculousness of these scenes by carrying the exaggeration a step further: two weak women dispatch a host of warriors with pinches, slaps, and sharp words. The villains' braggadocio and cowardice are exaggerated to the level of the absurd.

Only the devotion of Tora, Shōshō, and the Soga mother remained free from Chikamatsu's acid brush. Tora's traditional goodness is mocked in but a single scene in *Soga tayū zome.* Chikamatsu's always straightforward and sympathetic treatment of the three leading women is further evidence of his firm belief in the essential virtue of women who love.

276. Highet, *The Anatomy of Satire*, 80–83, makes this point. An example is *The Battle of the Frogs and Mice*, a classic Greek parody that employs Homer's heroic meter but replaces human heroes with vermin.

That parody and comedy came to play such an important part in Soga literature demonstrates changing attitudes toward the story and its characters. *Dōke Wada sakamori* and *Takenoshita Mago Hachizaemon* tell us that the change began as early as the 1660s. The cult of the Soga brothers was concentrated in eastern Japan and was tied to the agricultural cycle, so it played little role in the lives of the urban Kansai population. Neither audience nor playwright would have worried about offending the Soga spirits with satiric characterizations. Light romantic stories and parodies of traditional tales were standard fare in the fiction of the 1600s, and avid readers must have been delighted to see the same kind of material presented on the puppet and Kabuki stages. In chapter four we saw that *dōke* actors exercised a strong influence on the tone of both Kabuki and *jōruri*, and Chikamatsu wrote his Soga plays for the kind of theater they created.

Chikamatsu's Soga plays were exciting, emotional, and comic entertainment, but they were not entirely cut off from the religious roots of the story. Soga plays were sometimes presented as a kind of offering. The *bon* Kabuki plays are examples, and Chikamatsu wrote *Uchiwa Soga/Hyakunichi Soga* to honor the five-hundredth anniversary of the brothers' deaths. Unfortunately, it is very difficult to say what meaning memorial or *bon* plays carried in the religious lives of Kansai audiences, performers, or Chikamatsu himself.

Spirits and ghosts appear in several Soga plays. They are inevitably the spirits of good characters: Asagao in *Honryō Soga*, the brothers' father in *Soga nanatsu i ro ha*, and the brothers themselves in *Uchiwa Soga*. The presentation of ghosts and spirits involved *karakuri* manipulations, and the main purpose of spirit scenes was to startle and thrill audiences. But in each case a good spirit kills an evil character or resolves an outstanding conflict. This portrayal of righteous revenge after death derives from *goryō* belief.

CHIKAMATSU'S IMPACT ON SOGA DRAMA

Chikamatsu's Soga story plays were successful on stage. The performance records in appendix F show that most plays were staged repeatedly within a few years of their first performance. But the popularity of his Soga plays was limited to his day. Only *Soga Kaikeizan* was performed more than twenty-five years after his death. Like most of his history plays, Chikamatsu's Soga plays have not withstood the test of time. Using imitation as a measure of a play's success, his Soga plays were only marginally popular even while he was alive. Only two complete Soga plays were adapted for the Kabuki theater.[277]

From the peak of his career Chikamatsu had only one important rival *jōruri* playwright, Ki no Kaion (1663–1742), who was inspired by Chikamatsu and used many of his themes, sources, and dramatic techniques. In a few cases Kaion's plays were equal to those of his more famous rival.[278] Kaion wrote but one Soga play, further evidence that Chikamatsu's Soga plays were not the most popular of his works.

Kaion's play, *Soga sugata no Fuji* (*Soga Images in the Smoke of Mount Fuji*), was performed in 1714 by Toyotake Wakadayū (1681–1764) at the Toyotake Theater, an Osaka theater that was the rival of Gidayū's Takemoto Theater. The play's plot and style are much like that of Chikamatsu's last four plays, but it does not include any surprising or unique *shukō* (it does include some tried and true *shukō*) or any parody scenes. It concludes with the vendetta scene and the interrogation of Gorō, both straightforwardly told in the spirit of the traditional tale.

Kaion's lack of interest in the Soga theme, the adaptation of only two plays to Kabuki, and the short performance lives of Chikamatsu's Soga plays might seem to indicate that the plays represented an interesting but uninfluential reinterpretation of the Soga story. In fact, their influence was considerable.

After the death of Tōjūrō, the Kabuki *bon* Soga tradition in the Kansai gradually died out. Soga puppet plays continued to be performed in Osaka after Chikamatsu's death, but in fewer numbers and with little apparent acclaim, although puppet plays about vendettas enjoyed popularity there throughout the Edo period. In the 1700s a tradition arose of performing vendetta plays in the summer season, and Soga plays were included. The custom may have derived from the earlier *bon* Soga tradition in Kansai Kabuki.

Plays dealing with contemporary vendettas were more popular than the story of the Soga brothers. Contemporary samurai ven-

277. Chikamatsu himself rewrote *Yotsugi Soga* as *Daimyō Soga*. *Hyakunichi Soga*, presented as a Kabuki play under the same title in Osaka in 1701, was a big success. The allocation of roles suggests that it was a relatively faithful presentation of the puppet play. See Yūda Yoshio and Torigoe Bunzō, eds., *Kamigata kyōgen bon* (Koten Bunko, 1977), 3:9.

278. See Keene, *World Within Walls*, 269–72, for a brief discussion of Ki no Kaion's works.

dettas had to be concealed within the framework of an historical cover story in order to escape censorship, but audiences recognized the real subjects of vendetta plays and enjoyed their topicality. The first play about the revenge of the forty-seven retainers of Ako was disguised as a Soga play.[279] Authors of vendetta plays created many scenes as parallels to, or in opposition to, famous episodes from the medieval Soga tradition or from Edo-period Soga plays. The Soga brothers were model avengers, and their real and fictional Edo-period counterparts strove to emulate them.

Chikamatsu's influence on Edo-period Soga theater is not apparent at the level of complete plays, but the episodes, motifs, and characters he created and his overall attitude toward the Soga tradition had a considerable impact both in his own time and later. Numerous Kabuki plays presented parts of Chikamatsu's plays. The play *Jinji Soga* (The Soga Rites), presented in Kyoto in 1701 as a *bon* play is an example. It is not a revision of any single Chikamatsu play, but it includes a *fushigoto* scene from act 1 of *Soga gonin kyōdai*, and a "villain killed in a chest" scene deriving partly from *Yotsugi Soga*, act 4, and partly from *Soga gonin kyōdai*, act 5.[280]

In fact, most of the important innovations that Chikamatsu brought to the story lived on in Edo Kabuki. This further attests to the power of printing in Edo-period Japan. By reading printed editions of plays, Edo Kabuki actors and playwrights could benefit from Chikamatsu's genius without ever having seen his plays performed. He created characterizations that would never be abandoned. After *Yotsugi Soga*, Tora and Shōshō became contemporary courtesans—never again would their main role be as religious paragons. Asahina became an active ally of the brothers, rescuing them or their mistresses on countless occasions,[281] and his test of strength with Gorō became a matter of pride between two friends who respect and admire each other. In Kabuki the "armor-pulling" scene became a spectacular piece of acting. Kabuki authors and actors followed Chikamatsu's lead in *Soga gonin kyōdai* and freely changed the circumstances of the scene.

Many of Chikamatsu's motifs were repeated again and again in Kabuki. After *Yotsugi Soga*, killing villains in chests became a ludicrously regular feature of both puppet and Kabuki drama. Chikamatsu

279. Keene, "Introduction," 3.
280. Yuda and Torigoe, *Kamigata kyōgen bon*, 3:9.
281. Kitano, "Chikamatsu Soga jōruri," 33.

was among the first to replace scenes traditionally played by men with women characters. Kabuki presented complete "women's plays" in which the heroes were converted into heroines. In this way it was easy for Kabuki playwrights to create novel scenes and plays that contained erotic appeal, parody, colorful spectacle, or a combination of all three.

The essence of Chikamatsu's art, as we have seen, was conflict and contrast at all levels. Kabuki authors and actors recognized the appeal of Chikamatsu's drama and included numerous scenes of contrast in their works. In particular, Kabuki exploited three thematic contrasts: (1) tradition versus novelty, (2) high-minded morality versus erotic love or depravity, and (3) tender emotions versus light-hearted violence.

The most important gift that Chikamatsu bestowed on fellow authors, both his contemporaries and successors, was his free and imaginative handling of a traditional story. After Chikamatsu's plays were published and performed, others continued to rewrite the story thoroughly and to radically recast its most important characters. Of course there was never absolute freedom in either plot or characterization: in no play did Kudō kill the Soga brothers, and in no play were Tora, Shōshō, or the brothers portrayed as venomously evil characters. Nevertheless, Chikamatsu had expanded the parameters of possible stories and characters to an extent barely conceivable in 1680.

Playwrights' freedom in handling Soga material was tightly constrained in one crucial way—by the presentational techniques and conventions of Kabuki and *jōruri*. Chikamatsu rewrote the Soga story in order to provide works that would best display the various talents of Kaganojō, Tōjūrō, and Gidayū. Several of Chikamatsu's Soga plays were extremely successful, attesting to a threefold genius: his own creative imagination, his accurate assessment of the abilities of collaborating performers, and his empathetic understanding of audiences' knowledge and tastes. Later playwrights operated under the same constraints as Chikamatsu but rarely possessed his genius. When we speak of the freedom to reinterpret the Soga story, perhaps it would be better to speak from the point of view of the performer: after Chikamatsu, if a performer had any special talent—whether in dance, acting, singing, or puppetry—the Soga tradition could be freely and radically modified to suit that performer's talent.

Chapter Six: Ichikawa Danjūrō's *Aragoto* Kabuki

In its successive incarnations on stage we have seen the Soga story become more and more secular in its message and appeal. In the Kansai Chikamatsu and Tōjūrō continued to secularize the story and to contemporize it fully, so much so that in *Soga tayū zome* the uninformed viewer or reader would not know that the Soga brothers and their ladies were characters from the medieval past. At the same time in Edo, Ichikawa Danjūrō (1660–1704), the most influential Kabuki actor of all time, created a different persona for the role of Soga Gorō, influenced by an approach to religion that was new to Japanese experience. Although there is nothing religious in *wagoto* characters, nor do *wagoto* acting or costuming borrow from religious ceremony or iconography, the plots and imagery of Danjūrō's *aragoto* (wild acting) plays are deeply indebted to esoteric Buddhism. It was Danjūrō's transformation of Soga Gorō into an archetypical *aragoto* hero that would begin the rise of the Soga brothers to their pinnacle of popularity. For a century and a half no Edo New Year's celebration would be complete without new Soga Kabuki plays running at all of the city's major theaters.

The records indicate that several actors contributed to the development of *wagoto* acting, but the creation of *aragoto* Kabuki is attributed to one man, Ichikawa Danjūrō. His origins and childhood are uncertain and obscured by legend. Family traditions maintain that the Ichikawas descend from samurai retainers of the Takeda clan, whose lands were in the region north of Mount Fuji. By the time of Danjūrō's father, the Ichikawa family was living in the city of Narita, northeast of Edo. Various theories have it that Danjūrō's father in his early years was a successful merchant or a wandering entertainer, but Danjūrō II wrote that his grandfather moved to Edo, prospered there, and gained a reputation as a generous and popular man about town.[282] Danjūrō I was born in downtown Edo, and his house was very near two of the city's four Kabuki theaters. What is of crucial importance is that the Ichikawas remained parishioners of the Shinshōji in Narita and worshipers of the temple's chief deity, the Fudō Myōō (The Immovable Bright King), an alternative form of the Dainichi Nyorai (The Great Sun Buddha), central to the esoteric sects of Buddhism.

We know nothing of Danjūrō's life before his first appearance in Kabuki in 1673, when at age fourteen he performed the role of Sakata Kintoki in *Shitennō osanadachi* (The Youth of the Four Guardian Kings). The text of this play does not survive, but it is part of the Shitennō/Kinpira thematic corpus. In Edo in the 1670s, *kinpira jōruri* was at its height of popularity, and Danjūrō contrived to achieve a *kinpira* style performance as an actor. He wore red and black makeup, carried a battleaxe, and fought a demon in a spectacular battle on a mountain top.[283]

In 1675 and 1676 Danjūrō performed Soga Gorō in *Kachidoki homare Soga* (The Soga Battle Cry) and *Soga ryōsha akebono* (Dawn at the Soga Shrine).[284] His first four roles were energetic and martial,[285]

282. According to Toita Yasuji, *Kabuki jūhachiban* (Chūō Kōronsha, 1969), 21, Danjūrō's father became a successful merchant and lived in Izumi-chō in Edo. Kanazawa Yasutaka, "Aragoto ni kiku kami no ashioto," *Kokugakuin zasshi* 57.5 (1956): 73, states that the Ichikawas had long been wandering entertainers. Danjūrō II wrote about his father and grandfather in a book called *Chichi no on* (In Gratitude to My Father). In it he wrote that his grandfather had been a popular Edo *otokodate* who composed *haiku* under the name Otokodate Tōgen Jūemon and who went by nicknames such as "Reed Jūzō" and "Pockfaced Jūzō" (Hattori Yukio, *Ichikawa Danjūrō*, vol. 20 of Nihon o Tsukutta Hitobito [Heibonsha, 1978], 6). Hattori notes that there is no evidence to corroborate what Danjūrō II wrote about his grandfather.

283. Misumi Haruo, "Soga no buyō oyobi aragoto," in *Soga kyōgen buyō shū*, edited by Hattori Yukio, vol. 50 of Kokuritsu Gekijō Jōen Shiryō Shū (Kokuritsu Gekijō Geinō Chōsa Shitsu, 1970), 22. The description of Danjūrō's first play is based on family records that are uncorroborated by other sources.

284. Ichikawa Danjūrō II wrote that his father performed in these two plays, but no independent records confirm that the first one was performed, and the date and location of the second play remain uncertain. Danjūrō II wrote that *Kachidoki homare Soga* was Kabuki's first multi-act Soga play, but other records show that the 1665 play *Soga* deserves that distinction. All Kabuki plays prior to 1664 had been short, one-act plays known as *hanare kyōgen*. Multi-act plays were called *tsuzuki kyōgen*. The writing of Danjūrō II about his father's roles is in his *Kin no sai*, with the entry on *Kachidoki homare Soga* excerpted in Ihara, *Kabuki nenpyō*, 1:123.

285. In 1689 Danjūrō played the hero Fuwa Banzaemon in *Yujoron* (The Courtesans' Dispute), and in 1684 he played the thunder god Narukami in *Kadomatsu Shitennō* (The Four Guardian Kings' New Year).

and he and his descendants would perform Soga Gorō, the thunder god, and other energetic heroes repeatedly during the next three hundred years. In the Genroku period, accounts began to refer to his performing art as *aramushagoto,* "wild warrior business," or simply *aragoto.*[286] We do not know if Danjūrō coined the term himself, or if it was invented by fans or critics, but Danjūrō was termed the "creator of *aragoto.*"[287]

In traditional *aragoto* plays the leading actor is the obvious center of attention. The other actors, the words and music of the play, and even the gorgeous sets fade into insignificance; their role is to reinforce the image of strength and valor presented by the *aragoto* character, and to bring the virtuosity of the main actor into clear focus. The *aragoto* character is spectacular even in immobility. Every aspect of his appearance is exaggerated. His bold costume makes him seem larger than life. Concealed stage assistants often hold out the actor's huge sleeves to enlarge his physical presence. Most *aragoto* roles call for the actor to use oversized weapons or to carry three swords instead of the samurai's usual two. The most striking features of the *aragoto* actor are his face and limbs, which are painted with bright stripes (first used by Danjūrō II) that accentuate musculature and natural lines of anger and tension.

The acting in an *aragoto* role is as stylized and overstated as the actor's appearance. *Aragoto* plays are an early form of *shosagoto* or dance play. The performer's movements follow a complex choreography, and his gestures and postures illustrate the lyrics of the play. The actor's movements are expansive and full of vitality: he stamps loudly on the stage, makes great sweeping strokes with his oversized sword, crushes foes beneath his feet or tosses them lightly away, and expresses his anger or joy in a swaggering *roppō* exit. Dynamic postures that demonstrate heightened emotion or resolve culminate with a *mie,* in which the actor rolls his eyes and opens his mouth in a fierce grimace. The action of the *mie* rivets the attention of the audience. The malevolent glare of an *aragoto* character is often enough to terrify an enemy and send him off in full flight.

286. See Suwa Haruo, "Goryō shinkō to aragoto gei," *Bungaku* 47.8 (1979): 10–11 for reference to early uses of the terms *aragoto* and *aramushagoto.* The earliest reference to *aragoto* appears in 1694, in the *hyōbanki* (guide to actors) entitled *Yakusha ikazuchi* (Actors' Thunder).

287. The quote is from *Yakusha kuchi jamisen* (The Actor's Vocal Shamisen), a *hyōbanki* of 1699 (Genroku 12).

Aragoto lines, usually delivered in a strong, guttural voice, can be part of the dialogue or simply another demonstration of the predominance of the leading actor. The actor may accompany his own physical effort with onomatopoetic descriptions of his actions, and sometimes he even bellows a brisk series of nonsense syllables to show the strength of his voice. Many lyrics are in a heroic vein; the hero recalls the immortals of Chinese and Japanese martial lore and vows to outdo their feats. *Aragoto* plays often demonstrate the pride and prestige of Edo-period leading actors when the actor steps out of his onstage role and plays himself, addressing the audience directly.

Danjūrō wrote almost all of the plays he performed in, and in each of them an *aragoto* hero was the major character. Danjūrō always took the leading *aragoto* role in his plays, and in most of them the main character is contrasted with a *wagoto* character played by a secondary actor. Facial makeup for *wagoto* actors is pale, and the actor's movements are small and restrained. The *wagoto* actor, far from making powerful gestures, often keeps his arms tucked in the sleeves of his kimono. His voice is high and effeminate; today, female impersonators sometimes play *wagoto* roles. The kimonos worn by the *wagoto* actor have few layers and are of ordinary design; they are usually black or pastel shades, as opposed to the bold patterns and primary colors of *aragoto* costumes. *Wagoto* characters often carry a fan or a pipe; if they carry weapons, they are suited to their station in society rather than being symbols of their strength. The tone of *aragoto* acting is bombastic, heroic, and often somewhat comic; the *aragoto* hero is ready to take on the world with a laugh. *Wagoto* characters are subdued, melancholy, and sensitive, often beset by worries.

Early accounts of the Soga brothers, beginning with the *manabon*, describe their contrasting personalities—Jūrō and Gorō correspond roughly to the *wagoto-aragoto* descriptions above. Soga Gorō was a proto-*aragoto* character in medieval works like the Noh plays *Hitsukiri Soga* and *Wada sakamori* and the *kōwakamai* play *Wada sakamori,* and in them the contrast in personalities between the two Soga brothers was enhanced. The dramatization of the brothers' contrasting natures was continued in early Edo plays, especially those based on the "Wada's Banquet" episode.

The leading role in Genroku-period Soga Kabuki plays in the Kansai was invariably Jūrō, the *wagoto* brother. We have seen that Sakata Tōjūrō played Jūrō on several occasions. Nevertheless, almost every Kansai Soga play featured at least a few heroic, martial deeds performed by Gorō, Asahina, or Zenjibō. During the years Danjūrō was formulating his *aragoto* art, there were popular *wagoto* actors in Edo as well. The first "true *wagoto*" portrayal of Jūrō is credited to Nakamura Shichisaburō (1662–1708) in *Kamakura kōshoku gonin onna* (Five Women of Kamakura Who Loved Love), presented in 1682. Shichisaburō was Edo's other great actor of leading roles, and he was often rated higher than Danjūrō in actor evaluation books. Danjūrō began playing a heroic and martial Gorō early in his career. In Danjūrō's first two Soga plays, Jūrō was certainly a less important character than Gorō, and he was likely portrayed as weaker and less impetuous than his younger brother. Danjūrō's meteoric rise to a dominant position in Edo Kabuki led to a process of development of Soga plays in Edo very different from what took place in the Kansai. In Edo a bombastic Soga Gorō, not a romantic Soga Jūrō, took center stage as the most important character in Kabuki versions of the Soga tale.

The origins of *aragoto* Kabuki are linked with the Soga tradition as well as with other religious and literary traditions. This is clear from Danjūrō's portrayals of Soga Gorō early in his career while he was in the process of formulating his art. The relationship between the Soga story and *aragoto* Kabuki is a complex one. The Soga story as it already existed in drama and in fiction helped inspire Danjūrō's creation of *aragoto* acting, but Danjūrō's later *aragoto* acting irrevocably changed popular conceptions of and attitudes toward the Soga tradition.

On what sources did Danjūrō draw to create his new stage art? This question has intrigued specialists in such diverse fields as literature, cultural history, religion, and anthropology. In the Soga tradition danced combat and displays of martial prowess were presented in the earliest Noh plays. Dances in these plays were vigorous and sometimes even acrobatic.[288] Noh dance undoubtedly contributed to the choreography of *aragoto* Kabuki:

288. Examples of acrobatics in Noh dance include somersaults (in *Shakkyō* and *Youchi Soga*) and the *hotoke daore* or "Buddha fall," a difficult fall flat on the back, which represents death in battle. The most vigorous dances, *hataraki,* contain jumps of various types.

1. The Kabuki "pillar *mie*" probably derives from the similar *hashiramaki* (pillar coil) used in demon dances in Noh.
2. The *tachimawari* fight dances of Kabuki probably derive in part from combat scenes in Noh (including the very exciting fight choreography of *Youchi Soga*).
3. The Kabuki *danmari*, fights in which the protagonists mime groping in the dark, have a precedent in the *tachimawari* of *Youchi Soga*, in which Gorōmaru captures Gorō in the dark.

Scenes in some of the medieval Soga plays that are no longer performed are striking in their resemblance to Kabuki *aragoto*. In the Noh play *Hitsukiri Soga*, Gorō's loud, rash words, and his thoughtless, exuberant violence are reminiscent of *aragoto* characters in Kabuki. Gorō even carries a very long sword, the mark of *aragoto* heroes. Shimazu Hisamoto claims that the first *aragoto* acting in the history of Japanese theater is found in the portrayal of Gorō in the *kōwakamai* play *Wada sakamori*.[289] The text of the armor-pulling scene in this play (translation pp. 74-75), and Gorō's ride to rescue his brother (p. 196) suggest that this is proto-*aragoto*, even though we have no idea how the scenes were performed. Yet the claim that *Wada sakamori* is the first occurrence of *aragoto* theater is hard to prove because we have no choreographic records for medieval *kōwakamai* performance, and because it is so difficult to date this and other proto-*aragoto* Noh and *kōwakamai* plays. Danjūrō's Kabuki play texts make it abundantly clear that he read a large number of Noh and *kōwakamai* texts. While commoners could not often see full Noh plays performed, they had access to teachers of singing and dance, and thus Danjūrō is likely to have been well informed in these areas as well.

Most theater histories state that Danjūrō drew his inspiration from *kinpira jōruri*. In the 1660s and 1670s *kinpira jōruri* was very popular in Edo, and Danjūrō's first play presented characters from the *kinpira* world. The violence and power of early *aragoto* acting were exaggerated beyond any counterparts in medieval theater, and this aspect of *aragoto* clearly derives from the special effects used in puppet fight scenes.

The costuming and characterizations in both *kinpira jōruri* and Danjūrō's *aragoto* derive in part from the images of folklore. *Aragoto* costumes resemble Kintarō's outfit as it appears in illustrated

289. Shimazu Hisamoto, "Kōwaka no Soga mono," *Kogugo to kokubungaku* 10.4 (1943): 465.

editions of folk tales.[290] The various *aramusha* (wild warriors), like Kintarō and other heroes of folk tales, are youthful and have simple, straightforward characters. Their only role is to run amok and kill demons.

Medieval warrior and demon plays and Edo puppet theater surely influenced Danjūrō's *aragoto* style, but the true origins of *aragoto* are to be found in the images and ritual performances of popular religion—mostly as experienced by Danjūrō himself in the rites of the Shingon (True Word) and the syncretic Shugendō sects of Shinshōji in Narita.[291] The appearance of Fudō Myōō, the temple's principal deity, is terrifying: "One eye glares downward, the other squints divergently upward. His mouth is twisted into a snarl, revealing protruding fangs. His long hair hangs in a coil over his left shoulder. He stands not on a lotus or animal mount, as do many Buddhist divinities, but on an immovable rock. Always he is ringed with fire."[292]

The doctrine of Shugendō contains elements taken from both Buddhism and Shinto, and its most important adherents were mountain ascetics (*yamabushi*), who retired from society for long periods to practice austerities in the mountains. Even in the temple their religion required rigorous, sometimes painful devotions. Their rituals included dances called *aramai* (wild dances),[293] in which they portrayed violent warriors and deities, including Fudō. The action in *aramai* includes stamping, glaring, twirling, and acrobatics, and dancers use swords and sticks in fight dances.[294] Several kinds of evidence link Shugendō practices and Fudō worship to the Kabuki of the Ichikawa family: (1) the movements in *aragoto* and *aramai* are similar; (2) some lines in *aragoto* and the actor's powerful, droning delivery may derive from *yamabushi* prayers[295]; (3) Fudō is an important character in the *aragoto* repertory—Danjūrō I played the role often, and

290. Toita, *Kabuki jūhachiban*, 27.

291. For a good description of the beliefs and modes of worship of Shugendō, see Hori, *Folk Religion in Japan.*

292. Carmen Blacker, *The Catalpa Bow: A Study of Shamanistic Practices in Japan* (London: George Allen and Unwin, 1975), 175.

293. *Yamabushi aramai* is still performed in some sections of Hokuriku and Tōhoku. See Misumi Haruo, *Sasurai bito no geinōshi* (NHK Books, 1975), 125.

294. Ibid., 124.

295. Ibid., 129. *Yamabushi* prayers are satirized in *kyōgen* plays about *yamabushi*. In *kyōgen*, *yamabushi* prayers are *tsurane*-like run-on lines, the contents of which include boasting, rhythmical gibberish, and silly wordplay. See Carolyn Anne Morley, *Transformation, Miracles, and Mischief: The Mountain Priest Plays of Kyōgen* (Ithaca, NY: Cornell East Asia Series, 1993), 49–51, 74–77.

his son Danjūrō II made his debut as Fudō; and (4) The Ichikawa family may have chosen the color persimmon for its ceremonial kimono because that is the color of *yamabushi* robes.[296]

The purpose of *yamabushi aramai*, like that of many powerful ritual dances, is to drive away evil spirits that cause sickness and disaster. *Yamabushi* performed *aramai* in private houses to cure the ill or insane, and at festivals to protect communities from calamity. Vigorous dances such as the *aramai* were intended to please the deities by demonstrating their great strength, but festival participants also believed that divine power could enter the performers of dances and that performers could cure illness or torment caused by evil spirits.[297]

The concept that demons or wrathful deities, presented on stage at festivals, can destroy evil spirits is basic to Japanese folk belief. The *kami* of early Japan often had malevolent intentions and a demonlike aspect and so inspired fear in believers. As we have seen, the Japanese believed that violent and dangerous gods, if supplicated, respected, and entertained, could be won over to protect the community from lesser evil spirits.[298] Buddhist iconography reinforced this belief in the coexistence of the terrible and the benevolent in a single god. Fudō, for example, appears ferocious, but "according to popular belief, Fudō is a Buddha who has been changed into a being of frightening aspect in order to act as a guardian of men in a world filled with evil spirits."[299] He smites demons with the sword in his right hand but pulls lost souls to paradise with the rope in his left hand. The dynamic and awesome appearance of statues of the Five Great Bright Kings (*Go Dai Myōō*—Fudō is one of them), the Shitennō, and *niō* (guardian kings)[300] strongly influenced *aragoto* costuming, posture, and makeup. A few examples follow:

296. Misumi, *Sasurai bito nogeinōshi*, 129. Kanazawa ("Aragoto," 75) states that the choice of the color persimmon reflects the Ichikawa family's status as wandering outcast entertainers: "butchers and slaughterers used the color, and it was used for the entry curtains at brothels." Danjūrō I used light blue for his ceremonial robes, but his son changed the color to persimmon.

297. This can still be seen at Setsubun festivals. For example, at the Rōzanji Setsubun festival in Kyoto, after the demon dance is over the dancers sit on the veranda and spectators line up before them to be cured. The performers rub the part of the "patient's" body that gives pain.

298. Masaya, "*Soga monogatari* no minzokutei kiban," 41–49.

299. Thornbury, *Sukeroku's Double Identity*, 39.

300. *Niō* statues are placed on either side of temple gates or halls.

1. Costuming: *Niō tasuki*, cords with two intertwining colors, are used to hold up the actor's sleeves when he fights.[301]
2. Posture: When *aragoto* actors strike a defiant pose, they assume the posture of guardian statues, even raising their toes in imitation of deities treading on demons.[302]
3. Makeup: Many scholars believe that the red and blue lines painted on the actor's face and limbs derive from protruding *chikara suji* (sinews of strength) found in Buddhist statuary.

In addition to Fudō worship, worship of *arahitogami* (violent gods who are the spirits of powerful men who died harboring feelings of rancor and hate) is part of Shugendō practice. *Aramai* dances portrayed Soga Gorō. Gorō trained at Hakone Temple, a Shingon institution, but in *The Tale of the Soga Brothers* Fudō is only mentioned once, and that is in a tale tangential to the core story of the Soga brothers' vendetta. Fudō and Gorō were first linked in the Noh play *Chōbuku Soga*. This play, which shows the first meeting between Hakoō and his father's murderer, Kudō, has a unique plot. In the first half of the play the *shite* takes the part of Kudō. Hakoō, played by a child actor, is a strong-willed lad who is too young and weak to consider attacking his blood enemy, and Kudō publicly humiliates him.. In the second part of the play the *waki*, who is the Hakone abbot, performs a fire service (*goma*), in this case a ritual to place a curse on Kudō. The abbot summons Fudō (the *shite* in the second act), who performs a violent and impressive dance that comes to a climax when he pierces an image of Kudō with a sword, thus promising Hakoō eventual success (see fig. 12). "Hakoō is metaphorically transformed into Fudō. Neither Hakoō nor Kudō appear in the second act, but Hakoō's resolve through the long years is embodied in the Fudō of *Chōbuku Soga*."[303]

Danjūrō created an even closer relationship between Gorō and Fudō in *Tsuwamono kongen Soga*. In this play Danjūrō I enacted Soga Gorō, and his son made his stage debut as a manifestation of Fudō. When Danjūrō began his career in Kabuki, deities such as Fudō, and *arahitogami*, among whom Soga Gorō was the most prominent, were frequently portrayed in popular ritual performances in rural areas,

301. Toita, *Kabuki jūhachiban*, 33.
302. Ibid., 32.
303. Thornbury, *Sukeroku's Double Identity*, 40.

especially in the Kantō and Tōhoku. Danjūrō's *aragoto* art added contemporary dramatic flair to medieval gods and heroes. The association of Soga Gorō with Fudō that Danjūrō created was historically credible and dramatically exciting, and Danjūrō's influence on Edoites was so great that Soga Gorō became an urban cult deity in the city of Edo.

Aragoto's roots in popular religion have been amply documented, but for Genroku-period spectators was *aragoto* Kabuki a secular or a religious performance? This is a question that is still being debated by scholars. Records from the period tell us that when Danjūrō I and his descendants played the role of Fudō, members of the audience threw coins onto the stage as an offering to Fudō. When Danjūrō and his son performed in *Tsuwamono kongen Soga,* people from Narita flocked to the show. They brought money to Danjūrō[304]: "it was as if the people of Narita viewed Danjūrō and his son as manifestations of Soga Gorō and Fudō."[305] After presenting the play and receiving offerings, the Kabuki actors led a pilgrims' procession to Shinshōji, and the Ichikawa family made generous contributions to the temple in thanks for the success of the play.

Several performers and spectators went to Danjūrō I, and later to his son, to be cured of illness or possession. The most remarkable account is of an acting colleague of Danjūrō II who was ill due to possession by a fox:

> Danjūrō seized the patient, glared at him in *aragoto* fashion, and shouted, "If you don't go away now, you'll have to deal with me!" The patient's face changed color, and he suddenly jumped from the second floor balcony into the street. The leap was the fox spirit in flight, and the patient was cured.[306]

Many other accounts corroborate the exorcistic power of the Danjūrō glare, which was believed to be a gift of Fudō. The gift did not come without effort—actors had to perform austerities and rites dedicated to Fudō—but every actor named Danjūrō has used the famous glare.[307]

304. Nishiyama Matsunosuke, *Ichikawa Danjūrō* (Yoshikawa Kobunkan, 1960), 18.
305. Thornbury, *Sukeroku's Double Identity,* 54.
306. Toita, *Kabuki jūhachiban,* 29.
307. See C. Andrew Gerstle, "Flowers of Edo: Kabuki and Its Patrons," in *18th Century Japan: Culture and Society,* edited by C. Andrew Gerstle (Sydney: Allen and Unwin, 1990), 37, for other accounts of the spiritual power of the Danjūrō glare. The present Danjūrō XII performed austerities at Shinshōji prior to assuming the Danjūrō name, and demonstration of the glare was the highlight of his name-taking ceremony.

Ukiyo-e prints became the artistic icons of *aragoto*.[308] Prints of Danjūrō II as Gorō in *Ya no ne* (like the one on the jacket of this book; see pp. 195–217 for a detailed discussion and translation of the play) were placed above door frames to ward off evil spirits. In the era of Danjūrō V parents were told, "Hang a picture of Danjūrō over a crying child and it will be more effective than a charm."[309] Today, when Danjūrō XII goes to the countryside on tour, parents bring children to see him, hoping that his touch will bring their children strength and good health.[310]

For Danjūrō I religious life and work on the stage were intimately connected. In his autobiographical writing he recorded his prayers and acts of devotion to numerous esoteric Buddhist deities, and many of his prayers were for professional success. In 1692 he wrote:

> Look at myself. Among all the arts, there is not one I have mastered, that I am better at than anyone else. I am not naturally skilled in martial arts, nor am I exceedingly clever. It is Sanbōkōjin, Ganzan Daishi, Dainichi, Aizen Myōō, Fudō Myōō, and Nitten who shine on me, and, because the deities protect me, I am called "unrivaled in Japan," "the finest actor," "the founder of a new temple of Kabuki in the modern age." My name is revered, but this is not the work of a mere mortal.[311]

He repaid the kindness of the deities who had aided him by turning them into heroes on the Kabuki stage, by serving the deities and their temples publicly and privately, and by bringing many new worshipers to his sect. For many years Danjūrō's wife failed to bear him a son, and Danjūrō prayed fervantly and persistently to Fudō for assistance. When the boy who was to become Danjūrō II was born, his father called him "Fudō's gift." Danjūrō petitioned and thanked the Fudō with offerings and gifts, but he also honored his deity by portraying him on stage, and by having his son debut as Fudō.

Records of the lives of townsmen in seventeenth- and early-eighteenth-century Edo show a new attitude toward religious worship. People poured into the shogun's capital, but the Bakufu had made

308. For the relationship between *aragoto* Kabuki, *ukiyo-e*, and religion, see Hattori Yukio, *Edo kabuki ron* (Hōsei Daigaku Shuppankyōku, 1980), 286–96.

309. Ibid., 294.

310. Conversation with Ichikawa Danjūrō XII, 19 March 1987.

311. Ichikawa Danjūrō I, "Gansō Danjūrō no zangeroku," in *Danjūrō no shibai*, edited by Ihara Seiseien (Waseda Daigaku Shuppanbu, 1934), 117.

few provisions to meet the spiritual needs of a large urban commoner population. Commoner immigrants to Edo found themselves in a competitive, socially underregulated environment, very different from the secure but highly structured and repressive rural communities they had left behind. Their spiritual needs changed dramatically with their changed social situation. Records show lively competition between purveyors of religion, both Buddhist and Shinto, with the measure of success for a given sect corresponding to the extent its worshipers' prayers were perceived as being met. Evidence attesting to the efficacy of offerings and prayers was the key to the success of religious sects. Diaries show that the prayers of most commoner Edoites centered on the desire for material success, and, if a given deity did not follow through, worshipers quickly changed allegiances.[312]

In the early 1600s the Shinshōji was a rural temple with a small, local following, but by the nineteenth century it had become a grand complex, the wealthiest and most popular pilgrimage site in the Edo suburbs. The temple's association with successive Danjūrō actors was a major cause of its prosperity. The abbot Shōhan, a contemporary of the first two Danjūrōs, was the first to actively proselytize in the city of Edo, and he found both actors willing allies.[313] Shōhan, in turn, may have written some portions of the plays of Danjūrō I that relied heavily on Buddhist scripture.[314] For out-of-town temples a major means of proselytization and income were *degaichō* in Edo, temporary exhibitions (usually for one or two months) for worship of divine images from sponsoring temples or shrines. *Degaichō* became focal points for extended festivals, attracting thousands of merry makers,

312. For examples, see Hattori, *Edo kabuki ron,* 304. The new relationship between Edo Japanese and their gods is explained by Mary Douglas' grid and group theory of religion. In rural villages Japanese were in "high grid, high group" societies, which experience continuity in religious worship and congruity of social and religious hierarchies. For commoners, Edo in the 1600s and early 1700s was a "low grid, low group" social environment. In these societies people follow charismatic leaders who seem to appear from nowhere. Danjūrō I was such a figure, and he exerted considerable religious impact even though in the eyes of the authorities he was a social outcast with no formal connections to religion. For grid and group theory of religious worship and symbolism, see Mary Douglas, *Natural Symbols: Explorations in Cosmology* (London: Barrie and Rockliff, The Cresset Press, 1970), 53–59, 103–29.

313. Hattori Yukio, "Danjūrō no aragoto to shomin shinkō," *Ichikawa Danjūrō,* edited by Kanamori Kazuko (Shōchiku, 1984), 54.

314. Asahi Jūzan, *Naritasan to Ichikawa Danjūrō narabi ni Geinōjin no Shinkō* (Narita: Narita-shi Bunka Zaidan, 1968), 13.

who would also stop to pray and throw coins before the statue. Danjūrō I and his descendants scheduled plays about esoteric Buddhist deities to coincide with, and in effect to advertise, Edo *degaichō* sponsored by Shinshōji and related temples, and all served as official greeters (*torimochi*) at Shinshōji *degaichō* in Edo.

There is strong evidence that Danjūrō I and many in his audience regarded his *aragoto* depictions of divine power as religious experiences of some kind, but Suwa Haruo, an important Kabuki historian, refutes the argument that *goryō shinkō* beliefs were part of Danjūrō's *aragoto* art.[315] Suwa believes that the essence of *aragoto* was the presentation of an exciting and ostentatious acting style deriving from traditional villain roles. Villains, of course, were never the main characters in Kabuki plays, and Danjūrō, an egotistical and ambitious man, could never tolerate working as a supporting actor. When Danjūrō I played a "dark *aragoto* hero," a hero moved to acts of violence by lust or pride, that hero was invariably rescued by or reincarnated as a deity in the last act of the play, and the deity put to rights all of the discord sewn by the hero. According to Suwa, "the sense of the undeserved, tragic outcome essential to *goryō* belief is not to be found in Danjūrō's plays, and it is impossible to find a sense of piety in them."[316] Suwa concludes that "the current of the history of performing arts, which turns belief into amusement, ran swiftly in the Genroku period."[317]

Certainly the attitudes of Ichikawa Danjūrō and his urban audiences toward *arahitogami* must have differed from those of medieval farmers who lived in fear of insect infestations that might be caused by Soga Gorō's vengeful spirit. *Aragoto* plays about Soga Gorō do not convey the idea that anyone except his onstage enemies need fear him, and in this sense *goryō shinkō* beliefs were not operative for Kabuki audiences. But the awe and power we sense in Danjūrō's *aragoto* Gorō suit an *arahitogami*. Without doubt Danjūrō I and Danjūrō II converted fear and propitiation of Soga Gorō into awe, excitement, and celebration. The exorcisms by actors and offerings by audience members demonstrate that for many the awe inspired by the *aragoto* portrayals of Gorō and Fudō were more than mere amusement. And in the Edo period, even more than in earlier ages, spirituality and

315. Suwa, "Goryō shinkō to aragoto gei," 1–16.
316. Ibid., 15.
317. Ibid., 16.

amusement went hand in hand—many clearly religious activities seem to lack a "sense of piety." The Ise Shrine pilgrimage phenomenon is just one, though perhaps the best example. Records make it clear that Edo-period Japanese believed wholeheartedly in the efficacy of the pilgrimage in terms of protecting families and communities, but it is also clear that the experience was the most enjoyable one in the lives of many Japanese commoners. Pilgrims made new friendships, encountered exotic people and places, and indulged in spendthrift shopping and irresponsible love affairs. *Degaichō* and expanded festivities for holidays such as *bon* and the New Year were further examples of the merging of religion and amusement. Going to a Danjūrō *aragoto* play was an experience very much in tune with the new tenor of popular, urban religion—fun and good for you too.

TSUWAMONO KONGEN SOGA: DANJŪRŌ'S NEW SOGA GORŌ

Although Danjūrō I played Soga Gorō many times, the *e-iri kyōgen bon* for Danjūrō's *Tsuwamono kongen Soga* is the only surviving text of a performance of this role. The play was probably first staged in 1697.[318] The three main roles, Gorō, Jūrō, and Asahina, were played by Danjūrō, Murayama Shirōjirō, and Nakamura Denkurō, respectively. The four-act play featured *aragoto* scenes with Asahina in act 1, Gorō in act 3, and Asahina and Gorō together in acts 2 and 4.

The high point of the play, and the scene from which the play takes its name, occurs in act 2 when Gorō meets Kudō for the first time and is magically transformed from a weak child into a powerful warrior. The setting for the scene is Hakone Temple (see fig. 20).[319] Hōjō Tokimasa comes to the temple, where he officiates at Gorō's coming-of-age ceremony, and the Hakone abbot gives Gorō his blessing to seek revenge as a samurai. Kudō Suketsune comes to the temple

318. In his autobiographical writings Danjūrō I wrote that he was in a production of *Tsuwamono kongen Soga* in 1695. No other source corroborates the 1695 production date. According to Danjūrō the 1695 version was a play in five acts (the 1697 version was four acts long), but no mention is made of Fudō appearing as a character in the play, or of Kuzō making a stage appearance, or of whether the play was a success or a failure. Danjūrō wrote some of his autobiography years after the events he describes, and the 1695 production date may be in error, or there may have been a less than successful play in 1695 that Danjūrō rewrote and restaged to achieve his 1697 success.

319. The plot summary of *Tsuwamono kongen Soga* comes from Akashi Seizaburō and Ichikawa Danjūrō, "Tsuwamono kongen Soga," in Hattori, *Kotobuki kongen Soga*, 82–98.

Fig. 20. Gorō meets his enemy Kudō Suketsune for the first time at Hakone Temple. Kudō is seated in the right panel, holding two swords. Gorō is bowing in the left panel; the abbot looks on. Gorō's robe is decorated with the Ichikawa family's three-rice-measure (***mimasu***) crest. From the ***e-iri kyōgen bon*** of ***Tsuwamono kongen Soga***, 1697. Illustration attributed to Torii Kiyonobu and Torii Kiyomasu. Courtesy of the Tokyo Geijutsu Daigaku Collection.

as part of Yoritomo's entourage and is introduced to Gorō. He presents Gorō with a sword, with which Gorō promptly attacks him, but Kudō easily disarms Gorō. Gorō tries to attack Kudō two more times, but Kudō pins him to the ground, releasing him only at the earnest request of Hōjō and the abbot. Gorō leaves the scene, angry and humiliated. This was the "confrontation" or *taimen* scene, and it would be rewritten and restaged again and again throughout the Edo period (for a detailed discussion of the appeal and significance of Soga confrontation scenes, see pp. 187–92).

After Kudō leaves the temple, Gorō secretly prays to Fudō that he be turned into a powerful demon, strong enough to kill Kudō. Later, when Gorō rejoins the abbot and Hōjō, his face turns a livid red, his body develops powerful muscles, and his demeanor becomes ferocious and wild. Gorō does three weeks of "wild training" (*aragyō*), an exaggerated parody of *yamabushi* austerities. Gorō's training consists of ripping apart hoes, pulling up bamboo by the roots, and smashing stone stupas (see fig. 21). Smashing bamboo is an actual, if rarely performed, *yamabushi aragyō* practice, but in the play Gorō rips up bamboo by the roots, a truly prodigious feat. The image of this feat of strength is the most memorable one from this play because of an impressive woodblock print of the scene done by Torii Kiyomasa, who based the print on the illustration he did for the *e-iri kyōgen bon* text. Thanks to the power of this image, *aragoto* heroes created for later Kabuki and puppet plays were sometimes given bamboo staves to use as weapons.[320]

When Gorō has finished his wild training, a little *yamabushi* approaches, played by Kuzō, the son of Danjūrō I and the future Danjūrō II. The little *yamabushi* dances and then disappears in a flash just as Gorō is about to attack him. Gorō hurries to a nearby river, where he spies Asahina, a powerful comic *aragoto* (*dōke aragoto*) warrior. The two heroes challenge each other and begin to fight, only to be stopped by the little *yamabushi*, who reveals that he is in fact Fudō (see fig. 22). Fudō reminds the two warriors that they are related by blood and must act as allies. The act concludes with a dance by Fudō and his promise that he will give Gorō tremendous strength to carry him through the confrontation with his blood enemy.

320. Two examples are Watōnai, the *aragoto* hero of Chikamatsu's 1714 puppet play *Kokusen'ya kassen* (The Battles of Coxinga), and the "Oshimodoshi" hero, created by Danjūrō II in 1727.

In this act Danjūrō I used a well-known incident from the traditional Soga story to create a classic *aragoto* scene. Antecedents for the scene include the *rufubon* and *kōwakamai* versions of the first meeting between Hakoō and Kudō Suketsune. The Noh play *Chōbuku Soga,* in which the *shite* played Fudō, was Danjūrō's most important source work. In all previous versions of the episode Hakoō (he has not yet come of age) recognizes the fact that as a child he is unable to harm his enemy, and he therefore does not attack Kudō. In the Kabuki play Gorō's weakness is demonstrated by physical action on the stage—his three fruitless attempts to kill Kudō. This visual presentation of his helplessness is essential for the audience to appreciate Gorō's strength after he is transformed into a powerful *aragoto* warrior.

In Danjūrō's *aragoto* scene the symbolic transformations of the Noh play *Chōbuku Soga* are actually presented on stage. Gorō is magically transformed into a powerful warrior before the eyes of the audience. Danjūrō probably put on *aragoto* costumes and makeup in "quick changes" when he ran offstage. In *Chōbuku Soga* Hakoō is played by a child actor, and Fudō is played by the *shite,* but in the Kabuki play the casting is opposite: Gorō is played by the leading adult actor (Danjūrō I), and Fudō is played by a child. This makes it possible for Gorō to appear convincingly onstage as a physically strong adult warrior. Fudō's power is expressed by both characters—in the magical powers (transformation, instant disappearance and reappearance, the power to control two wild warriors) of the little *yamabushi* and Fudō himself, and by Gorō's transformation, "wild training," and fight with Asahina.

Fudō is further linked to Gorō by the "armor-pulling" scene in the last act of the play (see fig. 24). Gorō of course remains immovable, like Fudō whose name literally means "the immovable one." The scene relies not on *aragoto-wagoto* contrasts but on a conflict between two powerful *aragoto* heroes. It is important that the two heroes are friends, not enemies, so that their tug-of-war is not a martial combat but a ritualistic test of strength, much like a *sumo* bout performed to entertain the deities. The primacy of Fudō is established by having Gorō, his proxy, defeat the man who was heretofore the strongest warrior in Japan. Jūrō is a *wagoto* character, but the first act concludes with a fight scene in which Jūrō injures several minor villains and chases the rest away. Perhaps Jūrō fought in a *wagoto* style; in contemporary Kabuki there are many fight scenes featuring nonmartial heroes. In these fights the hero stands in the center of stage languidly

Fig. 21. Right panel: Gorō's *aragyō*. He has already smashed hoes (fragments are visible in the lower right) and is currently uprooting bamboo. A stupa awaits destruction in the right foreground. Left panel: The little *yamabushi* appears and dances. From the *e-iri kyōgen bon* of *Tsuwamono kongen Soga*, 1697. Illustration attributed to Torii Kiyonobu and Torii Kiyomasu. Courtesy of the Tokyo Geijutsu Daigaku Collection.

Fig 22. Fudō (right panel, top) appears to break up the fight between Gorō (right panel, bottom) and Asahina (left panel). From the *e-iri kyōgen bon* of *Tsuwamono kongen Soga*, 1697. Illustration attributed to Torii Kiyonobu and Torii Kiyomasu. Courtesy of the Tokyo Geijutsu Daigaku Collection.

Fig. 23. Hakoō (Gorō by his childhood name) holds aloft a statue of Fudō and writes prayers in Sanskrit. This is not a Kabuki print, but it demonstrates how *aragoto* Kabuki added Fudō to the Soga legend as the source of Gorō's strength. Woodblock print (ca. 1844–47) by Utagawa Toyokuni III (Kunisada). Courtesy of Odawarashi Kyōdo Bunkakan.

Fig. 24. The "Armor Pulling" scene. Right panel: Wada Yoshimori, Tora, Shōshō, and the Soga mother look on. Left panel: Asahina tugs on Gorō's armor. From the *e-iri kyōgen bon* of *Tsuwamono kongen Soga*, 1697. Illustration attributed to Torii Kiyonobu and Torii Kiyomasu. Courtesy of the Tokyo Geijutsu Daigaku Collection.

waving his arms, and his foes scatter and toss themselves this way and that, indicating that they have been thrown by the hero. Unfortunately there is no way to know how Jūrō's fight was staged in *Tsuwamono kongen Soga*. The mixed *wagoto* and traditional portrayal of Jūrō is reinforced by his two very different prayers: one, a traditional arrow-shooting prayer at the *yatate no sugi*[321] expressing his desire to kill Kudō, and the other a prayer that women "return his love."

The opening of the third act of *Tsuwamono kongen Soga* is set in the dilapidated Soga house where Oniō is making straw sandals to help support the brothers. It is the the day of the Iris Festival (the fifth day of the fifth month), and Jūrō weeps because of his poverty. His spirits are restored by an unexpected present of sweets from Oniō and by the arrival of a letter from Tora. Tora visits Jūrō and they have a simple love scene, including a section called *kamisuki* in which Tora combs Jūrō's hair.[322]

As in most of Chikamatsu's plays, the most important *shukō* in Danjūrō's *Tsuwamono kongen Soga* restages Gorō's pardon in a most outlandish way. The Soga brothers and their mistresses decide to persuade the Soga mother to forgive Gorō during a big ceremony to be held at Hōjō Tokimasa's mansion. The mother refuses even to set eyes on Gorō, so they disguise him as a huge Boy's Day doll.[323] Hōjō's guests are amazed at the lifelike appearance and movements of the doll. This scene is a bit of human *karakuri*, and Danjūrō imitated puppet movements in his acting. Finally, Gorō cannot restrain himself and speaks to his mother. She, of course, refuses to pardon him. Finally Hōjō's guests stage a mock attack on the Soga brothers. Jūrō appears to be in grave danger, so his mother orders Gorō to rescue him, but Jūrō refuses to be aided by a "stranger." When his mother pardons Gorō so

321. The *yatate no sugi* ("the arrow-studded cryptomeria") was a cryptomeria tree (resembling a Douglas fir) in Hakone. Samurai prayed by shooting arrows into it. If the arrow stuck (as it was almost certain to) one's prayer would be granted.

322. The *kamisuki* or "hair-combing love scene" is based on the episode entitled "Tora's Sorrrow at Parting from Jūrō," in book 6 of the *rufubon*. It was first used in Soga *wagoto* scenes and later adapted for non-Soga plays. In these scenes a man and woman express their love for each other and their sorrow at parting while the woman dresses the hair of her beloved.

323. Dolls representing warriors were displayed in samurai households on the fifth day of the fifth month. This was also the day of the Iris Festival. In Meiji Japan many samurai customs were introduced to all Japanese, and May fifth became a national holiday called Children's Day. Today most families display samurai dolls or fly carp banners on Children's Day.

that he may assist Jūrō, all combat ceases, the ruse is revealed, and a congratulatory banquet follows.

Tsuwamono kongen Soga is no longer performed today, but it had a tremendous impact on the Soga story in Kabuki. The illustrations from the *e-iri kyōgen bon* are among the finest Kabuki prints extant from the Genroku period, and they illustrate the play's most dramatic moments.[324] Ritualized conflict between Gorō and Asahina became the *aragoto* centerpiece of most Soga plays, and specific scenes from *Tsuwamono kongen Soga* were parodied or restaged as *shukō* in play after play. Soga Gorō became one of the most frequent roles played by the eleven successors to Danjūrō I, and to Edoites Gorō became a surrogate of the deity Fudō.

KEISEI ASAMA SOGA: EDO *ARAGOTO* IN A *WAGOTO* PLAY

The plot summary for *Tsuwamono kongen Soga* shows that secondary *wagoto* and *dōke-aragoto* actors had significant parts in Danjūrō's *aragoto* plays. In *wagoto* Soga plays written for Shichisaburō's leading role of Jūrō, there are subordinate but important *aragoto* parts for Gorō. In *Keisei Asama Soga* (The Sogas and the Mount Asama Courtesan, author unknown), presented in 1703, Shichisaburō played Jūrō, a well-meaning but weak and indecisive character resembling Tōjūrō's Jūrō. *Keisei Asama Soga* took characters from the Soga world and put them in a story that derived from Shichisaburō's most successful and influential play, *Keisei Asama Dake* (The Mount Asama Courtesan). In *Keisei Asama Soga*, Shichisaburō's most important scenes include: (1) a confrontation with Inubōmaru in which Jūrō is afraid to fight, (2) a scene in which Jūrō takes off his over-kimono, (3) a hair-combing love scene with Tora, (4) a parting from Tora, and (5) a scene in which Oniō's wife, sold into prostitution, makes advances to Jūrō, but Tora catches the pair in a compromising position. All of these are typical Tōjūrō-style *wagoto* scenes set in the pleasure district.

Oniō and Gorō are the two most important roles after the *wagoto* lead. Oniō is a "realistic" or *jitsugoto* part. In the first act he prevents

324. In the Genroku period, artists did not sign the work they did to illustrate theatrical texts. Based on stylistic evidence, scholars believe that the illustrations in the *Tsuwamono kongen Soga e-iri kyōgen bon* may have been a collaboration by the two leading Kabuki print artists of the day, Torii Kiyonobu and Torii Kiyomasu. See Howard Link, *The Theatrical Prints of the Torii Masters* (Honolulu: Honolulu Academy of Arts Riccar Museum, 1977), 24.

Gorō from engaging in a foolish fight, and in the third act he convinces Jūrō to give up his philandering. In the same act Oniō sells his own wife into prostitution to aid his master's vendetta. In the last act Oniō engineers the pardon of Gorō in the play's climactic scene.

The many scenes of trickery and concealed identity in *Keisei Asama Soga* remind us of Chikamatsu's Soga Kabuki plays. One humorous trick involves Ōtōnai's bringing a trained horse to the Soga mother. He tells her that it is the reincarnation of her late husband, Kawazu Saburō, the brothers' father. Ōtōnai and the horse perform a stunt routine intended to convince her that Kudō did not in fact kill Kawazu Saburō. Shinkai Arashirō, an important villain in the play second only to Kudō himself, enters the Soga household disguised as a poetry teacher, kills Oniō's daughter, and steals twenty *ryō* in cash. The daughter's ghost takes revenge by turning into a great snake and killing Shinkai while he is sporting in the pleasure district, spending the stolen money. There are several other supernatural and occult scenes in the play. The title derives from an incident following Jūrō's decision to break with Tora so he can devote himself to the vendetta. He burns Tora's love letters in a brazier, and the smoke of the fire reminds him of the volcano, Mount Asama. An apparition of Tora appears in the smoke and expresses in words and dance Tora's resentment of Jūrō's fickleness (see fig. 25).

Gorō is the third most important character in the play, and his *aragoto* portrayal clearly derives from Danjūrō's acting, especially his portrayal of Gorō in *Tsuwamono kongen Soga*. In act 2, Gorō does "wild training" at a Fudō temple. In a parody of Danjūrō's Hakone Temple scene, Shinkai dresses up as the deity Fudō, but Gorō and Dōsaburō discover the deception.[325] They rip off Shinkai's disguise in a scene contrasting with the immediately previous one in which Jūrō delicately removes his kimono in the pleasure district (see fig. 26). This parody of *Tsuwamono kongen Soga* six years after it was performed shows that playwrights were confident that audiences remembered Danjūrō's play and that they had come to regard Soga Gorō and Fudō as a linked pair.

The fourth act features an *aragoto* conflict and exciting stage effects. The Soga mother has disowned both Jūrō and Gorō. Gorō

325. The description of this section of the play is too incomplete to determine what activities constituted "wild training" or to determine the charlatan Shinkai's motives in dressing up as Fudō. See Takano Tatsuyuki and Kuroki Kanzō, eds., *Genroku kabuki kessaku shū* (Waseda Daigaku Shuppanbu, 1925), 555.

sneaks back to the family house, only to be caught and severely chastised by his mother. Gorō answers her, "If you consider me to be an evil man, then I might as well sink to the very depths of Hell!"[326] Gorō heaps abuse on his mother and pursues her upstairs, as if intending to kill her. Suddenly a fissure opens in the earth, splitting the house in two, and Gorō falls into the flames of Hell. Gorō's mother is aghast that her punishment has led to such a tragedy, and when Oniō asks her if she would pardon Gorō were he alive, she responds with a heartfelt "Yes!" Oniō then says, "All right, Gorō, you can come out now!"[327] and the two men reveal that they staged the entire hellfire scene as a means to gain Gorō's pardon. Oniō and Gorō explain the trick to Gorō's mother, and to the audience, which was undoubtedly fascinated by the mechanics of the stage.

In the above scene Gorō's violent temper is carried to the extreme of matricidal fury. The fact that in this play Gorō can even feign an attack on his mother attests to the power of previous *aragoto* portrayals. The hellfire scene is an absurd exaggeration of Gorō's character and therefore a parody of Danjūrō's heroic *aragoto* Gorō.

The *e-iri kyōgen bon* version of *Keisei Asama Soga* is little more than a plot summary with excerpts of dialogue from the play, but it clearly demonstrates the impact of Chikamatsu's plays and Danjūrō's *aragoto* on other Soga drama. The play uses or parodies earlier characterizations, dramatic motifs, and acting techniques, but also adds its own innovations in plot and stage mechanics. Comparing its inserted pictures with those in *Tsuwamono kongen Soga,* it is clear that many of the best moments in *Keisei Asama Soga* were parodies of scenes and routines borrowed from Danjūrō's play. It is probably representative of a "typical" Soga Kabuki play of the first half of the eighteenth century in its reliance on Danjūrō's *aragoto,* Tōjūrō and Shichisaburō's *wagoto,* and Chikamatsu's freedom to parody or reshape the events and characters of the Soga story. New disguises, plot tricks, and "thrills" provided the novelty in most new Soga Kabuki plays of this period.

ARAGOTO ACTING, THE ICHIKAWA FAMILY, AND EDO KABUKI

Danjūrō I drew upon archetypes deeply rooted in the cultural imagination of the Japanese when he created his *aragoto* heroes and

326. "Keisei Asama Soga," in ibid., 563.
327. Ibid., 566.

Fig. 25. Above right: Oniō and his wife come to rescue Jūrō who is being beaten by Inubōmaru's thugs. Above left: Tora's apparition appears in the smoke of love letters burning in the brazier. Two-page lower panel: A pleasure district scene with Oniō and his wife on the left. Jūrō (Nakamura Shichisaburō) converses with Tora as the villain Shinkai Arashirō eavesdrops from the far right. The costume bearing the family crest in the design of two interlocking squares identifies Nakamura Shichisaburō. From the *e-iri kyōgen bon* of *Keisei Asama Soga*, 1703. Illustration attributed to Torii Kiyonobu and Torii Kiyomasu. Courtesy of the Tokyo Geijutsu Daigaku Collection.

Fig. 26. Above: An attendant removes Jūrō's robe as Inubōmaru looks on. Tora and Shōshō (between Jūrō and Inubōmaru) enjoy the view but cover their faces with their hands to conceal their excitement. Below: Gorō pursues Shinkai Arashirō, who has been impersonating Fudō. Jūrō watches from the extreme left. From the *e-iri kyōgen bon* of *Keisei Asama Soga*, 1703. Illustration attributed to Torii Kiyonobu and Torii Kiyomasu. Courtesy of the Tokyo Geijutsu Daigaku Collection.

plays. The popularity of *aragoto* acting made him the preeminent actor in Edo. By 1692 he was the highest paid actor in that city, and in 1693–94 he performed for a year in Kyoto. After meeting Tōjūrō, Danjūrō refused to appear with him, saying that as long as Tōjūrō was active, no other actor could be successful in Kyoto.[328] Such deference was uncharacteristic of the man. Danjūrō cast his plays so that he would dominate the stage and all other actors would remain in his shadow. Tōjūrō was well known for his ability to cooperate with lesser actors and elicit their best efforts, but Danjūrō engaged in continual conflicts with subordinate and rival actors. By 1693, after a series of poorly received plays, the Edo theater owners refused to employ him. Danjūrō took his family with him to the Kansai and worked the next season in Kyoto. After his return to Edo in 1694, he worked without a break until his death, which was very much in character with the life he had lived. In 1704 a rival actor, Ikushima Hanroku, used his stage sword to kill Danjūrō in a fight in the theater. The exact motives of the murder remain obscure.

The last *hyōbanki* to evaluate Danjūrō was *Daijin mitsu sakazuki* (Three Sake Cups for Millionaires), and the author (probably the fiction writer Ejima Kiseki) concludes as follows: "For a long time I have known that all men must take this road, but for *this* to happen now . . . the deities we worship should be impervious to harm. From now on, whenever I pray to the Narita Fudō, it will be him that I see."[329] It is significant that the author sees Danjūrō as invested with the divinity of the Fudō and suggests that he himself is a worshiper of Fudō.

Ichikawa Danjūrō II (1688–1758) was a brilliant successor to his father. He brought to the stage many of the plays that became classics of *aragoto*, and he performed in more than forty different Soga plays. Soon after his father's death he performed *wagoto* roles in several plays, including Kabuki adaptations of Chikamatsu's love suicide plays, and in 1711 he used "realistic" makeup to portray Gorō in *Yunzei yomeiri Soga* (The Soga Bowman's Wedding).[330] In this play he gave Soga Gorō's character a romantic side. In 1716 his Soga Gorō, alias Sukeroku, was a

328. Toita, *Kabuki jūhachiban*, 28.

329. Attributed to Ejima Kiseki, "Daijin mitsu sakazuki," in *Kabuki hyōbanki shūsei*, edited by Kabuki Hyōbanki Kenkyūkai (Iwanami Shoten, 1973), 3:576.

330. Atsumi Seitarō, "Sukeroku no yūrai," *Engei gahō*, March 1925. Reproduced in *Kokuritsu gekijō jōen shiryō shū* 164 (January 1977): 38–39.

commoner, *otokodate* hero, popular among all the women in the pleasure district and beloved of the district's most sought after courtesan (see chapter seven for a discussion of *Sukeroku*). Danjūrō II performed Soga Gorō more often than any other character, and his portrayals of Gorō ranged from the "gentle *aragoto*" of Sukeroku to the classic, pure *aragoto* of *Ya no ne* (see pp. 199–217 for a discussion and translation of the play).

Like his father, Danjūrō II was the leader of Edo Kabuki, both in the influence of his acting style and in the authority he exerted on other actors, playwrights, and producers. After his father's death, his mother told him that she would not consider him his father's equal until he made 1,000 *ryō* a season in Edo. One thousand *ryō* would have constituted a sizable sum, roughly equivalent to a quarter of a million dollars today. It took the young actor some years to accomplish this, and later, in 1742, on a one-year tour in Osaka, he received the unprecedented salary of 2,000 *ryō*, probably the highest salary ever paid a Kabuki actor in the premodern age. His work in Osaka that year demonstrated that Kansai audiences would throng to see the best Edo *aragoto*.

In 1832 Danjūrō VII (1791–1859) selected the "Eighteen Great Plays" (*Kabuki jūhachiban*) from among the works of his predecessors. Most of the plays were first performed by Danjūrō I and Danjūrō II. Danjūrō VII felt that these plays best represented the *aragoto* traditions of the Ichikawa family, and that regular performance of the "Eighteen" would maintain his family's prestigious position in the world of Edo Kabuki. Three of the eighteen great plays featured Gorō as the main character. In fact, eighteen was considered a lucky number, and Danjūrō VII chose some mediocre works and fragments of plays to round out his list, but the best plays have been performed continually until the present day, and the "Eighteen Great Plays" have ensured the Ichikawa family's continuing stature as the premiere acting line in Tokyo Kabuki.

Chapter Seven: The Soga Story As Festive New Year's Kabuki

The performances of *Kachidoki homare Soga* and *Soga ryōsha akebono* in 1675 and 1676 by Ichikawa Danjūrō I helped launch his career as an *aragoto* actor and also established Soga Gorō as a leading *aragoto* character in Kabuki. Acting in Soga plays also helped two of Danjūrō's contemporaries in Edo to achieve eminence. In 1682 Nakamura Shichisaburō (1662–1708) pioneered the *wagoto* portrayal of Jūrō. He did this independently of, and apparently earlier than, Tōjūrō in Kyoto, but no scripts survive to tell us more of his early work as Soga Jūrō. Shichisaburō's popularity in Edo was second only to Danjūrō's, and Shichisaburō had successful seasons in the Kansai where he was regarded as Tōjūrō's equal.[331] The comic actor Nakamura Denkurō (1662–1713) played his first Asahina in 1683, and he played the role repeatedly thereafter, sometimes as a comic/heroic lead and sometimes, as in *Tsuwamono kongen Soga*, as an *aragoto* rival and comic foil to Danjūrō's heroic *aragoto* lead as Soga Gorō. These actors established the three central roles in Soga Kabuki: *aragoto* Gorō, *wagoto* Jūrō, and *dōke/aragoto* Asahina.

In 1688 these three actors played the leading roles in three Soga plays that ran concurrently at three of four Edo theaters during the first month of the year. After 1688 Soga plays were performed about every other year, and following the success of *Tsuwamono kongen Soga*, a Soga play or plays were presented in Edo every year (except 1725) until the turn of the twentieth century.

331. Dunn and Torigoe, *The Actor's Analects*, 184. The ninth item of the "Kengai Collection," the *dōke* actor Azuma Sanpachi's (d. ca. 1735) record of the conversations of the leading actor Somekawa Jūrōbei (d. 1708 or 1711), is a relatively lengthy account of Shichisaburō's experiences in Kyoto. Tōjūrō and Shichisaburō admired each other's art, and the two became close friends. See pp. 133–36 for this item.

In 1709 three Edo theaters again performed Soga plays in the first month,[332] and the Edo "Spring Kabuki" (*haru kyōgen*) tradition continued for almost two hundred years. The Kansai *bon* Soga tradition began some twenty to twenty-five years earlier but was never as faithfully followed as the Edo New Year's tradition. *Bon* Soga *kyōgen* plays were discontinued in the mid-eighteenth century.

In 1709 each Edo theater's New Year's play was a popular success and enjoyed a long run. The prime motivation for theater owners' perpetuation of the New Year's Soga tradition was the profits brought in by consistently high attendance figures. Why were Soga plays more popular at New Year than in other seasons? Traditional New Year's customs included (and still include) ceremonies believed to ward off evil spirits and ensure good health and safety throughout the coming year. *Kagura* and various demon dances are included in these ceremonies. Many New Year's dances involve stamping, glaring, and dramatic postures—precisely the kind of presentation in *aragoto* Kabuki. The *aragoto* Gorō was a powerful godlike character, reminiscent of rural gods upon whom common folk relied to drive off evil spirits. In rural Japan both the performing and visual arts were intimately associated with religion. Painting, sculpture, and performance could be seen only at temples and shrines, where they were efficacious as well as beautiful and entertaining. Newcomers to Edo transformed the meaning of Kabuki thanks to their belief in the religious power of art. As we have seen, many audience members saw Danjūrō as invested with spiritual power, and *ukiyo-e* prints of *aragoto* heroes (see frontispiece) were hung on doors and in alcoves to ward off evil spirits.[333]

Following the lunar calendar, New Year's day was considered to be the beginning of spring, and in rural Japan it was a time of cyclical renewal in the agricultural year. Many rural New Year's dances are intended to drive off evil spirits (as above), but others supplicate the gods for good harvests or reaffirm the social and economic life of the community. In some rural dances, for example, middle-aged men

332. In 1688 the three Edo theaters that staged Soga plays were the Yamamura Theater, the Ichimura Theater, and the Nakamura Theater. In the first month of 1709 the Morita Theater put on a Soga play, and the Nakamura Theater did not. The Yamamura Theater was closed permanently in 1714 after the exposure of an illicit love affair between one of the theater's actors and a senior lady-in-waiting on the shogun's staff.

333. Toita, *Kabuki jūhachiban*, 155.

imitate the teaching of farming skills to youths.[334] Noh and *kyōgen* preserve their rural origins in ritual New Year's presentations of *Okina* and *Sanbaso* dances. The main characters in both are old men, symbols of fertility and longevity. The words accompanying the *Okina* and *Sanbaso* dance-plays are an archaic mixture of felicitations and sexual and agricultural imagery. The cyclical renewal represented by the New Year is also seen in the universal symbol of a youth or baby (the New Year) who replaces, chases away, or even kills an old man (the Old Year). In *aragoto* Kabuki, Gorō was always portrayed as a youthful upstart and his enemy as a crafty old man.

Theater owners continued the *haru kyōgen* tradition because Soga New Year's plays brought financial success, but the custom soon came to be accompanied by a sense of reverence. Migrants from the countryside to the cities prayed to the old gods of Japan, as they had in their villages, but the goals of their prayers changed from good harvests to personal wealth and success in business ventures.[335] In Edo the Soga spirits, like many other deities, saw a change in the class and livelihoood of their worshipers, and in the prayers directed to them. Theater owners and actors gave thanks to the Soga spirits for providing the material that brought artistic and commercial success. Kabuki management believed, as Japanese have believed from the very beginnings of ritual performance, that what entertains people must invariably entertain the gods as well. A diary entry demonstrates this conviction: "The Umewaka Soga *kyōgen* was an unprecedented smash hit. It must certainly have pleased the *arahitogami*."[336] The author of the diary used the traditional term *arahitogami*, but in the Edo-period theater world a sense of fear had left the cult, replaced by a sense of gratitude for providing the theater with inspiration for literary creativity and entertaining acting.

The New Year's Soga tradition became an important part of Edo holiday celebrations. The very word "Soga" came to have felici-

334. One example is the Shirotori *Ennen*, held every January fifth in Shirotori, Gifu Prefecture. The festival dances are said to date from the fifteenth century. In one dance a middle-aged man imitates turning the soil with a mattock, and he is followed in the dance by a youth.

335. Inari was originally an agricultural fertility deity, and in the countryside people pray to the god for good rice harvests. In Japan's cities Inari has become the patron god of success in commerce and business ventures. The Inari sect has perhaps the largest following of any Shinto sect. The "Seven Gods of Happiness" similarly aid worshipers with either agricultural or commercial aspirations.

336. Aoe, "Nihon geinō no genryū," 158. Umewaka is an acting family.

tous connotations,[337] and posters advertising Soga Kabuki performances, and prints depicting Gorō in *Ya no ne* added visual splendor to traditional New Year's decorations.

THE SOGA FESTIVAL IN EDO KABUKI THEATERS

The Soga cult in the Edo theater world reached its pinnacle with the establishment of the Soga festival, observed at the three Edo theaters. The festival began as a backstage ceremony, held on the twenty-eighth day of the fifth month, the anniversary of the brothers' vendetta, to express thanks to the Soga brothers' spirits when the Soga play that year had enjoyed a long run.[338] Until 1753 it was a private or "shadow" festival (*kage matsuri*) involving the erection and decoration of an altar, the preparation of banquets, and the rendering of offerings.

The first Kabuki Soga festival to include ceremonies open to the public was held at the Nakamura Theater in 1753 to give thanks for the long run of *Otokodate hatsukoi Soga* (Gallant Soga's First Love). Soga festivals that included public ceremonies and attractions continued at all Edo theaters until the third decade of the nineteenth century, if the Soga plays of the given year had been successful.

A typical Soga festival began with private celebrations. Actors and others connected with the theater worshiped in the morning at a temporary altar dedicated to the Soga brothers' spirits. The public Soga festival began with a procession around the neighborhood of the theater, during which actors performed various "side show" entertainments. Sometimes a play about the Soga night raid replaced the regularly scheduled Kabuki play on the day of the Soga festival. Gala festival dances were added to the day's Kabuki program. When the curtain closed on the last Kabuki play, the theater owner came on stage and announced the beginning of the "Soga Festival." All the actors reappeared on stage wearing cotton kimonos decorated with patterns of butterflies or plovers. They bore a *mikoshi* (a sacred palanquin that houses a deity during a festival). After a procession on stage, the actors performed various group dances. To conclude the public festival, the theater owner, dressed as a Shinto priest, rode a horse onto the

337. Koike Shotarō, *Kōshō Edo kabuki* (Miki Shobo, 1979), 50, sets forth several passages demonstrating the role of Soga traditions in Edo New Year's customs.
338. Misumi, "Soga buyō oyobi aragoto," 20.

stage and announced, "That's all for today!" Finally, the performers returned to the backstage area where a concluding banquet was held before the Soga altar.[339]

The Soga festival became a popular event for Edo commoners, and the parade became larger and more boisterous, including a *mikoshi* that careened through the city streets. In 1795, during the Kansei reforms, a campaign against corruption and licentiousness, the government banned one theater's Soga festival on the grounds that it was a nuisance to traffic and commerce.[340] By the early nineteenth century the Soga festival had become, in most years, a relatively quiet affair celebrated onstage and backstage in the theaters.

THE STRUCTURE OF SOGA *HARU KYŌGEN* AND ITS ROLE IN THE KABUKI PERFORMANCE CALENDAR

In the first few decades after 1709, Soga plays were performed beginning in the first month, but the contents of the plays and the duration of performances varied considerably. Performance duration depended entirely on popular response. The longest run for a Soga play was *Ōtaka nigiwai Soga* (Joyous Sogas and the Great Hawk), which in 1721 played for 280 consecutive days. Leading actors strongly influenced the content of early New Year Soga plays, but as the example of *Ya no ne* will demonstrate in the next section, plays invariably included references to New Year rituals and customs, and a felicitous tone prevailed.

The establishment of the Soga New Year tradition was part of a general process of consolidation of the Kabuki repertory and codification of performance practices that took place throughout the eighteenth century. By the middle of the century the *shibai nenjūgyōji*, or "theatrical calendar of events," was well established; plays were written to fit its thematic requirements, and performance durations were controlled by special "Kabuki calendar" dates.

The "Kabuki calendar" year was divided into four main seasons: (1) *Kaomise* (Face Showing), opened the Kabuki year and lasted from the first day of the eleventh month to the tenth day of the

339. Atsumi Seitarō, "Soga matsuri," in *Soga kyōgen buyō shū*, edited by Hattori Yukio, vol. 50 of *Kokuritsu gekijō jōen shiryō shū* (Kokuritsu Gekijō Geinō Chōsa Shitsu, 1970), 88–90.

340. Gunji Masakatsu, *Kabuki mon*, vol. 1 of *Gunji Masakatsu santei shū* (Hakusuisha, 1990), 226.

twelfth month. The Kabuki New Year actually began two months before the end of the normal year. (2) *Haru* (Spring) lasted from the fifteenth day of the first month through the sixth day of the seventh month. The Spring season was the longest and was subdivided into three subseasons. (3) The *bon* season ran from the fifteenth day of the seventh month to the middle of the eighth month. (4) *Wakare* (Farewell) ran from the ninth day of the ninth month to the fifteenth day of the tenth month.

In *Sukeroku's Double Identity* Barbara Thornbury has presented a detailed summary of the events of a typical Edo Kabuki year, so here let us investigate only the role of the Soga plays in the Spring season. During the first fourteen days of the New Year, Kabuki theaters presented ceremonial dances, including *Okina* and *Sanbaso*, and actors paid New Year's calls on teachers, patrons, and tea houses—establishments that played an important role in theater life and finances.[341] From the fifteenth of the first month ("Little New Year," the last day of the two-week New Year holiday) through the second month, Soga plays were performed. The day's performance often began with a felicitous but nondramatic grand opening scene in which characters from the Soga world paraded before Tsurugaoka Hachiman Shrine. Typically, two Soga plays were presented. One portrayed the poverty of Oniō, Dōsaburō, and Oniō's wife and their devotion to the brothers' cause; *Tsuwamono kongen Soga, Keisei Asama Soga,* and several of Chikamatsu's plays set precedents for this theme.

The second Soga play was a *taimen* or "meeting" play in which the brothers confront Kudō before the vendetta. The *taimen* scene, the climax of the early Spring program, was considered best suited to conclude the ceremonial New Year program for several reasons: (1) Visiting relatives and benefactors played an important role in New Year customs and ritual. In the Soga *taimen* the brothers visit their uncle, Kudō Suketsune. In the Edo period a *taimen* between leading daimyo and the shogun was the main New Year event at Edo Castle. The palace had a special *taimen dokoro* (meeting hall) for this ceremony.[342] (2) The formality of the meeting scene allowed actors to extend New Year greetings directly to the audience.[343] (3) The

341. Thornbury, *Sukeroku's Double Identity*, 8.

342. Gunji Masakatsu, *Kabuki ronsō*, 543. In some years the *taimen* scene was performed on the second day of the first month to correspond exactly with the celebratory meeting between the daimyo and the shogun in Edo Castle.

343. Ibid.

confrontation between brash young heroes and an old enemy particularly suits New Year symbolism of the new replacing the old. (4) The Soga *taimen* is tied to the agricultural renewal and fertility prayers of traditional New Year's ritual in that it is a dramatic coming together of opposites. An early *taimen* in Japanese theater is found in *Okina* and *Sanbaso*, the coming together of black and white.[344] (5) According to tradition, Hakoō's actual first encounter with Kudō at Hakone Temple took place on the fifteenth day of the first month.[345] (6) A homonym of *taimen* means "sea bream noodles." Because the sound *tai*, which can mean "sea bream," is part of the felicitous word *medetai* (congratulations), sea bream has long been eaten on festive occasions. Humorous puns using the word *taimen* became an important part of Soga *taimen* plays in the late Edo period.[346]

The *taimen* and "Oniō in Poverty" plays were rewritten every year using new *shukō*. The process of reworking these plays was known as *kakikae* (rewriting), and since *kakikae* plays were meant to be used just once each, few of them were published. The first surviving Soga *taimen* scene in Edo Kabuki is the second act of *Tsuwamono kongen Soga*. Variations on the *taimen* theme were innumerable. In some Gorō or Jūrō appeared alone, but in most both of them appear, together with Asahina. In most *taimen* Kudō was a typical villain, but variations included: a false Kudō, a meeting with Kudō's wife, Kudō disguised as a woman, a sick Kudō, and Kudō who is really a fox.[347] In the 1750s to 1760s leading actors began to take the role of Kudō.[348] In these *taimen* Kudō is an honorable man who presents the brothers with passes to the Fuji hunt and challenges them to try to kill him. This version is performed today. A variation, *Uiro uri*, is included among the "Eighteen Great Plays." In it Gorō appears before Kudō disguised as a medicine seller and reveals his true identity only after he recites a virtuoso imitation of a medicine peddler's spiel. Settings for *taimen* plays have included: Hakone Temple, Kudō's Mansion (the setting for the currently performed *Kotobuki Soga no taimen* (see figs. 27–29), the Tama River, the Umairi River, the Ōiso pleasure district (the setting for *Uiro uri*), traveling in the snow, and during an earthquake.[349]

344. Ibid., 545.
345. Ibid., 546.
346. Koike, *Kōshō Edo kabuki*, 57, and Gunji, *Kabuki ronsō*, 543.
347. Gunji, *Kabuki ronsō*, 550.
348. Koike, *Kōshō Edo kabuki*, 55.
349. Gunji, *Kabuki ronsō*, 550.

Fig. 27. At Kudō's mansion, Gorō (Nakamura Kashō) crushes a New Year's present stand to express his hatred for Kudō. Jūrō (Nakamura Karoku) tries to restrain Gorō. Tora (Sawamura Tanosuke), stage left, and Shōshō (Nakamura Matsue) look on. From *Kotobuki Soga no taimen*, Kyoto Minami Theater, December 1981. Courtesy of the Shochiku Co., Ltd.

Fig. 28. Jūrō (Nakamura Karoku) restrains his brother from attacking Kudō (Kataoka Nizaemon XIII), who is seated on a dais at the right. Gorō (Nakamura Kashō) still holds a splinter from the crushed present stand. From *Kotobuki Soga no taimen,* Kyoto Minami Theater, December 1981. Courtesy of the Shochiku Co., Ltd.

Fig. 29. Gorō (Nakamura Kashō) holds a pass to the Fuji hunt given to him by Kudō. Jūrō (Nakamura Karoku) restrains his brother. Asahina (Kataoka Gatō) is on the left. From the final scene of ***Kotobuki Soga no taimen***, Kyoto Minami Theater, December 1981. Courtesy of the Shochiku Co., Ltd.

In no Soga *taimen* is Kudō killed; the scene always concludes with the promise or knowledge that the same foes will meet again.

The *taimen* scene must have had a special appeal for commoner audiences, for in almost every case it involved brash but virtuous heroes disrupting a staid ceremony presided over by an evil and corrupt, but powerful, authority figure. The discomfiture of the authority figure in situations like this is deliciously entertaining to anyone of lower social status. The two currently performed *taimen* plays, *Kotobuki Soga no taimen* and *Uiro uri*, serve also to showcase Kabuki's major role types in a dazzling array of costumes, wigs, and makeup styles. Like *kaomise* plays, these *taimen* plays served as a formal display of the theater cast for the upcoming season.

In the third and fourth months the daylight hours increased, enabling theaters to stage longer shows, and thus new material was added to Kabuki programs. These were the "flower months"; theater decor and play titles reflected the season, but new plays were tied, at least in name, to the Soga tradition. Some new pieces were short dances, but many new plays were *sewamono.* Plays from the world of Yaoya Ōshichi[350] were particularly popular additions to the second and third months. Because servants in the Edo daimyo residences were given days off during the third month, theaters presented plays about rivalry in feudal houses, which were incorporated into the Soga world.[351] Final changes in the Spring production were made on the fifth day of the fifth month, the day of the Iris Festival and the Boys' Day Festival. After 1753 special performances were held for the Soga Festival on the twenty-eighth day of the fifth month.

Of the four main seasons, the Spring season had the strongest thematic requirements. Although the *Shibaraku* ("Wait a Moment!") scene was standard fare for the Ichikawas' *kaomise* productions, the thematic "world" of the *kaomise* was decided in the tenth month and was often different at the three Edo theaters.[352] The material for the *bon* and Farewell seasons was also more flexible than for Spring.[353]

350. Koike, *Kōshō Edo kabuki,* 51. Saikaku's version of the story of the green grocer's daughter is available in English translation in W. Theodore de Bary, *Five Women Who Loved Love* (Rutland, VT and Tokyo: Tuttle, 1956) and also in Ivan Morris, *The Life of an Amorous Woman, and Other Writings* (London: Chapman and Hall; New York: New Directions, 1963).

351. Thornbury, *Sukeroku's Double Identity,* 12.

352. Ibid., 3–4.

353. Ibid., 13–14.

The uniqueness of the Spring season poses the question of why Soga Kabuki was codified and tied to seasonal ritual in a way not true of the other historical and thematic "worlds" of Edo Kabuki.

The answer to the question is not simple and is best approached by studying the interplay between Edo theater managers and the attitudes of their patrons. In 1709 the three Edo theaters were engaged in intense competition. Soga plays at the New Year were so popular that no theater could afford to present another theme and risk losing its audience to rival theaters. Why were Soga plays so much more popular in Edo than in the Kansai? (1) The three great Edo actors of the day made the Soga brothers and Asahina their favorite roles. (2) According to folklorists and anthropologists, vigorous dancing is a more important part of popular rural religion in eastern and northern Japan than in the Kansai region.[354] And (3) the Soga brothers' spirits naturally played a greater role in rural religion near the geographical setting for the Soga legend than they did in the distant home provinces.

The Edo population of the Genroku period and a few decades later was different from the urban population in the Kansai. Because Edo expanded so rapidly, most Edoites were country-born, or at most a generation or two removed from their rural origins. Festivals played an important role in rural Japan: they marked the changing seasons, provided continuity between generations, protected the community from misfortune, and were the major social and entertainment events in villages. Newcomers to Edo found that the natural rhythms of agricultural life and their attendant festivals were irrelevant to urban life; they nevertheless sought the sense of seasonal change and communal celebration that festivals had provided in their rural homes. Numerous religious cults and institutions stepped in to provide these needs. The Edo period saw the growth of urban cults (including the Fudō cult) and urban festivals, and the Kabuki calendar was part of the process. In Edo, in particular, Kabuki was something of an ongoing festival.[355] In the Kansai, and especially in Kyoto, urban religion and communal bonds were comparatively well established before the late-seventeenth century, and the new Kabuki and puppet theaters did not have to play the same role in molding a new urban community.

354. Aoe, "Nihon geinō no genryū," 161.
355. See Gerstle, "Flowers of Edo," passim.

The cult of the Soga brothers was popular in Edo, not only among theater people, but also among the citizenry at large.[356] Soga spirits worshiped in rural shrines were on several occasions transferred temporarily to Edo shrines (*degaichō*) where they received the offerings and prayers of urban believers. The frequent appearance of the Soga brothers on the Kabuki stage helped to transform the character of the Soga spirits from fearsome *arahitogami* into gods of good fortune and celebration. As we will see in *Ya no ne*, the Soga brothers' participation in commoners' New Year's customs in Kabuki plays brought the god-heroes into the lives of the audience and produced a sense of identification that had not been part of medieval *goryō* worship.

FROM MEDIEVAL NARRATIVE TO THE *ARAGOTO* NEW YEAR'S PLAY, *YA NO NE*

Ya no ne by Murase Genzaburō (dates uncertain) was first performed at the Nakamura Theater in 1729, and it was the most popular scene in a long play entitled *Suehiro ehō Soga* (The Soga Fan and the Lucky Direction).[357] Danjūrō II performed the leading role of Soga Gorō, and the play was so well received that it ran for five months and the proprietor of the Nakamura Theater erected two "*Ya no ne* storehouses" from the profits made during its long run.[358] Despite the fact that new Soga plays were usually presented every year, *Ya no ne* was shown eleven times in the Edo period,[359] and it is one of the seven or eight plays of the "Eighteen Great Plays" that are regularly performed today.

The plot of the play is based on a small part of *The Tale of the Soga Brothers*. *Ya no ne* embellishes the story and interweaves all man-

356. Similarly, actors worshiped not only the Soga deities but also the same gods their audience did. For example, private Inari festivals were held in all Edo theaters in the second month (Thornbury, *Sukeroku's Double Identity*, 11–12).

357. Ernst translates *Ya no ne* as "The Arrow Maker," but *ya no ne* literally means "arrowhead." Gorō sharpens arrows and does not make them, and thus "The Arrow Sharpener" is better than "The Arrow Maker." Although Murase Genzaburō is considered to be the author of the play, most scholars assign credit for the play's concept and form to Danjūrō II. The two collaborated on many of Danjūrō's plays.

358. Misumi, "Soga buyō oyobi aragoto," 22.

359. For a record of performances of *Ya no ne* from 1729 through 1918, see Hattori Yukio, ed., *Ya no ne sannin Kichisa kuruwa hatsugai*, vol. 74 of *Kokuritsu gekijō jōen shiryō shū* (Kokuritsu Gekijō Geinō Chōsa Shitsu, 1972), 1–5.

ner of Edo-period New Year customs. Some scholars consider the text to be "incoherent and impossible to comprehend," even to an Edo-period audience.[360] It is true that one cannot find a well-crafted story in this play; such is not the purpose of the text. First and foremost the words of the play provide opportunities for the *aragoto* actor to display his virtuosity. Second, they delight the audience with their irreverent and sarcastic wit. The play pokes fun at the values and symbols that the Edo-period elite held in respect, and that dashing Edo townsmen therefore took pride in debunking. Puns twist the sayings of Confucius into calls for lechery, and Gorō heaps abuse on the gods of happiness in a satiric monologue. Much of the humor in the play derives from incongruities created by the juxtaposition of "contemporary" Edo-period vocabulary with the traditional Soga story. Edo-period audiences were familiar with both vocabularies, so the contrasts in meaning and tone were apparent and amusing. For the modern reader and Kabuki viewer, unfortunately, both languages are archaic. *The Tale of the Soga Brothers* naturally had nothing to do with the Edo New Year celebration, so the contrasts between those two worlds are obvious to all readers and viewers. The intrusion of New Year foods, gifts, and superstitions lightens the tone of the Soga story and brings Soga Gorō into the lives of ordinary spectators.

The original source for *Ya no ne* is found in the "Wada's Banquet" episode of the *rufubon.* In the narrative, after Tora has served sake to Jūrō rather than Wada Yoshimori, the two men exchange heated words, and Yoshimori's retainers prepare to assault Jūrō. Jūrō wishes that his brother were on hand to help out, and Jūrō's thoughts are so intense that Gorō senses Jūrō's danger and hurries off to rescue his elder brother. The "Armor-Pulling" scene ensues, and the brothers leave safely. *Ya no ne* is concerned solely with Gorō's premonition and hasty departure. In the *rufubon* it reads as follows:

> Shortly before this Gorō was at home in Soga. He sat in front of the altar reading the *Lotus Sutra* and praying for the salvation of his father's spirit. Suddenly a premonition of danger came to him. "I know that Jūrō went to Ōiso. The warriors of the eight eastern provinces are probably there by now, on their way to the Fuji hunt. Tora is a courtesan, and she might well be the cause of some disturbance." He rushed into his room, put on his armor, and thrust in his belt the

360. Misumi, "Soga buyō oyobi aragoto," 17.

> four-foot six-inch long red-handled sword that had belonged to the family for generations. With no time to saddle his horse, he jumped on bareback and galloped more than twenty *chō*, riding as if taking a single turn around the training ground.[361]

In this version Gorō is depicted as a filial, religious, decisive, and vigorous young man whose virtue is rewarded by a premonition that will enable him to rescue his brother.

A *kōwakamai* and several *ko-jōruri* versions of the same incident were performed and published prior to 1729. The text of Satsuma Jōun's *ko-jōruri* play *Wada sakamori* is virtually identical to the earlier *kōwakamai* play of the same title. Tosa no Shōjō modified the Soga story considerably in *Fūryū Wada sakamori*, but the most dramatic sections of his play, including the section corresponding to *Ya no ne*, still very much resemble the *kōwakamai* version. A summary of the *kōwakamai* version follows, with translations of sections particularly relevant to the text of *Ya no ne:*

> Gorō was at the "Old Well"[362] sharpening arrows. He became very sleepy, and, pulling up a *go* board to serve as his pillow, he fell into a deep slumber. His elder brother Jūrō approached his pillow, "Listen, Gorō! Even though you studied Zhang Liang's *Kakō biyō* (Scroll of Forty-Two Chapters) on the martial arts,[363] you have drunk too much sake and are helpless. If you stay fast asleep the plans of a thousand days will be destroyed in a single night. Get up! Get up!" Jūrō repeated, "Get up!" four or five times in Gorō's dream to rouse him. Gorō awoke with a start, looked around, but saw no one. Thinking it strange, he summoned a serving woman and inquired about Jūrō. She told him that Jūrō said he would spend the evening at Ōiso.

(Gorō speculates on Jūrō's predicament. He thinks that the danger must be Kudō's doing, and he says he will permit no one to "tread on

361. One *chō* is 119 yards, so twenty *chō* is about one and one-third miles. The last phrase in the translation means "riding without halting." The passage is taken from Ichiko and Ōshima, *Soga monogatari,* 256.

362. "Old Well" (*furui*) is another name for Soga Village (near present-day Odawara). This name first appears in the Soga tradition in this play.

363. Zhang Liang (?-168 B.C.) was a general who served the first Han emperor. He is credited with one treatise on the martial arts, *Kakō biyō.* The story of how he learned the secrets of martial arts from a sage is told in the Noh play *Chōryō* (Zhang Liang).

Jūrō's shadow." There follows a lengthy description of Gorō arming himself, more detailed than in the narrative version, dwelling at length on the histories of swords and armor.)

> Gorō ran to the stable. There stood a fawn-colored horse that he had recently washed. Since there was no time to saddle it, he pulled some reins off a hook, put an iron bit in the horse's mouth, led it from the stall, and mounted. If he took the roundabout route, it would be three *ri*, but if he went straight it would be fifty *chō*.[364] "If I go around, it will take too much time," he thought, and pressed on for Soga Nakamura. He spurred his horse and struck with his crop, "*Shitoto, hatato!*" He struck with his crop, "*Shitoto, hatato!*" and spurred on his horse, which was soon bathed in white foam.[365]

The *kōwakamai* author secularized the story. No longer is Gorō chanting the *Lotus Sutra* before his premonition; instead, he is sharpening arrows. The playwright added considerable detail about the nature of the dream premonition and the manner in which Gorō armed himself and rode off to rescue Jūrō.

The *ko-jōruri* play *Dōke Wada sakamori*, performed in the 1670s, also describes the scene in which Gorō rides off to rescue his brother. It is a parody of the *kōwakamai* text above, retaining some of the lines from that text, but adding jokes and humorous references to contemporary Edo life and customs:

> At a place called "Old Well" Gorō was engaged in the scrap-metal business. He grew drowsy while polishing some arrowheads that he had bought at Asakusabashi[366] in Edo as part of a bulk-metal purchase, and pulling up an iron tea kettle to serve as a pillow, he dozed off and was soon fast asleep. A moment later his elder brother, Jūrō, stood above his pillow, "Hey, listen, Gorō! Forty-two robbers can join together and snatch wallets and steal scrolls, but, if they commit too many crimes, they'll be discovered even if they try to hide their deeds. And if you stuff yourself with too much sake and noodles, you'll be completely useless. If you stay fast asleep, the plans of a thousand days will be ruined in a single moment. And what do you think you're doing sleeping at noon

364. One *ri* is 2.44 miles, and thus three *ri* equal 7.3 miles.

365. "Wada sakamori," in Sasano, *Kōwaka bukyoku shū,* 473–74.

366. Asakusabashi would not have existed in the days of the historical Soga brothers when Edo was a fishing village, and there was no bridge (*hashi*) over the Sumida River.

when there are so many sneak thieves about nowadays?[367] Get up! Get up!" he repeated four or five times in Gorō's dream to rouse him.

Gorō awoke with a start, looked around, but saw no one. When he went around to the kitchen, there was the girl, Kazuya, doing the laundry. Gorō caught sight of her and shouted, "Hey, servant, servant!" Then he shouted backwards, "Hey vantser, vantser!"[368] Gorō asked her about Jūrō, and she replied, "Master Jū[369] said he wanted to go to Ōiso this evening, so he'll be away from home."

(Gorō's speculation that Kudō is responsible for Jūrō's plight, and the arming scene, are parodied in the same manner as the above section.)

Gorō ran to the stable and saw nearby the unloaded pack horse he had sent that morning to Odawara with a load of freight.[370] It was being used to plow a rice field. There was no time to saddle it, so he pulled some reins off a hook, clanked an iron bit into its mouth, and swung onto its back. "Kyuroku, don't drop the money bag, I'm depending on you."[371] If he took the roundabout route, it would be three *ri*, but the straight road was fifty *chō*. "If I go around, it will take too much time," he thought, and he hurried toward Soga Nakamura. He spurred his horse and struck with his crop, "*Shitoto, hatato!*" He struck with his crop, "*Shitoto, hatato!*" and spurred on his horse, which was soon bathed in white foam.[372]

367. In the preceding monologue Jūrō rebukes his younger brother but never asks for help. When Gorō awakens, the situation returns to the traditional one in which Gorō must hasten to rescue Jūrō. Because the audience knew the traditional story so well, such inconsistencies were unimportant. Puns based on the *kōwakamai* version in this dialogue suggest that the audience was very familiar with the traditional play: "forty-two thieves" replaces "forty-two chapters on the martial arts," "stolen scrolls" replaces "martial arts scroll," and "hiding" thieves (*kakusu*) replaces "studying" (*gakusu*).

368. Gorō plays with words in a very silly way. First he calls his servant in the normal way, *gejo*, and then he merely reverses the syllables, creating a nonsense word, *joge*.

369. Kazuya refers to Jūrō in an affectionate way using the dialect of the pleasure district, "Jū-sama."

370. The city of Odawara would not have existed at the time of the historical Soga brothers.

371. This line is cryptic. Kyuroku is an Edo-period servant's name, but Kyuroku appears in no other work about the Soga brothers. Presumably it was Kyuroku who led the horse to Odawara and is using it to plow the rice field. The money may be what Gorō earned with the freight delivery.

372. "Dōke Wada sakamori," in Yokoyama, *Ko-jōruri shōhon shū,* 6:418–19.

Uji Kaganojō made further modifications in his depiction of the scene in *Yoritomo hamaide* in 1686. Kaganojō's plays were performed in Kyoto, but it is likely that published texts of his plays were available to Edo actors and playwrights. He returned to the more serious tone of the *kōwakamai* text but created a new season for the scene, early spring, the time of year that would later be established as the "Soga season" in Edo Kabuki. He also made his play less fanciful in that there is no dream premonition. Instead, a servant tells Gorō about his brother's plight. Kaganojō also gave Gorō a friend and ally, Hatakeyama Sukenobu, to aid him in his mission. True to Kansai theatrical tastes, Gorō is depicted as a sensitive person who weeps several times during the scene.[373]

Several modifications found in all three early theater versions provide two essential premises for every Kabuki version of *Ya no ne*: (1) Gorō is not praying; instead, he is sharpening arrows. (2) Jūrō is endangered by Kudō Suketsune, their father's murderer, not by Wada Yoshimori.

The wit and humor in *Ya no ne* owe much to *Dōke Wada sakamori*. In the Kabuki play we find the same facetious puns, and the same juxtaposition of crude colloquialisms and classical heroic words alongside the jargon of tradesmen and bandits. The puppet play was a purely comic piece, but *Ya no ne* is an *aragoto* play with a stronger emphasis on Gorō's heroism. Much of the wit of the latter is more intellectual than that of *Dōke Wada sakamori* (hence harder to follow today), and *Ya no ne* does not make use of gratuitously silly wordplay like the *gejo/joge* (servant/vantser) line. Since Gorō in the Kabuki play is a true hero, Jūrō does not taunt him in the dream as he does in *Dōke Wada sakamori* but calls for help in the traditional way. Several motifs from the comic play continue in *Ya no ne*: Gorō engages in the scrap-metal trade (in the Kabuki play he sells old metal to pay his New Year's bills), and he rides off on a pack horse.

A major innovation in *Ya no ne* is its New Year's setting. The New Year's Soga tradition was of course well established by 1729. Kaganojō's play may be the first in which Gorō's ride to the rescue is set in early spring: there is a scent of plum, and a caller brings Gorō a present, although not specifically a New Year's gift. Danjūrō and Murase ostensibly based Gorō's arrow sharpening on a ceremony performed for

373. Uji Kaganojō (attributed), "Yoritomo hamaide," in Chikamatsu, *Chikamatsu zenshū*, 3: 28–31.

the New Year by official armorers to the shogun,[374] but the rest of the many New Year references in the play derive from the customs of Edo commoners. In Chikamatsu's Soga Kabuki plays and his puppet play *Soga nanatsu i ro ha*, the Kansai performance tradition provided a *bon* setting for a few scenes, but Chikamatsu's plays told the story of the vendetta. In the case of *Ya no ne* the New Year's performance context is dominant, completely overwhelming the story of the Soga brothers' revenge, and Gorō is more like a New Year's decoration or talisman come to life than a character in a story.

The most important modifications in the Kabuki version serve to emphasize the strength and determination of Gorō and the virtuosity of the actor portraying him. Danjūrō's Gorō would of course never shed tears in the manner of Kaganojō's *wagoto*-like portrayal.[375] In *Ya no ne*, when Bundayū,[376] a leading musician, appears to offer New Year's congratulations, the leading actor is in fact playing two roles—Soga Gorō and himself, the head of an acting troupe. Jūrō's brief appearance provides a *wagoto* contrast to the *aragoto* lead: Jūrō's voice is thin and quavering, his form slender and insubstantial.

The play includes several dramatic monologues that give the leading actor opportunities to assume dynamic postures and demonstrate his powerful voice. Even when Gorō falls asleep, the actor assumes a striking position, with arms and legs outstretched, a posture that requires considerable effort to maintain even with the help of a stage assistant. The arming scene is deleted and replaced by an encounter with a *daikon* seller[377] in which Gorō shows his physical strength and martial prowess. The vigorous onomatopoetic descriptions of Gorō's ride in pursuit are replaced in *Ya no ne* by action on stage; thanks to the dancing horse and Gorō's use of the *daikon* as a whip, the play concludes on a light note suitable to a felicitous New Year play.

The costumes and accoutrements of *Ya no ne*, like the text and the actor's actions, mark the play as classic *aragoto*. The actor's face and limbs are covered with bold, red lines. His costume is large and

374. See Toita, *Kabuki jūhachiban*, 153, for a description of the ceremony.

375. It is only in the Kaganojō version that Gorō weeps during this scene. While *aragoto* dominated the Edo stage, in Kyoto and Osaka love plays and pathos plays were popular. Kaganojō modified the story to suit his audience.

376. Bundayū is the name of the chanter. His surname, Ōzatsuma, is a style of music and chant now performed by *nagauta* musicians. It is the style of music used to accompany *Ya no ne* today.

377. The *daikon* is a large white tuber in the radish family, usually one to two feet long.

brightly colored, and he wears *niō tasuki* from his first appearance to the end of the play. Gorō's three huge swords are displayed on a rack at the back of his room.

Ya no ne is the only play in which an *aragoto* character handles huge arrows. The arrow plays an important symbolic role in Japanese religion. Blind men or children shot arrows for divination; arrows were shot into the sky to quell violent storms or to determine holy boundaries when shrines or temples were founded; and arrows with white feathers represented gods or the will of gods in numerous religious stories.[378] During the New Year's holiday people bought arrows at shrines and hung them in their houses. By means of these arrows the god of a shrine defeated evil spirits that might cause illness or accidents in the house in the coming year. In the Edo period people hung pictures of "Ya no ne Gorō" for the same purpose.[379] Gorō was depicted in two common poses: in profile, ready to loose an arrow, and in a front view, holding an arrow (see frontispiece). Soga Gorō and the Fudō were the only heroes in the "Eighteen Great Plays" to be depicted in full face in *ukiyo-e* prints. Toita writes that the full face pose of "Ya no ne Gorō" derives from traditional representations of Fudō: Gorō's arrow represents divine power, and the raised brazier on which he sits corresponds to Fudō's pedestal of stone.[380]

YA NO NE: TRANSLATION AND COMMENTARY

Ya no ne is above all a visual experience. The bold costumes and makeup, the actor's grandiose gestures, and the ease with which he handles his long arrows and carries the huge whetstone create the *aragoto* character. While a translated text does little justice to the theatrical experience, it does demonstrate the energy and irreverent humor typical to felicitous New Year's plays. The photographs provided by Mr. Morita Tōshirō, staff photographer of the National Theater, will help the reader picture the living *aragoto* of *Ya no ne.*

378. Toita, *Kabuki jūhachiban,* 154. In the story of the founding of the Kamo Shrine in Kyoto, the thunder god took the form of a white feathered arrow; see the Noh play "Kamo" in Koyama Hiroshi, Satō Kikuo, and Satō Ken'ichi, eds., *Yōkyoku shū* 1, vol. 33 of *Nihon koten bungaku zenshū* (Shōgakkan, 1963), 76–86.
In Chikamatsu's play *Uchiwa Soga*, the Soga brothers' spirits rescue Tora and Shōshō from demons by shooting the demons with white feathered arrows.

379. Toita, *Kabuki jūhachiban,* 155.

380. Ibid.

YA NO NE
(THE ARROW SHARPENER)

CHARACTERS: Soga no Gorō Tokimune
Soga no Jūrō Sukenari
Mago no Hataemon, a farmer
Ōzatsuma Bundayū
(Stage Assistants)

SETTING: Soga Village, New Year

Text	Commentary: Literary and Performance
NARRATOR: Now Soga no Gorō Tokimune faces in a lucky direction and offers a Shinto prayer. He cannot live with his father's murderer under the same heaven. . . . "the brush of heaven and the dance of peace, luck, and happiness and ten thousand blessings of fortune!" North of the "strategy treatise window" this morning patches of snow remain, but pale green are the breezes and waters. A branch of plum bursts into bloom; flowery spring is here. Although his hermitage has been redecorated, Tokimune begins this year too in his old hut, on old *tatami* mats, at a place called the "Old Well." He sits sharpening arrowheads.	The curtain opens to the staccato beat of wooden clappers. The setting is a house in the country. The whole stage is covered with a *shosa butai*.[381] The *shamisen* players and *jōruri* chanters (usually two each) sit on a *jōruri* dais to stage left. The lively music is in the *ōzatsuma* style, often used to accompany *aragoto* scenes. A felicitous New Year's greeting, this line was also written for the first calligraphy of the New Year. According to a poem from *Wakan rōeishū* (A Collection of Japanese and Chinese Poems for Intoning), samurai read strategy treatises at the north window.[382] It is still a custom to clean, repair, and replace certain household items for the New Year. The *shōji* enclosing the main room on stage are raised abruptly, revealing Soga Gorō.

381. The *shosa butai* is placed in sections on the main stage for use in dance plays. Its surface is smoother and cleaner than the main stage surface.
382. See Gunji Masakatsu, *Kabuki jūhachiban shū*, vol. 98 of *Nihon koten bungaku taitei* (Iwanami Shoten, 1965), 52, n. 11.

Fig. 30. Full-stage view of the beginning of *Ya no ne.* Gorō (Onoe Shōroku II) is in the middle. National Theater, January 1972. Photo by Morita Tōshirō.

Tales tell of the arrows of Yang Yu in far off China and Korea, and here in the land of Japan there were Chinzei Hachirō Tametomo and Genzanmi Yorimasa, whose feats of archery are unrivaled in ages past and present. "Yet I will be their equal or surpass them!" he says, a stout-hearted bowman of natural valor.

Yang Yu was a general of the state of Chu in the Spring and Autumn period of China. His exploits are described in the *Shiji* and other sources. It is said that in one hundred shots at willow leaf targets at one hundred paces, he could make one hundred hits. Tametomo (1139–70) was the eighth son of Minamoto Tameyoshi (1096–1156). Tametomo distinguished himself fighting in defense of his father in the Hōgen Insurrection (1156). Defeated in 1156, he was exiled to Ōshima, but he defied the terms of his exile and took possession of all seven Izu Islands. In 1170 an imperial expedition went to kill him. According to legend, Tametomo sank one attacking ship with an arrow from his mighty bow, then committed suicide. Genzanmi Yorimasa (Minamoto Yorimasa, 1104?–80) figures prominently in *Heike monogatari*, which states that in 1153 he shot down a flying monster that was attacking the imperial palace. He was the first Genji general to defy the Taira. He died in the Battle of Uji in 1180.

GORŌ: He saw a tiger in the stone and shot . . . raw oyster and *daikon* salad!

The first part of the sentence derives from a story about Li Huang, a Han general, recounted in the *Shiji*. Li sought to slay the tiger that had killed his mother, but when he fired in the gloom at a tigerlike form, he found he had struck a boulder. Blood dripped from the boulder, signifying that heaven had granted his revenge. The second part of the sentence derives from a New Year dish. *Ishi ni tatsu* (strikes the rock) and *tazukuri* form a pun. *Tazukuri* is a kind of salad made with a long radish known as *daikon*.

Fig. 31. Gorō (Onoe Shōroku II) poses as if shooting an arrow as the chanter sings of the exploits of the renowned archer Genzanmi Yorimasa. From *Ya no ne*, National Theater, January 1972. Photo by Morita Tōshirō.

NARRATOR: The arrow strikes, "bur-dock!" ... in vinegar with boiled *daikon.*

The first part of this line refers to the custom of praying at the *yatate no sugi* by shooting the tree. The sound of the word "burdock" (*gobō*) resembles the sound of an arrow striking wood. I have attempted to let the pun stand in English.

A one-inch carp has a soul of kelp.

This is a takeoff on a Buddhist saying, "A one-inch insect has a half-inch soul."

GORŌ: Even if Suketsune is as powerful as the whale in my New Year's soup, I'll be a killer whale disguised as the decorative lobster, for my lobster-red face was handed down to me by my father.

A model lobster was used as an alcove ornament for the New Year. In Japanese "shrimp" is *ebi* and "lobster" is *ise ebi.* The leading or second leading Ichikawa actor has been called Ebizō from the time of the second Danjūrō. The stripes on a shrimp or lobster are compared to *aragoto* makeup. *Aragoto* acting and makeup were passed down to Danjūrō II from his father.

Drowsily he views the world in the kettle lid ... the sake warming pan, the *bunbuku* teapot, even broken pieces of tweezers and scissors go to the old metal sale.

Apparently people sold old metal to raise money to pay debts and to pay for New Year's festivities. The *bunbuku* teapot was an iron pot used to boil water for tea. The word *bunbuku* may derive from the sound of boiling water. The term first appears in a medieval story about a priest who owned a magic teapot that was actually a badger.[383]

In the shuttlecock dawn after but a single night, last winter's shirt of mail and shin guards have become dried bream and skewered shellfish.

This refers to the shuttlecocks used in the game of battledore that girls play on New Year's morning.

Adding it all up and including trips to the sake shop, it comes to 17 *kan* and 864 *mon.*

These are units of coinage.

383. See Nihon Kokugo Daijiten Kankōkai, ed., *Nihon kokugo daijiten* (Shōgakkan, 1972), 17:577, for information on the *bunbuku* teapot.

"On the first day of the rat, sleep on your side, and don't blow happiness by eating blowfish."

Since I'm a poor man, I'll declaim an abusive monologue for the fickle gods of happiness:

These are New Year's proverbs based on puns.

Ne means both "sleep" and "rat." "Happiness" is *fuku* and "blowfish" is *fugu.*

"First, how about the rascal Daikoku—well, you know he never removes his head scarf. How about Ebisu—he looks so bedraggled—carrying his sea bream, his armpit reeks worse than fish from the Edo shore. Better not befriend him on an abstinence day!

Daikoku, Ebisu, Bishamonten, Hotei, Fukurokuju, and Benzaiten are six of the Seven Gods of Happiness (*shichi fukujin*). The *akutai* was an abusive monologue popular in Edo. This particular one derives from the *tsukushi* tradition. In the play the phrases of the *akutai* are declaimed alternately by the actor and the reciter, but it would destroy the continuity of the translation to indicate the different parts here. Worshipers of Daikoku were called "Daikoku rascals" (*Daikoku no ryōgai mono*).

Bishamonten wears his octopus cowl so carefully it makes me depressed. Hotei is a clay figure, and Fukurokuju takes a long time to shave his head. Benzaiten is for boat whores: 'The boat riding the waves brings in the pennies,' but whether or not they make a profit, they work hard for love of their nation, or is it for love of dissipation?"

Most of the disparaging comments are based on the physical appearance of the gods.

This line, *nami nori no zeni mōke,* is a takeoff on a poem commonly written on New Year's scrolls depicting a treasure ship: "How fine the sound of the boat riding the waves" (*nami nori no oto no yoki kana*). The poem does not follow normal poetic meter.

This pun uses *gokudō* (dissipation) and *kokudō* (the nation).

"Heaven controls wealth and rank, and destiny controls life and death," but anyway I've got no reason for praying.

This line is quoted from *The Analects of Confucius.*

Truly Yan Hui of the slums ate but a single dish of food and drank but a single gourd of water. If you eat brown rice, drink water, and use your elbow as a pillow . . .

Yan Hui was a disciple whom Confucius greatly admired and who was content to live a life of poverty and virtue. The original in *The Analects of Confucius* reads: "How admirable was Yan Hui. He ate a single dish of food and drank a single gourd of water, and lived in the slums." The next sentence derives from an admonition in the *The Analects of Confucius*: "The Master said, 'He who seeks only coarse food to eat, water to drink, and bent arm for a pillow will without looking for it find happiness to boot.'"[384]

NARRATOR: "You will find true happiness with a young courtesan!"

Gorō takes out some of the cheap tobacco that he happens to have on hand, puts it in his pipe, and lights up. He relaxes, gazing at the "spring haze at the tip of his nose."

Now a New Year's caller appears at the gate, carrying a fan box and a *shamisen* box. He calls in a high voice, "Hello, there!"

This pun uses the word *shinzō*, which can mean either "true" or "junior grade courtesan."

This line derives from a *kyōka* or humorous poem by Teiryū (1636–1717) on the subject of smoking: "It looks like a cloud—the thin smoke from Yoshino tobacco rising before my nose."

GORŌ: Who is it?

BUNDAYŪ: Ōzatsuma Bundayū. Congratulations on the New Year.

In 1729 the chanter Bundayū would have left his dais to approach and talk with Gorō. When *Ya no ne* is peformed today, an actor plays Bundayū.

GORŌ: My, my, you've come so early. I appreciate your thoughtfulness. And you brought New Year's presents: a fan, a treasure ship scroll, and a *kamishimo*. Well, come in and let's celebrate!

The *kamishimo* is a ceremonial over-robe. The other gifts are traditional *toshidama* or New Year's gifts.

BUNDAYŪ: No, I'm afraid I can't. I have to make calls all over town. I look forward to a more relaxed time when I can comply with your request.

GORŌ: In that case, just stay for a cup of sake.

384. The translation is from Arthur Waley, trans., *The Analects of Confucius* (New York: Vintage Books, 1938), 126.

Fig. 32. Gorō (Onoe Shōroku II) smokes his pipe, "gazing at the spring haze at the tip of his nose." From *Ya no ne*, National Theater, January 1972. Photo by Morita Tōshirō.

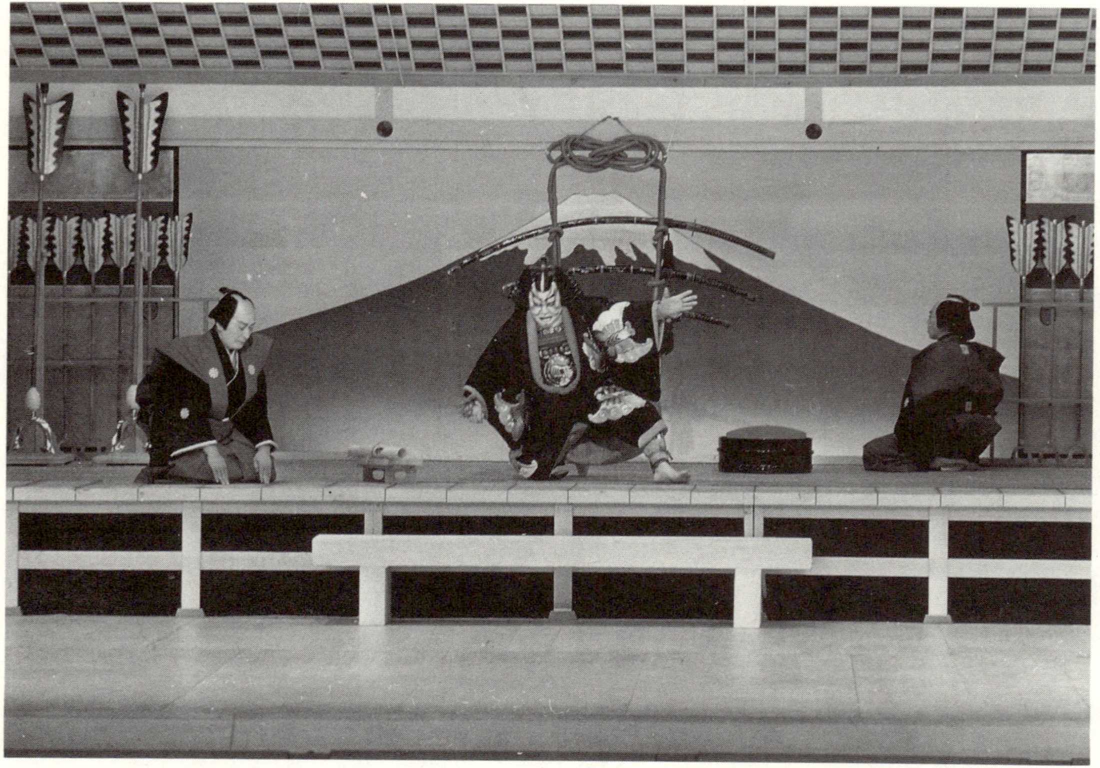

Fig. 33. Gorō (Onoe Shōroku II) converses with Ōzatsuma Bundayū (Bandō Mitsugorō VII): "Well, come in and let's celebrate!" From *Ya no ne*, National Theater, January 1972. Photo by Morita Tōshirō.

BUNDAYŪ: No, I'm sorry. "'Til we meet again," he says, and takes his leave.

In the first part of this line Bundayū is an onstage character; in the second part he again becomes the narrator of the play.

GORŌ: So the great Bundayū came to wish me a happy New Year. My, what an admirable man he is.

NARRATOR: Now Tokimune opens his New Year's presents. "A fan and a treasure ship scroll. These are fine gifts," he says, full of the youthful spirit of the New Year. "It says 'Ages Eternal' whether read from the top or the bottom." He is already dozing off because his belly is full of the New Year's soup that he drank too heartily.

New Year's scrolls were often inscribed with palindromes.

Soup prepared for the New Year is called *zōni*. It is eaten all over Japan, but ingredients differ in different regions.

"If I put this under my pillow, maybe I'll dream of ripping off Suketsune's head. I'll relax and take a little nap after my meal." He wipes off the whetstone and effortlessly arranges it as his pillow. "This is the pillow of Kantan," he says, and falls backward.

There was a popular belief that, if one put a ceremonial picture under one's pillow the second night of the New Year, one would have a good dream.

This refers to the magic pillow of Kantan (Chinese, Handan) of Chinese legend. "A young man seeking his fortune in the world stops at an inn where a sage lends him a pillow. In a moment's dreaming he lives through the vicissitudes of a long public career. Convinced that worldly striving is in vain, he follows the Way."[385] When Gorō calls his whetstone the "pillow of Kantan," it means he expects to have a remarkable dream, which in fact he does.

GORŌ: *Yattoko cha, untoko na!*

These sounds are a combination of three sound sequences Japanese might say when making a physical effort, or upon resting after tiring effort: (1) *yattoko na*, (2) *dokkoi sho*, (3) *untoko sa*. Gorō's lines are an exaggeration of normal speech.

385. This is a summary of Arthur Waley's version of the story of the pillow of Kantan (*The Nō Plays of Japan* [New York : Grove Press, 1935], 193).

NARRATOR: Soon he is asleep, emitting loud, bounteous snores. But what a strange nap. From one side come weird footsteps. Suddenly his older brother, Jūrō Sukenari, appears.

Drums play a soft "wind drum roll" as Jūrō, standing on a concealed, rolling platform, is pulled onstage near the plum tree at stage left.

JŪRŌ: Tokimune! I have unexpectedly been taken captive in Suketsune's mansion. I'm like a bird in a cage or a fish in a net. I want to fight but am powerless. Come quickly and rescue me from this calamity! Come, brother! Wake up, Tokimune!

NARRATOR: Right after saying, "Gorō Tokimune, wake up!" the figure suddenly fades and disappears from sight.

Tokimune wakes from his dream and springs to his feet. He looks around.

Gorō awakes from his dream and springs to his feet. He looks around and sees no one; he is still in a daze.

GORŌ: So, does that mean that my brother's thoughts came to me in a dream and that he told me to save him from danger? Even if Suketsune climbs up to heaven, I'll climb up after him. If he enters the bowels of the earth, I'll dig my way down to him. The sixty-odd provinces of Japan are before my eyes: to Sotogahama of Ōshu in the east, to Kikaigashima of Chinzei in the west, to the Kumano shore on the Kii Road in the south, to the rough seas of Echigo in the north, even to where men have never been, I'll walk 1,000 *ri*, I'll fly 10,000 *ri*! Now for the pursuit!

These lines derive from a scene in *The Tale of the Soga Brothers* that takes place right after the brothers have assassinated Kudō. Jūrō suggests that they flee, but Gorō graphically describes the wide bounds of the shogun's authority and says that, since they cannot fly into the sky or hide under the ground, there is no escape for them.

Very similar lines are used in other ceremonial *aragoto* plays and, according to Gunji, have a "demon-quelling ring to them."[386] Danjūrō II used virtually the same lines in the closing scene of *Narukami Fudō kitayamazakura* (Saint Narukami and the God Fudō).

386. Gunji, *Kabuki jūhachiban shū,* 387.

Fig. 34. Jūrō (Onoe Kikugorō VII) appears in Gorō's dream. From *Ya no ne.* Photo by Morita Tōshirō.

Fig. 35. Gorō (Onoe Shōroku II) performs a "pillar *mie*" during the delivery of his vow to pursue Kudō to the ends of the earth. From *Ya no ne*, National Theater, January 1972. Photo by Morita Tōshirō.

Gorō does a "pillar-entwining" *mie.*

NARRATOR: When Tokimune shows his strength, he looks terrifying.

Now, from a different direction, approaches a horse laden with *daikon* for the New Year's trade, and the seller comes, shouting, "*Daikon! Daikon!*" Tokimune thinks, "It's a pack horse, so it will be cheap," and he looks sharply at the *daikon* seller. "I'll pay you whatever price you ask."

GORŌ: Rent me your horse! Rent me your horse!

NARRATOR: He approaches, shouting, "Rent me your horse!" The owner thinks him a ruffian.

HATAEMON: Ride a market horse? No way, damn you! No way, I tell you!

NARRATOR: As he says, "No way, I tell you!" Gorō seizes him, and with an "Ei, ei, ya!" throws him about fifty feet, like a human stone. Gorō grabs the reins and nimbly mounts; the *daikon* at hand will serve as a whip for 1,000 *ri.*

GORŌ: If I go straight it will be fifty *chō.* The long way is three *ri* through the three manors; Usami, Kuzumi . . . and Kawazu's second son will show you the art of riding a horse to musical accompaniment!

In this line "Kawazu" has two meanings: (1) one of the hereditary Itō family manors, and (2) Gorō's father, Kawazu no Saburō. The three manors, Itō, Kawazu, and Usami, made up the estate of Kuzumi whose ownership had been disputed before the Soga revenge. At the time of the vendetta Kudō had title to the estate.

NARRATOR: How brave he looks as he hurries off to Kudō's mansion![387]

387. The text is "Ya no ne" in ibid., 52–57.

Fig. 36. Gorō (Onoe Shōroku II) seizes the market horse from Mago Hataemon (Ichimura Uzaemon XVII), a radish vendor. From *Ya no ne*, National Theater, January 1972. Photo by Morita Tōshirō.

Fig. 37. Gorō (Onoe Shōroku II) rides off on the market horse to rescue Jūrō, using a *daikon* as a whip. From *Ya no ne*, National Theater, January 1972. Photo by Morita Tōshirō.

SUKEROKU: A DOUBLE IDENTITY PLAY

Edo audiences enjoyed the seasonal rhythms of Kabuki, but they also demanded novelty and excitement in their theater. In the Soga tradition the response to the demand for novelty took three basic forms: (1) *shukō*—the variations in the *taimen* scene are examples; (2) *naimaze*—the intermingling of literary worlds, that is, putting Yoshitsune and Shizuka, or Ōshichi, the green-grocer's daughter, into Soga plays; and (3) double identity plays—plays in which new leading characters in original plays are in fact disguised characters from the Soga story. By the early eighteenth century the use of disguises and characters with double, or even multiple, identities had become common in Kabuki plays. By the middle of the century leading Kabuki actors had to be *kaneru yakusha*, "versatile actors" who could demonstrate mastery of a wide range of character types. Multiple identities made it easier for playwrights to introduce new *shukō* into their plays and provided opportunities for leading actors to display the breadth of their talent. Chikamatsu's success at the Takemoto Theater led to the establishment of the playwriting profession in Kabuki as well as puppet theater. Actors for the most part ceased writing their own plays, but the leading actor at a given Kabuki theater was designated "producer" (*zagashira* in Edo, *zamoto* in the Kansai),[388] and he consulted with staff playwrights on the creation of new plays. Multiple identities for main characters served the needs of both playwrights and *zagashira*.

The most famous Soga double identity play is *Sukeroku yukari Edo zakura* (Sukeroku: The Flower of Edo).[389] It is one of the "Eighteen Great Plays" and is currently the most frequently performed Soga Kabuki play. The original Sukeroku was a hero of prose fiction, a dashing commoner and *kabukimono*-like character known as *otokodate*.[390] Unreliable historical accounts say that a man named Sukeroku,

388. In Edo the *zagashira* was usually the highest paid actor of male lead roles (*tachiyaku*) employed by a given theater. In the Kansai *zamoto* received high salaries, but they were also part of the management team and received a percentage of profits from successful productions.

389. A good translation is available in James Brandon, trans., *Kabuki: Five Classic Plays* (Cambridge, MA: Harvard University Press, 1975).

390. Thornbury contends that *otokodate* is a theatrical term only, corresponding to *machi yakko*, actual commoners. Other specialists assume that *otokodate* referred to actual townsmen as well.

and his lover, Agemaki, killed themselves in Osaka in 1673.[391] Sukeroku and Agemaki had been used in Kabuki plays beginning in 1675. Danjūrō II played his first Sukeroku in 1713 in *Hana yakata aigo zakura* (Protection of the Cherries of Flower Mansion) by Tsu'uchi Jihei II and Tsu'uchi Han'emon.[392] In this play Sukeroku was depicted as a commoner hero, but his true identity was the samurai Daidōji Tahatanosuke. He is depicted as more popular with the pleasure district courtesans than his samurai rivals, and in the course of the play he defeats many samurai in sword fights.

Danjūrō's acting style combined elements from both *aragoto* and *wagoto* traditions. After the death of his father, Danjūrō II played many *wagoto* roles, including Chikamatsu's love suicide heroes, and this experience in both *aragoto* and *wagoto* acting gave him the expertise he needed to create a new, romantic acting style and a new type of swashbuckling romantic hero.

Danjūrō's second performance of Sukeroku was in 1716 in *Shikirei yawaragi Soga* (Ceremonial Gentle Soga), a revision of *Hana yakata aigo zakura* by Tsu'uchi Jihei II. It was a second month "flower" addition to the Spring program, and the seasonal setting of the play has remained constant since 1716 despite changes in text and staging from one performance to the next.[393] As the title indicates, the second Sukeroku play was part of the "gentle" Soga Gorō tradition of Danjūrō II: Sukeroku is portrayed as a dashing and handsome commoner–nothing in his dress or vocabulary suggests he is a samurai. In fact, his makeup and costume suggest a *wagoto* hero. Yet his martial prowess, defiant attitude, and dramatic movements (including a modified *roppō* entrance) relate the character to *aragoto* traditions. Sukeroku carries a short sword (the only weapon allowed to commoners), but he baits and challenges samurai all over the pleasure district as part of his search for the stolen hereditary sword of the Soga clan. Of course he defeats all opponents. Sukeroku's true identity is revealed in a scene with his mother and Jūrō, who also have dual identities as commoners.

391. Brandon, *Kabuki*, 51.
392. For more information on these playwrights, see ibid.
393. See ibid., 52, for a brief performance history of the Sukeroku tradition after 1716. The 1749 version, starring Danjūrō II, used cherry blossom decor to commemorate the placing of cherry trees in the Yoshiwara pleasure district, and that decor has been maintained in all versions of the play until the present.

Fig. 38. Sukeroku (Ichikawa Danjūrō XII) entering on the *hanamichi* at Tokyo's Kabuki Theater (Kabuki-za), January 1995. Sukeroku is actually Gorō. Courtesy of Ichikawa Danjūrō XII.

In the third Sukeroku play of Danjūrō II, Sukeroku had yet another double identity. He appeared as a dashing middle-aged *otokodate* who helped poor people in distress, while he was actually one of Edo's wealthiest merchants.[394] It was the dual identity of Sukeroku and Soga Gorō that proved the most popular and that has been performed repeatedly until the present. The currently performed version, *Sukeroku yukari Edo zakura*, was first performed sometime after 1761. Even today the acting and staging of the play are considered to be close to the style of Danjūrō II because at least one Sukeroku play, and in most cases many more, have been performed by every generation of Ichikawa actors.

Soga Gorō's double identity as a commoner, like his participation in popular New Year's activities in *Ya no ne,* made it easy for the commoner audience to identify with the hero of the play, and transformed the god/hero of medieval times into a very different sort of figure. It is Sukeroku's commoner traits that endear him to the audience—his dress, his speech, his romantic flair, his remarkable aplomb. In all of these he is reminiscent of Tōjūrō's romantic dandies. But Sukeroku has a "tough" side too. The scene in which he humiliates the high-ranking samurai villain Ikkyū by putting a sandal on the villain's head would have provided vicarious wish fulfillment for Edo-period audiences. In terms of plot structure the Soga brothers' filial piety and selfless, heroic quest give sense and high moral purpose to Sukeroku's boastful challenges and seemingly gratuitous fighting with a host of characters. Sukeroku became the model for a new breed of romantic, swashbuckling heroes, and the acting style used to portray them was called "gentle *aragoto.*"

Shikirei yawaragi Soga was staged before the rules of New Year's Kabuki had been codified and canonized, but its popularity and dramatic quality certainly contributed to the use of double identities as a standard method of creating "original" Soga plays for the Spring season. Many other dual identity plays were performed, but no Soga Gorō double has ever approached the popularity of Sukeroku.

THE SOGA VENDETTA AS A MODEL FOR IMITATION

Edo-period theater had a remarkable impact on real life. In the medieval period, narratives and plays were based on historical

394. Thornbury, *Sukeroku's Double Identity*, 65.

events, but literary works occasionally inspired emulation by participants in subsequent historical events.[395] From the Genroku period onward, the Kabuki and puppet theaters not only reflected current trends and fashions, they actively stimulated and created them. New designs in kimonos moved from the Kabuki stage, to the tea shop and brothel, and to the daily life of commoners, as did conventions of feminine and masculine behavior and etiquette. Chikamatsu's *Sonezaki shinjū* documented and embellished an actual double love suicide, but his lovers' suicide plays were so popular that they undeniably inspired many deaths that might not have occurred had he not written in this dramatic genre.

There are several reasons why the theater contributed to the association of contemporary vendettas with the Soga story. It was illegal to describe in literature or to show onstage strife within contemporary samurai houses. Theatrical accounts of the contemporary warrior class were usually masked by being ostensibly medieval in setting. The degree to which medieval disguises were necessary depended on the severity of censorship enforcement at any given time during the Edo period. The Soga tradition was a convenient "world" in which to disguise recent vendettas; any significant deviations from the well-known traditional story were easily recognized by the audience, which could piece together the real events in terms of these changes. The Edo Kabuki theater required new Soga plays every New Year, and the story of a contemporary vendetta or upheaval in a samurai house, if set in the Soga world, satisfied the New Year's requirement, made it unnecessary for playwrights to invent new *shukō* by relying entirely on their imaginations, and responded to the audience's fascination with contemporary scandals.

It was only natural that Edo-period samurai turned to the legendary Soga brothers, the most frequently portrayed avengers in the theater, as model avengers suitable for emulation in actual vendettas. Would-be avengers prayed for success at Soga shrines. Plays and stories that openly described contemporary vendettas not only drew parallels between the Soga story and the main plot but also depicted the protagonists as consciously emulating the Soga brothers. In 1701 the Ishii brothers, Hanzō and Genzō, killed Akabori Gengōemon at the

395. Some examples include: warriors in *Taiheiki* who try to emulate (unsuccessfully) the actions of heroes in *Heike monogatari*, and courtiers and nobility described in *Towazugatari* (The Confessions of Lady Nijō) who endeavor to emulate the cultured pastimes they read about in *Genji monogatari*.

foot of Kameyama Castle. Twenty-eight years previously Akabori had killed the brothers' father. The Ishii brothers were immediately dubbed "the Soga brothers of the Genroku period," and their revenge was depicted in the puppet theater exactly one year after the actual assassination. Numerous puppet and Kabuki versions were performed, and in Edo Kabuki the Ishii revenge formed part of the Soga world.

The puppet play *Go Taiheiki Shiraishi banashi* (The Shiraishi Story: A Latter Day "Taiheiki"), by Ki no Jotarō, Yo Yodai, and Utei Enba, which first appeared on both puppet and Kabuki stages in 1780, embellished an actual vendetta carried out in 1723 by two sisters who were the daughters of a farmer. Their father had tried to organize a movement to lower rents and had been killed by a magistrate.[396] In the play, the elder sister sells herself to the pleasure district in order to raise money to support her father's campaign. After her father's murder, her younger sister comes to the pleasure district and tells the story of her father's tragic death. The two women resolve to avenge their father. The proprietor of the brothel overhears the whole conversation and supports the women in their endeavor, inspiring them by reading from *The Tale of the Soga Brothers* and pointing out the similarity of the sisters' situation to that of the young Soga brothers. When the proprietor gives the older sister documents releasing her from service, he says, "Here is your pass to the Fuji hunt," alluding to the Kabuki version of the *taimen* scene in which Kudō gives passes to Jūrō and Gorō. The sisters take service with a fencing master to the Date family (the daimyo of the Sendai region) and study secretly with him, learning even his secret dueling techniques. They kill their enemy at a public fencing match. The site and manner of the killing may be historically accurate; we know that the Date daimyo occasionally arranged public duels between avengers and their foes.[397]

The popularity of Soga plays and other revenge plays and stories contributed to a "revenge craze," a phenomenon of the late eighteenth and early nineteenth centuries, resembling the "double suicide craze" of some seventy years before.[398] Most participants were samurai, and successful avengers were rewarded by their masters. Some

396. The following plot summary and single quote come from "*Go Taiheiki Shiraishi banashi*," in Gunji Masakatsu et al., eds., *Meisaku kabuki zenshū* (Sogen Shinsha, 1969), 7:233–34.

397. Mills, "Kataki-uchi," 536.

398. Douglas Mills, "Gaikoku ni okeru Nihon koten bungaku kenkyū no kadai: Soga kyōdai no densetsu o megutte," *Tōhōgaku*. 12 (1975): 5.

even became celebrities. From the last decade of the eighteenth century, popular fiction describes numerous vendettas carried out by commoners, evidence that revenge had become a fad, divorced from the stern dictates of samurai honor.

SOGA KABUKI BECOMES DANCE DRAMA

Within the framework of the Spring Kabuki program, the "rewriting" (*kakikae*) requirement for Soga plays was meant to ensure yearly innovations in the Soga dramatic tradition. In fact, after the age of Chikamatsu and the first two Danjūrōs, few original, cohesive Soga plays were written. The mixing of historical worlds and the use of multiple identities for main characters led to the creation of all sorts of outlandish hybrid plays that featured the Soga brothers and their ladies as important characters in at least a few acts. At the end of the eighteenth century, handbooks were published with rules instructing playwrights and producers how to use multiple identities and *naimaze* to modify the Soga story for the Spring production.[399] Such codification indicates that truly original work on the Soga theme was no longer necessary. Soga *haru kyōgen* was firmly entrenched in Edo as ritual drama.

From the last decades of the eighteenth century through the mid-Meiji period, innovation in Soga Kabuki continued primarily in the form of dance drama (*shosagoto*). In the 1770s and 1780s Nakamura Nakazō (1736–90) established long dance dramas with complex plots as important vehicles for leading actors of male roles. Furthermore, the development of transformation dances (*hengemono*) and dances deriving from Noh and *kyōgen* (*matsubamemono*) made independent dance dramas much more important in Kabuki. Many actors achieved fame in the Kabuki world by specializing in dance. In most New Year's performances the plots and themes of the "Greetings at the Shrine," "Oniō's Poverty," and *taimen* scenes changed little, but new and original dances were presented as parts of these scenes or in addition to them.[400] Changes in musical modes, choreography, characters, and costuming were significant enough in the context of dance drama to constitute "new" Soga plays every year.

399. Thornbury, *Sukeroku's Double Identity*, 20.

400. Atsumi Seitarō, "Asahina tsurigitsune—kaisetsu," in *Soga kyōgen buyō shū*, edited by Hattori Yukio, vol. 50 of *Kokuritsu gekijō jōen shiryō shū* (Kokuritsu Geikijō Geinō Chōsa Shitsu, 1970), 108.

Many dance dramas were based on the "Armor Pulling" (*kusazuribiki*) episode. Early armor-pulling scenes had been performed to the accompaniment of music in *ko-jōruri, jōruri,* and early Kabuki. Testimony to the popularity of the motif are other Kabuki plays centering on tests of strength by pulling. These plays include, *Zō hiki* (Pulling the Elephant), one of the "Eighteen Great Plays," *Sotoba hiki* (Pulling Down the Stupa), and *Torii hiki* (Pulling Down the Shrine Gate).[401] Danjūrō I and Denkurō were the first famous armor-pulling pair in Kabuki, but their scenes were always part of a long play. The first independent dance drama version of the scene was *Kongen kusazuribiki* (The Original Armor Pulling), performed in 1759.[402] This play featured a female Asahina danced by a specialist in women's roles. The variations on the armor-pulling theme were numerous. Some followed the traditional pairing of Gorō with Asahina, but in others either Gorō or Asahina was replaced by a woman character, adding an erotic element to the dance. In still other plays a third character, often Shōshō or Wada Yoshimori, was added to the contest. In *Enoshimadai kusazuri sanmai* (Pulling Three Layers of Armor on the Enoshima Cliff), presented in 1763, six characters participated in three separate tests of strength.[403] Changes in staging were almost as important as choice of characters and choreography. In some dance dramas, including the currently performed *Kusazuribiki,* the armor was carried, not worn, and in others there was no armor at all and the aggressor pulled his rival's sash. Physical settings and lyrics for armor-pulling dance dramas were often totally original, with no connection whatsoever to the traditional Soga story. Lyrics were ornamental and poetic, following the formulaic expressions of dance lyrics, which include the specialized vocabulary and romantic mood of the contemporary Edo pleasure district.[404]

The "Armor Pulling" episode was the most important motif for Soga dance dramas, but almost every scene or theme presented in dramatic Kabuki was reworked in dance plays. Other important dance motifs included the ceremonial assembly at Tsurugaoka Hachiman

401. Misumi, "Soga buyō oyobi aragoto," 59.

402. Machida Hirozō, "Kongen kusazuribiki no hensen," in *Soga kyōgen buyō shū,* edited by Hattori Yukio, vol. 50 of *Kokuritsu gekijō jōen shiryō shū* (Kokuritsu Geikijō Geinō Chōsa Shitsu, 1970), 70.

403. Ibid., 62.

404. Machida does a line-for-line analysis of different versions of the "Armor Pulling" dance drama to study changing fashions and mores in the pleasure district.

Shrine, the *taimen*, and the brothers' visits to their mistresses in the pleasure district.

Felicitous New Year's symbols and references played an important role in the lyrics of most dance dramas just as they did in dramatic Kabuki. *Naimaze, shukō*, and "plays within plays" provided an inexhaustible supply of fresh literary material to accompany dance dramas, but dances relied even less on literary sense and quality for their success than did dramatic Kabuki plays. The quality and novelty of music, choreography, costumes, and setting, and the dancer's ability, not the lyrics, made the difference for dance dramas.

When women were banned from the Kabuki stage, they continued to perform popular dance in the brothels and tea houses. From the seventeenth century onward popular music and dance played an important role both in the Kabuki world and in the world of courtesans and geisha, and they were an important artistic link between the two worlds of pleasure. It is not surprising therefore that themes of romantic and erotic love dominate the lyrics of dance plays more thoroughly than any other form of Kabuki play, and it is in dance dramas that the Soga characters are most appealing and attractive as romantic archetypes.

About ten Soga dance dramas are currently performed.[405] The most popular is a solo piece entitled *Gorō,* danced to *nagauta* accompaniment. It was first performed in the seventh month of 1841 by Onoe Tamizō as the second of a nine-dance series, and it is now titled *Ame no Gorō* (Gorō in the Rain), *Kuruwa kayoi Gorō* (Gorō Going to the Pleasure District), *Gorō Tokimune,* or *Gorō.* The piece commemorates the temporary transfer (*degaichō*) of an image of the god Soga Gorō to Asakusa Kannon Nenbutsu Temple in Edo:

Text:	Commentary:
NARRATOR: Now Soga Gorō cannot live under the same heaven as his father's murderer and unceasingly strives to kill him.	Gorō's costume resembles Sukeroku's. Gorō wears a black robe with gold and silver embroidery. He carries an umbrella and a letter. Like Sukeroku, he is a "gentle *aragoto*" character.

405. Ibid., 81.

Yet his valiant heart is dampened in the spring rain so that he often turns astray to Ōiso. To the pleasure district of Kewaizaka he goes, on rainy nights and on snowy days too to visit Shōshō of high renown.

Spring rain is unpredictable and represents inconstancy and changeability; here it refers also to the changeability of Gorō's moods. "To become damp" and "to fall in love" are expressed by the same verb, ***nureru***. There is a further play on words: "to become damp" (***nurete kuru***) and "the pleasure district" (***kuruwa***).

One is easily hobbled by entanglements in the pleasure district: a casual letter sent on the wings of a wild goose, repeated letters containing boorish propositions, and sometimes one is tricked by worldly deceits.

The word play here uses ***kari***, which can mean either "temporary" or "wild goose." Su Wu sent tidings from his captivity in Tartary to China by tying a letter to the foot of a wild goose. "Wild goose" letters were to or from a loved one far away. The letter Gorō is carrying is used as a dance property here.

Drinking the wine of fickleness, were it better if tonight's moon shines clear or is clouded over? No matter. Mist is the way of spring.

The moon refers to love, or one's lover. "Clear moon" means one's lover comes, "cloudy" means he does not. The spring mist sometimes hides the moon and sometimes reveals it. Mist is a metaphor for the uncertainty a woman feels while waiting for her lover.

"I must be off! I must away! When will I kill my foe and cleanse my father's name?

Through this line the dance has been in a delicate, ***wagoto*** style. Here the dancer removes his purple head scarf and frees his arms for vigorous movement.

Here the dance is performed with strong ***aragoto*** movements.

Now, after eighteen years, the wind of heaven blows on the power of my determination. I'll not let my enemy escape!" Gorō's spirit, given form, would be as a butterfly spreading its wings over a peony blossom, brave and gallant.

Hareru means "to clear up" and "to cleanse a man's honor" or "to clear away a man's rancor." The wind imagery is associated with clearing weather; rain and damp thus indicate erotic feelings or love attachments, and clear weather means devotion to duty.

Fig. 39. Gorō (author) in the *buyō* dance drama *Gorō*, June 1990: "When will I kill my foe and cleanse my father's name?" Photo by Terry Tambara.

The butterfly is the pattern of Gorō's crest in all Kabuki plays. On one traditional lucky playing card (*hanafuda*) a butterfly hovers over a peony. Butterflies and peonies are also associated in Noh and Kabuki with the lion, the strongest animal.

"How I envy the warbler in the thicket, singing to its heart's content, then going to the plum in the garden.

The warbler and plum tree are natural and poetic companions. In this section of the piece the dancer reverts to a gentler, more *wagoto* style. Here the warbler represents Gorō; the plum, his lover Shōshō.

'That's the way it is. That's the way it is,' sighs the spring wind, and blows rumors of love affairs.

Soyo means "that's how it is," and *soyosoyo* is an onomatopoetic representation of a soft breeze.

Rushes and violets on the embankment together are dampened by the kindly dew. Though I compare the fruits of love making and yearning, in fact I'm alone in Nakanomachi."

This is a metaphor for making love.

A location in the Yoshiwara pleasure district.

But that's all right, for the merit of his incomparable bravery and filial piety has made him a violent god, feared and adored even in these latter days—this year at Asakusabashi in Edo as well, where people throng to visit his image now on display.

The tempo changes here to a stronger and more martial beat, and the dance changes to *aragoto* style. The dancer does a quick costume change into a scarlet robe decorated with a symbol deriving from Genroku-period *otokodate* jargon meaning "devil-may-care determination."[406] At the word "adored," the dancer executes a dramatic five-direction head movement, then does another quick costume modification.

The dancer concludes with a Genroku *mie*, a classic *aragoto mie*, and the curtain is closed.[407]

406. The expression *kamawanu*, meaning "I don't care," is represented graphically using a sickle (*kama*) inside a circle (*wa*) followed by *nu* in *hiragana*. In some versions of the dance the robe with this design is revealed earlier in the dance, after the words "brave and gallant."

407. Mimasuya Fumiji, "Gorō," in Matsumoto Kamematsu, "Gorō—nagauta kaisetsu," in *Soga kyōgen buyō shū*, edited by Hattori Yukio, vol. 50 of *Kokuritsu gekijō jōen shiryō shū* (Kokuritsu Geikijō Geinō Chōsa Shitsu, 1970), 114.

Gorō owes even less to the medieval Soga literary tradition than does *Ya no ne* of a century earlier, yet its lyrics demonstrate the persistence of certain motifs, associations, and character traits: (1) Gorō is a valiant man, duty bound to avenge his father, but torn between love and honor. (2) Gorō is associated with rain. (3) Gorō's spirit is referred to as an *arahitogami*. Although the lone dancer plays Gorō, many of the lyrics express the yearnings and sufferings of Shōshō, who in the end willingly releases her lover to death and glory. The language of *Gorō* is decorative and suggestive. It tells no story but rather ties images together by means of wordplay and emotional resonances, using connections somewhat reminiscent of linked poetry (*renga* and *haikai*). The song begins and ends in a narrative mode, creating an effective frame for the lyric main body of the text, which suggests Gorō's thoughts and feelings and a poetic love exchange between Gorō and his mistress.

The last few lines of the dance drama attest to the popularity of the Soga cult and show that the dance was an advertisement for the Asakusa Temple *degaichō*. The closing lyrics state that today people fear and adore Soga Gorō as a violent god (*arahitogami*), but the festive bustle at the temple, also mentioned in the song lyrics, was probably the real attraction for most visitors to the temple. This dance is representative of the late-Edo-period Soga tradition because of its commingling of secular and religious imagery, moral and erotic appeal, and its mixture of *aragoto* and *wagoto* costuming and choreography for a single performer. In this dance, although we can find vestiges of Soga Gorō, the medieval hero, he has been almost entirely transformed by the romantic values and decorative and metaphorical imagery of the late-Edo-period world of pleasure.

THE MODERN ERA: A "LIVING HISTORY PLAY" AND *SHINPA* ABROAD

In the 1850s foreign warships forced Japan to end her self-imposed isolation, and with the Meiji Restoration of 1868 Japan entered the modern age. It was a time of dramatic change: a strong central government abolished the samurai class and the warlords' feudal domains, universal education and universal military service were imposed on citizens of every class, and the country began its drive to become a military and economic world power. In the 1870s and 1880s intellectuals avidly studied the new ideas, technologies, and cultural accomplishments of the West and sought to better Japan with their newfound knowledge. Western art, fiction, music, and poetry vied for the affections of Japanese with the more familiar domestic and Chinese arts.

Despite the radical social, political, and cultural transformations of the Meiji period, Kabuki was slow to change. Soga plays continued to be staple fare for the Tokyo New Year's performance until the first decade of the twentieth century. The Japanese part reluctantly with ritual traditions, continuing to observe customs whose origins have long been forgotten. Soga plays for the Tokyo New Year were almost as important a part of the holiday as pine and bamboo door decorations and *zōni* soup.

The dramatic appeal of the Soga story, coupled with its prominence in Tokyo Kabuki, made it a natural choice for dramatists who sought to experiment with new theatrical genres in the Meiji period. One of the earliest reformers was Danjūrō IX (1837–1903) who invented the "living history play" (*katsureki geki*) for Kabuki.[408] Danjūrō IX aspired to act in historical plays that were true to their period and to human feelings and aspirations, plays free from the anomalies, absurdities, and burlesque humor of Edo-period history plays. The "living history" movement reached its peak in the decade between 1877 and 1887, when the greatest playwright of the nineteenth century, Kawatake Mokuami (1816–93), wrote for Danjūrō, the progressive Morita Kan'ya (1863–1925) produced his plays, and the movement received support from reform-minded officials and scholars. "Living history" playwrights were encouraged to do research into the periods of their subjects and to use appropriate language and character portrayals. Sets, costumes, and acting techniques were to be reworked in an attempt to accurately reflect different historical periods and believable human emotions and behavior.

The last important Soga Kabuki play was a "living history play" by Mokuami: *Youchi Soga kariba no akebono* (Dawn at the Hunting Ground after the Soga Night Raid). Danjūrō played the leading role of Gorō at the opening in June 1881. The play in five acts describes the Soga brothers' last two days alive. It consists almost entirely of dialogue, and each act presents a situation of conflict or suffering, using a well-developed *jo-ha-kyū* structure. There is a climax at the end of each act, taking the form of a scene of combat or high emotion. Mokuami followed Chikamatsu in creating stark contrasts between acts and

408. The term was coined by the critic and novelist Kanagaki Robun (1829–94) in 1878 (Hayashi Kyōhei, "Katsureki mono," in *Kabuki jiten* [Hyōronsha, 1993], 111).

within them. For example, the frenzied searching for Kudō, fierce combat, and unbridled hatreds and blood lust of act 4 contrast with act 5 in which Gorō suppresses his anger while talking with the shogun and struggles to control his emotions in successive confrontations with Kudō's son Inubōmaru, the villainous Kajiwara, and finally Nitta, who shows Gorō his brother's severed head.

The first act of the play was Mokuami's invention, set in the pleasure district, but the next four are faithful elaborations of important medieval sources: the *rufubon*, the Noh play *Youchi Soga*, and the *kōwakamai* play of the same title. The language contains no references to New Year's customs and is largely free of the puns, allusions, and ornamental devices that had been so much a part of the Kabuki Soga tradition for the previous 150 years. The makeup and costumes appeared surprisingly unfamiliar to the audience of 1881. Gorō's were subdued and realistically drawn, certainly in contrast to *aragoto* costumes and makeup.[409] But the "realism" of Danjūrō and Mokuami was a relative phenomenon. Tora and Shōshō remained Edo-period courtesans, and the actors spoke the language of the Edo and Meiji periods. They were all trained in a stylized, presentational art, and the conventions of Kabuki acting continued to be employed: exaggerated vocalization, bold posturing, and danced fight scenes.

Danjūrō's talent, enthusiasm, and popularity were responsible for the brief success of the "living history" movement in Kabuki, but "living history plays" were never very popular with Kabuki audiences. After about a decade, support for the new plays by intellectuals and the leadership elite also waned. In his later career Danjūrō IX returned to the traditional roles of his family: Ya no ne Gorō, Sukeroku, Benkei, and other *aragoto* heroes. Audiences still preferred ceremonial Soga plays and dances. To a modern reader *Youchi Soga kariba no akebono*, with its solid dramatic structure and plot and scenes of intense and believable emotion, seems far superior to *Ya no ne* or the dance drama *Gorō*, but the ties between the Soga story and traditional New Year's ritual and images were still so much a part of urban life that they were not easily abandoned. Nothing better demonstrates the fallacy

409. Gorō's costume consisted of a wide sash (*haramaki*), gloves, shin guards, a "realistic" warrior's robe (*hitatare*), and straw sandals. Sawamura Sōjūrō, playing Jūrō, wore a more decorative costume, and the disunity of the effect was criticized by both audience and critics. Sōjūrō could not work with Danjūrō and left the cast after the opening performance. See Kawatake Shigetoshi, ed., *Mokuami zenshū* (Shun'yōdō, 1925), 10:232.

of the assumption that literary and cultural change immediately follow new political and social conditions than the survival of Edo-period values and tastes in Kabuki even forty years after the Meiji Restoration.

By the mid-1880s it seemed clear to theater "modernists" that dramatic innovation would have to take place outside the Kabuki theater. Romantic literature expounding political views or philosophies was in fashion at the time, and the first break with Kabuki was made in order to present romances in which contemporary political issues were addressed. The new form was called *shinpa* (new faction). The strong influence of Kabuki was apparent in the flamboyant *shinpa* acting styles, the use of men to play female roles (*onnagata*), ever-present musical accompaniment, and staging techniques. In the 1890s women were introduced to the *shinpa* stage (the government first limited actresses to playing the parts of "virtuous women"), *jōruri* and *nagauta* accompaniments were dropped, and Western techniques such as darkened auditoriums and footlights were introduced. *Shinpa* repertories broadened beyond their earlier reliance on simple "political romances" to include contemporary Japanese plays, reportage of the Sino-Japanese War, adaptations of Western plays, and reworked Japanese classics.

At the turn of the century Kawakami Otojirō (1864–1911) took his *shinpa* troupe on two tours to the United States and Europe. This was the first time abroad for Japanese theater (not including the Noh troupes with mobile stages that Hideyoshi sent with his armies to Korea) although several Japanese dancers had performed in Europe during the last decades of the nineteenth century. Most of the plays Kawakami staged were adaptations of Kabuki and *buyō*, and his wife, Sada Yakko, a former geisha and excellent dancer, was the main attraction. She had to take over the female acting roles when, in Boston, one of the troupe's *onnagata* died and another quit the tour. Kawakami was forced to improvise new plays with fewer women's parts, and as an actress "Madame Yakko" rose to the occasion with performances that moved the likes of Sarah Bernhardt. One of the new plays Kawakami wrote while on tour was *Soga,* sometimes called "The Murder of the Soga Brothers."

The Japanese ambassabor to the United States, Kimura Jūtarō, invited the Kawakami Otojirō troupe to Washington to perform at the Lafayette Theater. The play *Soga* was on the program, and on 6 February 1900 Kawakami presented it in Washington, D.C., for an audience that included President McKinley. American critics were excited by Japanese martial acting and by Sada Yakko and gave the program rave reviews.[410] At a private reception given by government dignitaries Kawakami was amazed when he was asked to perform part of *Soga* and to add a *harakiri* scene. So, changing the plot and rewriting history, he inserted a double suicide by the Soga brothers.[411]

The Soga New Year's tradition in Kabuki would continue in Tokyo for a few more years. Finally, with Kabuki losing in a competition with *shinpa*, *yose*, and other arts that more successfully combined traditional and modern elements, Kabuki producers undertook major reforms in management, personnel relations, and program organization. The traditional Kabuki calendar ceased to regulate performances, with the result that Soga plays became much less prominent. The New Year's plays had been celebrational and virtually devoid of literary or dramatic content for 150 years. In order to keep its audience, Kabuki organizers found it necessary to present potpourris of the most famous acts and scenes from classic plays. The practice of writing new Soga scenes every year came to an end, and popular versions of the ceremonial *taimen* scene (*Kotobuki Soga no taimen* and *Uiro uri*) became formalized playlets presented outside of the context of a longer play. Today the two *taimen* scenes change very little from presentation to presentation. The two other Soga plays that had been performed most frequently before 1900, *Sukeroku* and *Ya no ne*, were carried into the twentieth century, retaining the presentation and acting styles of mid-eighteenth-century Kabuki.

OCTOCENTENNIAL CELEBRATIONS

The eight-hundredth anniversary of the death of the Soga brothers fell on 28 May 1993. No special events took place in the world of Noh drama, but Kabuki marked the occasion. Danjūrō XII takes very seriously his responsibility as preserver of Ichikawa family traditions, and in May 1993 at the Kabuki Theater (Kabuki-za), he played Soga Gorō in *Uiro uri* (see fig. 40). It was an expression of thanks to

410. Jonah Salz, "Intercultural Pioneers: Otojirō Kawakami and Sada Yakko," *The Journal of Intercultural Studies* (Kansai University of Foreign Studies Publication) 20 (1993): 53.

411. Ibid., 54.

Fig. 40. Gorō (Ichikawa Danjūrō XII) in *Uiro uri.* Performed as a memorial tribute to the Soga brothers on the 800th anniversary of their deaths. Tokyo's Kabuki Theater, May 1993. Courtesy of Ichikawa Danjūrō XII.

the Soga spirits, and Danjūrō made explicit the memorial nature of the performance in a speech (*kōjō*) that interrupted the action of the play. The set suggested the Kabuki stage of 1716 when Danjūrō II first performed *Uiro uri*. The pillars and facade were decorated with Fudō talismans from Shinshōji, a reaffirmation of the linkage between Fudō and Soga Gorō forged by Danjūrō I in 1697.

Two hundred years ago Edo celebrated the six-hundredth anniversary of the Soga brothers' deaths with Kabuki-sponsored Soga festival events taking place in the city streets. In 1993 the few provincial shrines and temples associated with the Soga brothers scheduled special memorial events. At Kōzenji in Shimo Soga village on the outskirts of Odawara, a Buddhist memorial service was held to yet again bring peace to the Soga brothers' spirits (see figs. 41 and 42). Nakamura Baigyoku took part in the funeral service as an official representative of Kabuki (see fig. 43), and laquered paper umbrellas bearing the names of leading actors were hung on the temple wall. Attendance at the annual umbrella-burning festival was larger than in usual years. As always two little boys took the parts of Jūrō and Gorō, being transformed into official avatars of the brothers during the course of the memorial service (see fig. 44). The boys set fire to a pile of umbrellas, symbolizing the brothers' abandonment of the temporal world on that first night of the monsoon rains eight hundred years ago. What attracted a huge throng in 1993 was the appearance of sumo's only active grand champion, the Hawaiian born Akebono (see fig. 45). It was a rare opportunity for provincial folk to see a popular celebrity. Temple officials instructed Akebono in Soga traditions, including the link to sumo in the form of the brothers' father, who was reputedly the strongest wrestler of his day. The crowd jammed the temple yard to see the huge wrestler and to receive talismanic items thrown to the throng by the wrestlers and priests.

The localized nature of the festivities and their relatively modest scope are indicative of how marginalized the Soga tradition has become in modern Japan. Outside the theater the situation is just as it was in the years immediately following the brothers' deaths—the Soga spirits are known only in locales where they lived and died. Even though Soga Noh plays are still performed today, the Soga theme is seen as peripheral to Noh drama, and no Soga plays are performed by the Bunraku puppet troupe. Only Kabuki and *buyō* proudly present their versions of the avatars of vengeance, who once were known to all Japanese and who inspired the writing of hundreds of plays, ballads, and dance dramas.

Fig. 41. The Soga brothers' graves at Kōzenji, Shimo Soga, taken on 28 May 1993 on the 800th anniversary of their deaths. Photo by author.

Fig. 42. Woman praying at an altar erected beneath the Soga brothers' graves at Kōzenji, Shimo Soga, on the occasion of the 800th anniversary of their deaths. Photo by author.

Fig. 43. Kabuki actor Nakamura Baigyoku offering incense at the memorial service for the Soga brothers held at Kōzenji, Shimo Soga, on 28 May 1993, commemorating the 800th anniversary of their deaths. Photo by author.

Fig. 44. Children dressed as a Soga brother and Tora for the umbrella-burning festival and memorial service for the Soga brothers held at Kōzenji, Shimo Soga, on 28 May 1993, commemorating the 800th anniversary of their deaths. Photo by author.

Fig. 45. Sumo Grand Champion Akebono (center) on the grounds of Kōzenji, Shimo Soga, on 28 May 1993, for the festival and memorial service commemorating the 800th anniversary of the deaths of the Soga brothers. Photo by author.

Appendix A: Major Characters of the Soga Story

HEROES

Soga Jūrō Sukenari (childhood name Ichiman)
Soga Gorō Tokimune (childhood name Hakoō)

IMMEDIATE FAMILY

The brothers' mother (never referred to by name in the narrative tale, sometimes called Mankō in later works)
Kawazu Saburō (the brothers' father)
Itō Sukechika (the brothers' grandfather)
Onbō (later called Zenji or Zenjibō. He was the youngest Soga brother, born after his father's death.)
Soga Sukenobu (stepfather to Jūrō and Gorō. The brothers left the Itō clan and were adopted into the lesser Soga clan when their mother remarried Soga Sukenobu.)
Kyō no Kojirō (half-brother to Jūrō and Gorō, their mother's son by her first husband, prior to marrying Kawazu Saburō)
Ōiso no Tora (Jūrō's mistress or fiancée, reputed to be the most beautiful courtesan in eastern Japan. After Jūrō's death she becomes a wandering nun.)
Kewaizaka no Shōshō (from the late medieval period onward, considered to be Gorō's sweetheart—in the narrative tale, Tora's companion nun, but with no relation to Gorō)
Oniō and Danzaburō (or Dōsaburō) (the Soga brothers' loyal retainers, brothers to each other)

VILLAINS

Itō Kudō Suketsune (succeeded to the Itō clan headship after the execution of Sukechika, his uncle, by order of Yoritomo. Kudō was responsible for the murder of Kawazu Saburō)

Ōmi and Yawata (Kudō's close retainers. Yawata actually shot Kawazu Saburō.)

Kajiwara Kagesue (a close retainer to the shogun)

Inubōmaru (Kudō's son, an important villain only in Edo-period drama, in which his adult name is Arai no Kotōta)

Ōtōnai (Kudō's companion. According to most literary works, he perished with Kudō during the Soga brothers' night raid.)

IMPORTANT SAMURAI AND FEUDAL LORDS

Minamoto Yoritomo (the shogun)

Hōjō Tokimasa (the second most powerful man in the country, and Gorō's "godfather")

Wada Yoshimori (a powerful warlord, generally sympathetic to the Soga brothers)

Asahina (real name, Kobayashi Saburō Yoshihide. He was Wada Yoshimori's son and a legendary strongman of the Kamakura period.)

Hatakeyama Shigetada (a warlord who always staunchly supports the Soga brothers)

Nitta Shirō Tadatsuna (the warrior who killed Jūrō in the fight after the vendetta)

Gosho no Gorōmaru (a page in personal attendance on the shogun. He captured Gorō some hours after the vendetta. In Edo-period drama he is sometimes a villain.)

Appendix B: Major Episodes in *The Tale of the Soga Brothers*

(Taken from the *rufubon*, or "Popular Version," and omitting tangential tales of Chinese and Indian origin and stories of the founding of temples and shrines.)

BOOK I

Itō Sukechika usurps the manors and Itō clan headship, which were the birthright of his nephew, Itō Kudō Suketsune.

Kudō becomes an adult and attempts to regain his lands and title by means of first a lawsuit and then a military expedition. Itō Sukechika thwarts both moves.

Sukechika's son Kawazu Saburō Sukeyasu has two boys; they will be the Soga brothers.

Kudō orders his retainers, Ōmi and Yawata, to assassinate Sukechika.

Sukechika holds a grand hunt. Kawazu Saburō, the most handsome warrior participating, is victor at a sumo match held during the hunt.

Kudō's retainers stalk and kill Kawazu Saburō as he returns home from the hunt. Yawata fires the fatal arrow.

Kawazu Saburō's last son, Onbō, is born. The widow remarries Soga Sukenobu and moves to Soga village. Soga Sukenobu adopts the two older boys, who become the Soga brothers, Ichiman and Hakoō. The youngest is sent to a temple.

BOOK II

Kawazu Saburō's brothers kill Kudō's two retainers, Ōmi and Yawata.

The exiled youth Yoritomo is in the custody of Itō Sukechika, a Heike loyalist. Yoritomo has a clandestine affair with Sukechika's daughter, who bears Yoritomo a son. Sukechika discovers the liaison, kills the baby, and Yoritomo barely escapes with his life.

Yoritomo rebels against the central govenment, which is controlled by the rival Heike clan. He becomes master of eastern Japan.

Yoritomo captures and executes Sukechika. He gives the Itō lands and clan headship to Kudō Suketsune who served him loyally.

Yoritomo becomes the first shogun to rule Japan.

BOOK III

Kudō convinces Yoritomo that he must execute the Soga boys because they are the grandsons of the hated Itō Sukechika.

Numerous feudal lords petition Yoritomo to spare the boys, but Yoritomo is unmoved.

Hatakeyama Shigetada's petition wins Yoritomo's pardon of the boys. They are saved just as they are about to be killed.

BOOK IV

Ichiman becomes an adult samurai, taking the name Soga Jūrō Sukenari.

The younger brother, Hakoō, is sent by his mother to Hakone Temple to become a priest. He spends several years there, and the abbot becomes like a father to Hakoō.

Kudō goes on pilgrimage to Hakone Temple, where Hakoō meets his father's murderer for the first time.

Hakoō runs away from the temple and becomes an adult samurai, taking the name Soga Gorō Tokimune. Hōjō Tokimasa presides over the coming-of-age ceremony.

Gorō's mother disowns him for disobedience.

Jūrō's affair with Tora begins.

The brothers have close calls in disputes with warlords. Several relatives refuse to aid the brothers in their quest for vengeance.

BOOK V

The brothers attend several hunts, hoping to get a chance to attack Kudō, but they are unable to approach him.

Gorō almost fights with Kajiwara Kagesue over a prostitute. The prostitute becomes a nun (she is never given a name).

BOOK VI

Jūrō visits Tora. She is called on to entertain the feudal lord Wada Yoshimori.

Tora offends Yoshimori by showing preference for Jūrō. Yoshimori's men are about to attack Jūrō, but Gorō rescues his brother in the famous "Armor Pulling" encounter with Yoshimori's son, Asahina.

Jūrō and Tora spend a last night together and then part.

BOOK VII

Jūrō persuades his mother to forgive Gorō.

The brothers part from their mother. She gives them each a robe (*kosode*) as a parting gift.

The brothers take their last journey, to the shogun's grand hunt at the base of Mount Fuji.

BOOK VIII

On the way to Mount Fuji the brothers stop at Hakone Temple to bid farewell to the abbot. He gives them two remarkable swords to use in their vendetta.

Various samurai perform daring feats at the hunt.

Jūrō gets a good shot at Kudō, but at the last second his horse stumbles over a fallen log. The attempted assassination goes unnoticed.

Jūrō spies on Kudō's camp but is spotted and invited in. During a tense conversation with Kudō, Jūrō divulges neither his feelings nor his plans.

BOOK IX

The brothers send their two retainers home with a letter and other keepsakes for their mother. The retainers are reluctant to leave and threaten suicide, but eventually obey.

As a precaution, Kudō changes the location of his camp, but late at night a retainer of Hatakeyama Shigetada helps the Soga brothers find their blood enemy.

The brothers wake Kudō and his companion, Ōtōnai, and then strike them down. They slit Kudō's throat to conclude the ritual of revenge.

They raise a great victory cry and then kill and injure numerous samurai who try to arrest them.

Nitta no Shirō Tadatsuna kills Jūrō.

BOOK X

Gorō enters Yoritomo's camp, hoping to kill him, but Gosho no Gorōmaru, disguised in a woman's robe, grapples with and captures Gorō.

The next morning Yoritomo interrogates Gorō. The shogun expresses admiration for the brothers' devotion to honor but orders Gorō to be beheaded.

The executioner, a friend of Kudō, uses a dull sword to kill Gorō. He is later exiled (for reasons other than the execution) and dies soon thereafter.

The Soga brothers' retainers inform the brothers' mother of her sons' deaths. The retainers become monks.

The Soga mother has memorial services performed for her sons.

Yoritomo summons the last brother, Zenji, for interrogation. Zenji tries to commit *seppuku* but only wounds himself. Yoritomo has him beheaded.

BOOK XI

Tora visits the brothers' mother.

Tora and the brothers' mother visit Hakone Temple. The abbot consoles them and conducts a memorial service for the brothers.

"Evil spirits" of the Soga brothers terrify travelers on the Fuji Plain. Yoritomo has bad dreams in which the Soga brothers appear.

Yoritomo establishes a shrine for the worship of the Soga brothers' spirits.

BOOK XII

Tora becomes a nun and sets out for Zenkōji to perform services for the brothers.

On the way Tora stops at the site of the brothers' deaths.

Tora befriends Shōshō and they become companion nuns.

Tora and Shōshō visit the Pure Land Buddhist saint Hōnen.

Tora and Shōshō become recluse nuns.

Tora and Shōshō console and teach the brothers' mother and sister.

The mother of the Soga brothers dies.

Tora and Shōshō see Jūrō and Gorō enter Maitreya's Palace in a dream that the two ladies share on the same night.

Tora and Shōshō die together in their late seventies and ascend to the Pure Land Paradise.

Appendix C: Soga Noh Plays

MUROMACHI PERIOD
(Listed in sequential order, corresponding to the plot of
The Tale of the Soga Brothers.)

1. *Kirikane Soga* (no longer performed). Anonymous.
2. *Chōbuku Soga* (performed by Hōshō, Kongō, and Kita schools) by Miyamasu (Miyamasu is cited as the author in both *Nōhon sakusha chūmon* and *Jika densho*). English translation: Laurence Bresler, "Chōbuku Soga: A Nō Play by Miyamasu," *Monumenta Nipponica* 29.1 (Spring 1974): 74–86.
3. *Genbuku Soga* (performed by the Kita School) by Miyamasu (Miyamasu is cited as the author in both *Nōhon sakusha chūmon* and *Jika densho*).
4. *Onbō Soga* (no longer performed), attributed to Miyamasu.
5. *Wada sakamori* (no longer performed). Anonymous.
6. *Hitsukiri Soga* (another version of Jūrō's last visit to Tora's brothel, no longer performed) by Miyamasu (attribution probably not correct).
7. *Kosode Soga* (performed by all schools of Noh) by Miyamasu or anonymous. Kōzai Tsutomu, "Kosode Soga—sakusha to honsetsu," *Kanze* 28 (May 1961), makes a strong case, based on stylistic and thematic analyses, that the play is not by Miyamasu.
8. *Tora okuri* (no longer performed). Anonymous.
9. *Hakone Soga* (no longer performed). Anonymous.
10. *Fushiki Soga* (no longer performed) by Miyamasu or Zeami (neither attribution is convincing).
11. *Youchi Soga* (performed by all schools of Noh), attributed to Miyamasu. Alternate titles: *Fuji no makigari, Kariba Soga,* and *Uchi-iri Soga.* English translation: Laurence Kominz, "The Noh as Popular Theater: Miyamasu's Youchi Soga," *Monumenta Nipponica* 33.4 (Winter 1978).

12. *Jūban giri* (no longer performed) by Konparu Zenpō.
13. *Fumisaki Soga* (no longer performed), attributed to Miyamasu.
14. *Zenji Soga* (performed by the Kita School) by Zeami (the attribution, in the *Jika densho,* is dubious).

EDO PERIOD
(Listed in alphabetical order; none are performed today, and the authors are unknown.)

15. *Akazawa Soga*
16. *Hanami Soga*
17. *Kariba Soga*
18. *Ōiso*
19. *Okkake Soga*
20. *Taimen Soga* (may date from late Muromachi period).
21. *Yūrei Soga* (alternate title: *Kusakari Soga*).

Appendix D: Soga *Kōwakamai* Plays

The texts for all extant *kōwakamai* plays can be found in the following volume: Sasano Ken, ed., *Kōwaka bukyoku shū*, vol. 2 (Daiichi Shobō, 1943). The texts are not provided with explanatory notes.

A list and plot summaries of the seven Soga *kōwakamai* plays follows. It is taken from James Araki, *The Ballad Drama of Medieval Japan* (Tokyo: Charles E. Tuttle, 1964), 136–39. The plays are listed in order of their occurrence in the legend.

1. *Ichiman Hakoō / Kirikane Soga* (Reluctance to Slay the Soga Brothers)

This play relates an episode in the lives of the Soga brothers that occurred when Ichiman was eleven and Hakoō was nine. One day when Yoritomo is reminiscing about the unsympathetic treatment he received at the hands of Itō Sukechika during his days in exile, Kudō Suketsune informs him that Itō's grandsons are being reared by Soga Sukenobu and warns that they may some day threaten his life. Yoritomo is alarmed and immediately orders their execution. However, the sight of the two condemned youths arouses such pity that the chief executioner is reluctant to see them beheaded. He rides back to Kamakura and exhorts Yoritomo to spare their lives. He is joined by others at court, but to no avail. Finally, Hatakeyama Shigetada, who is held in high esteem by all Genji, comes to court in order to plead for release of the children, but Yoritomo will not relent. He is vindictive, for the hated Itō not only had forced his wife to leave him and marry another man but had even murdered his infant son. Only when Hatakeyama threatens to take his own life rather than see such an injustice come to pass does Yoritomo consent to their release.

2. *Genbuku Soga* (The Adulthood Rites of Gorō Soga)

This play treats two themes—Hakoō's chance meeting with Kudō and his initiation into adulthood as a samurai. In the early spring of 1185 Yoritomo comes to worship at Hakone Temple, where Hakoō is serving as an apprentice monk. Hakoō knows that Kudō Suketsune, whom he has never seen, is among Yoritomo's entourage. He has someone point Kudō out to him, and he studies the face of the man who killed his father. Kudō recognizes the son of Kawazu. He addresses Hakoō with a feigned tenderness and gives him a sword as a token of "his affection." Hakoō restrains his urge to attack Kudō then, for he is only thirteen and could not possibly succeed in such an attempt. One day, three years after that incident, Hakoō learns that his mother has come to Hakone in order to arrange his formal entry into the priesthood. Should Hakoō take the tonsure, the brothers realize, they can no longer hope to avenge their father's death. They leave Hakone secretly so that Hakoō may be initiated not into the priesthood but into adulthood as a samurai. They have Hōjō Tokimasa, who was a close friend of their father, conduct the initiation rites, and Hakoō is thenceforth to be known by the name of Soga no Gorō Tokimune.

3. *Wada sakamori* (Wada's Banquet)

This is a spirited piece in which the contrasting personalities of Jūrō and Gorō are depicted vividly. After the brothers have agreed to attempt their revenge during the great hunt that will take place at the foothills of Mount Fuji during the fifth month of 1193, Jūrō goes alone to Ōiso to bid farewell to his paramour, the beautiful Tora. While he is visiting her at her father's mansion, the famed Genji warrior Wada Yoshimori arrives there with his clansmen, and a lively party ensues. Tora joins the party reluctantly, at Wada's insistence, but she ignores Wada and directs her attention only to Jūrō. Incensed by this affront, Wada abuses the gentle Jūrō. Just when trouble is about to begin, the powerful and belligerent Gorō arrives on the scene. He has been at home sharpening arrowheads but has somehow sensed that Jūrō is in trouble. The Genji strongman, Asahina Saburō, grabs the hip plate on Gorō's suit of armor and tries to drag him into the party room, but Gorō stands firm. So strong are the two men that the hip plate is ripped apart. Gorō proceeds to intimidate Wada and his men by gesticulating menacingly, which causes them to leave.

4. *Kosode Soga* / *Kosode koi* (The Sogas and the Robe / Pleading for the Robe)

This play depicts the scene in which Gorō is reconciled with his mother. Before embarking on the vendetta, the Soga brothers go to visit their mother for the last time. She has not seen Gorō since he violated her wishes by forsaking the priesthood. They do not tell her about their plan. Jūrō appears before his mother alone to tell her that he is leaving for the Mount Fuji foothills, and his mother gives him a *kosode* to protect him against the cold. Jūrō begs her to bestow a similar garment on Gorō, but she refuses even to see him. But Gorō talks to her through a screen, speaking of his loneliness when he was sent away to Hakone as a child and of his misery in being estranged from his own mother, and she can no longer repress her own longings for her son. She forgives Gorō and gives him a *kosode.*

5. *Tsurugi sandan* (Praising the Swords)

This play tells the legend of a fabled sword used by Gorō. When the Soga brothers visit the abbot of Hakone Temple in order to bid him farewell, each is given a sword by him. The sword that Gorō receives is one of the two swords made in the early ninth century from the blade of a famed Indian halberd. The swords were named *Onikiri* (Demon Cutter) and *Kumokiri* (Spider Cutter) because Minamoto no Yorimitsu (tenth century) had used one of them to slay a demon, and the other to kill a monstrous spider. *Kumokiri* was presented as an offering to the Kumano Shrine by Yoshitsune's grandfather. It later came into the hands of Yoshitsune, who called upon the sword's magical powers to destroy the Heike. Yoshitsune made an offering of the sword to the Hakone Temple in 1185, when he went there to pray that he might be reconciled with Yoritomo.

6. *Youchi Soga* / *Fuji no makigari* (Night Raid by the Soga Brothers / Grand Hunt at Mount Fuji)

This play tells the climax to the story of the Soga brothers. All the warriors of the eastern provinces, some sixty-six thousand strong, are participating in the great hunt on the plains below Mount Fuji. The brothers search the area frantically for Kudō. When at last they chance upon him, Jūrō is thrown from his horse, and their quarry rides off into the distance. At night as they search the various quarters, Jūrō is recognized by Kudō's child, Inubōmaru. He comes face to face with Kudō but hesitates to act, for he and Gorō have agreed that neither will act without the other. When he returns later with Gorō, Kudō is gone, and all seems lost. But a man comes to them secretly from their sympathizer, Hatakeyama Shigetada, and he leads them to Kudō's quarters. They awaken Kudō that he may defend himself and slay him as he draws his sword.

7. *Jūban giri* (Fighting Ten Men)

This play is the final chapter in the lives of the Soga brothers. Gorō administers the coup de grace to Kudō, using the very sword that Kudō had given to him many years earlier. The brothers accept the challenge of Genji warriors who are attracted by the commotion. They cut down nine men, but the tenth man slays Jūrō. Gorō, crazed with grief, dashes into the shogun's quarters and is finally overpowered by several men and taken captive. He is questioned by Yoritomo the next day. As he recounts the story of the grief they have borne and of the many ordeals they have suffered, everyone is moved to sympathy. During the questioning, Kudō's son Inubōmaru dashes up to Gorō and beats him with a fan; but Gorō takes compassion on him, for he has known the torment that now possesses Inubōmaru. Although Yoritomo decrees the death penalty for Gorō as required by his own laws, he listens willingly to pleas on Gorō's behalf; but Gorō is executed by his own choosing. The Soga brothers are enshrined at the foot of Mount Fuji and deified for posterity.

Appendix E: Plays and Acts of the Seven-Play, One-Week *Ko-Jōruri* Soga Story

(Some plays have multiple titles. An asterisk indicates titles of plays attributed to the chanter Inoue Harima no Jō by Edo-period sources.)

I. *Yuiseki arasoi* (The Inheritance Dispute)

1. "The Succession Dispute Following the Death of the Lay Priest Jakushin"
2. "The Conflict between Suketsune and Sukechika"
3. "The Hakone Abbot Curses Suketsugu"
4. "The Death of Suketsugu"
5. "Suketsune's First Trip to the Capital"
6. "The Confrontation between Sukechika and Suketsune"

II. *Kongen Soga monogatari** (Origins of the Tale of the Soga Brothers) / *Soga monogatari* (The Tale of the Soga Brothers)

1. "Yoritomo Hunts Deer at Akazawayama"
2. "The Sumo Bout between Kawazu and Matano"
3. "The Death of Kawazu Saburō"
4. "The Deaths of Ōmi Kotōta and Yawata Saburō"
5. "The Lay Priest Sukechika Abducts Yoritomo's Sweetheart"
6. "Yoritomo Enters Hōjō's Mansion"

III. *Yoritomo ondai hajime* (The Beginning of the Age of Yoritomo) / *Ishibashiyama kassen* (The Battle of Ishibashiyama) / *Ishibashiyama* (Ishibashiyama)

1. "Asahi no Mae Interprets the Dream of Manyo no Hime"
2. "Yoritomo's Secret Tryst with Manyo no Hime"
3. "Yoritomo Receives the Cloistered Emperor's Command and Bungaku Jōnin's Prediction"
4. "In His First Battle, Yoritomo Attacks Yamaki"

5. "Sasaki Shirō's Military Tactics at Sugiyama"
6. "Kajiwara Rescues Yoritomo and Yoritomo Meets Yoshitsune"

IV. *Kirikane Soga** (The Refusal to Execute the Brothers)

1. "Yoritomo Sends Kajiwara as a Messenger to Sukenobu"
2. "The Quarrel between Suketsune and Sukekiyo"
3. "The Fight between Suketsune and Sukekiyo"
4. "Sukenobu and the Brothers Part from Sukenobu's Wife"
5. "Petitions to Save Ichiman and Hakoō"
6. "Yoritomo's Pilgrimage to Hakone and Hakoō's Resolution"

V. *Kosode Soga monogatari* (The Sogas and the Robe) / *Tsurugi sandan* (Praising the Swords)

1. "Tokimune's Coming-of-Age Ceremony at Hōjō"
2. "Tokimune's Unfilial Behavior toward His Mother"
3. "Jūrō and Tora's Last Night Together, and Gorō Incurs Kajiwara's Ill Will"
4. "Jūrō's Suit to His Mother and Her Pardon of Gorō"
5. "The Brothers Part from Their Mother and Set Out for Mount Fuji"
6. "The Hakone Abbot Explains the Lineage of the Swords"

VI. *Fuji no makigari** (The Grand Hunt at Mount Fuji) / *Jūban giri* (Fighting Ten Men) / *Dai Soga monogatari* (The Great Tale of the Soga Brothers)

1. "The Procession of the Daimyo through Kamakura on the Way to the Hunt at Mount Fuji"
2. "The Unexpected Meeting between Suketsune and Sukenari"
3. "The Brothers Send Keepsakes to Their Home"
4. "Honda Jirō's Strategic Guidance and the Consummation of the Vendetta"
5. "Fighting Ten Men, and Sukenari's Death"
6. "The Death of Tokimune and His Apotheosis"

VII. *Zenji Soga** (The Soga Priest) / *Tsuizen Soga monogatari* (The Tale of the Soga Memorial Service)

1. "Tora Gozen, Oniō, and Dōsaburō Enter Monastic Orders"
2. "The Fight at Kugami Temple in Echigo"

3. "The Death of Zenjibō"
4. "The Mother's First Meeting with Tora Gozen"
5. "The Mother and Tora Gozen Pray for the Brothers' Spirits"
6. "The Brothers Ascend to Paradise, and Yearly Observances"

Appendix F: Chikamatu's Soga Plays

Title	Performance Dates	Location
1. *Yotsugi Soga*	1684	Osaka, Kyoto
	1696	Owari (Nagoya)
2. *Ōiso Tora osana monogatari*	1695?	Osaka
	1695?	Owari
3. *Soga tayū zome* (Kabuki)	1696	Kyoto
4. *Daimyō (Nagusami) Soga* (Kabuki)	1698	Kyoto
5. *Soga nanatsu i ro ha*	1698	Kyoto
6. *Soga gonin kyōdai*	1700?	Osaka
	1703	Ise
7. *Hyakunichi Soga / Uchiwa Soga*	1701	Osaka
	?	Kyoto
	1703	Nagoya, Ise
8. *Honryō Soga*	1707	Osaka
9. *Kazo Soga*	1707?	Osaka
10. *Soga ōgi hakkei*	1711?	Osaka
	1720	Osaka
11. *Soga Tora ga ishiusu*	1716	Osaka
12. *Soga Kaikeizan*	1718	Osaka
	1812	Osaka
	1818	Osaka

Bibliography

(Unless otherwise indicated, all Japanese titles are published in Tokyo.)

Abel, Lionel. "Is There a Tragic Sense of Life?" In *Tragedy Vision and Form*, edited by Robert Corrigan. New York: Harper and Row Publishers, 1981, 52–62.

Akashi Seizaburō and Ichikawa Danjūrō. "*Tsuwamono kongen Soga.*" In *Kotobuki kongen Soga*, edited by Hattori Yukio. *Kokuritsu gekijō jōen shiryō shū* 46. Kokuritsu Gekijō Geinō Chōsa Shitsu, 1970, 80–98.

Amano Fumio, "Miyamasu Sogamono kō." *Geinōshi kenkyū* 60 (1978): 18–34.

Aoe Shunjirō. "Nihon geinō no genryū." *Minzoku mingei* 61 (1971): 151–61.

Araki, James. *The Ballad Drama of Medieval Japan*. Tokyo: Charles Tuttle Co., 1964.

Araki Shigeru. "Sogamono no kōwaka bukyoku to *Soga monogatari.*" *Wakō daigaku jinbungakubu kiyō* 12 (1977): 117–30.

Asahara Yoshiko. "Kōwaka bukyoku kokō Sogamono o megutte." *Bungaku* 35.10 (1967): 1073–84.

Asahi Jūzan. *Naritasan to Ichikawa Danjūrō narabi ni geinōjin no shinkō.* Narita: Narita-shi Bunka Zaidan, 1968.

Asahi Shinbun Sha, ed. *Nō no furusato.* Asahi Shinbun Sha, 1964.

Asakura Haruhiko. "*Shintōshū* to *Soga monogatari.*" *Shintō shūkyō* 5 (1953): 27–30.

Atsumi Seitarō. "Asahina tsurigitsune—kaisetsu." In *Soga kyōgen buyō shū*, edited by Hattori Yukio. *Kokuritsu gekijō jōen shiryō shū* 50. Kokuritsu Gekijō Geinō Chōsa Shitsu, 1970, 108–9.

______, ed. *Nihon gikyoku zenshū, Soga kyōgen hen*, vol. 14. Shunyōdō, 1929.

______. "Soga matsuri." In *Soga kyōgen buyō shū,* edited by Hattori Yukio. *Kokuritsu gekijō jōen shiryō shū* 50. Kokuritsu Gekijō Geinō Chōsa Shitsu, 1970, 88–90.

______. "Soga no ishidan." In *Soga kyōgen buyō shū,* edited by Hattori Yukio. *Kokuritsu gekijō jōen shiryō shū* 50. Kokuritsu Gekijō Geinō Chōsa Shitsu, 1970, 75–81.

______. "Sukeroku no yūrai." *Engei gahō* (March 1925). Reproduced in *Kokuritsu gekijō jōen shiryō shū* 164. Kokuritsu Gekijō Geinō Chōsa Shitsu, 1977, 34–66.

Blacker, Carmen. *The Catalpa Bow: A Study of Shamanistic Practices in Japan.* London: George Allen and Unwin, 1975.

Bowers, Faubion. *Japanese Theatre.* New York: Hermitage House, 1952.

Brandon, James, ed. *Chūshingura: Studies in Kabuki and the Puppet Theater.* Honolulu: University of Hawaii Press, 1982.

______, trans. *Kabuki: Five Classic Plays.* Cambridge, MA: Harvard University Press, 1975.

Bresler, Laurence. "Chōbuku Soga: A Noh Play by Miyamasu." *Monumenta Nipponica* 29.1 (1974): 69–81.

Butcher, S. H. *Aristotle's Theory of Poetry and Fine Art: With a Critical Text and Translation of "The Poetics."* London: MacMillan and Co. Ltd., 1927.

Butler, Kenneth. "The Textual Evolution of the *Heike Monogotari.*" *Harvard Journal of Asiatic Studies* 26 (1966): 5–51.

Chikaishi Yasuaki, ed. *Jōruri meisaku shū.* 2 vols. Yūhōdō Shoten, 1922.

Chikamatsu Monzaemon. "Appendix D: Eleven Soga Puppet Plays." In *Chikamatsu zenshū,* 12 vols. Edited by Fujii Otoo. Asahi Shinbunsha, 1923–28.

______. *Major Plays of Chikamatsu.* Translated by Donald Keene. New York: Columbia University Press, 1961.

______. "Soga tayū zome," and "Daimyō nagusami Soga." In *Chikamatsu kabuki kyōgen shū.* 2 vols. Edited by Takano Tatsuyuki. Rinsen Shoten, 1926, 489–514 and 8–45.

Cogan, Thomas, trans. *The Tale of the Soga Brothers.* Tokyo: University of Tokyo Press, 1987.

Corrigan, Robert. "Tragedy and the Tragic Spirit." In *Tragedy Vision and Form,* edited by Robert Corrigan. New York: Harper and Row Publishers, 1981, 1–14.

Dōmoto Kansei. *Kamigata engeki shi.* Shunyōdō, 1944.

______. *Kamigata geinō no kenkyū.* Kyoto: Kawara Shoten, 1954.

Dorsch, T. S. *Classical Literary Criticism.* London: Penguin Books, 1965.

Douglas, Mary. *Natural Symbols: Explorations in Cosmology.* London: Barrie and Rockliff, The Cresset Press, 1970.

Dunn, Charles J. *The Early Japanese Puppet Drama.* London: Luzac and Co. Ltd., 1966.

______, and Torigoe Bunzō. *The Actors' Analects.* Tokyo: University of Tokyo Press, 1969.

Enami Yoku. "Sogamono yōkyoku no genkō." *Kokugakuin zasshi* 32.12 (1926): 37–52.

Ernst, Earle. *The Kabuki Theatre.* Honolulu: The University Press of Hawaii, 1956.

Frye, Northrop. *Anatomy of Criticism, Four Essays.* Princeton: Princeton University Press, 1947.

Fujimura Tsukuru, ed. *Nihon bungaku daijiten.* Shinchōsha, 1934.

Fukuda Akira. "Soga katari to shōdō." *Ritsumeikan bungaku* 1 (1977): 114–29.

______. "*Soga monogatari* bungaku sakuhin ni okeru seiai no tsuikyū." *Kokubungaku kaishaku to kanshō* 31.8 (1966): 80–82.

______. "Yoritomo ryūri setsuwa no seichō: *Heike monogatari, Soga monogatari* ni yori." *Kokugo to kokubungaku* 43.6 (1966): 37–53.

Gerstle, C. Andrew. *Circles of Fantasy: Convention in the Plays of Chikamatsu.* Harvard East Asian Monographs 116. Cambridge, MA: Council on East Asian Studies, Harvard University, 1986.

______. "Flowers of Edo: Kabuki and Its Patrons." In *18th Century Japan: Culture and Society,* edited by C. Andrew Gerstle. Sydney: Allen & Unwin, 1990, 33–50.

Gidayū Nenpyō Kinsei Hen Kankōkai, ed. *Gidayū nenpyō: kinsei hen.* 6 vols. Yagi Shoten, 1980.

Gunji Masakatsu. *Buyō: The Classical Dance.* Translated by Don Kenny. New York and Tokyo: Walker/Weatherhill in collaboration with Tankōsha, 1970.

______. *Kabuki.* Translated by John Bester. Palo Alto: Kodansha, 1970.

______, ed. *Kabuki jūhachiban shū.* Vol. 98 of *Nihon koten bungaku taikei.* Iwanami Shoten, 1965.

______. *Kabuki mon.* Vol. 1 of *Gunji Masakatsu santei shū.* Hakusuisha, 1990.

______. *Kabuki no hassō.* Kōbundō, 1959.

______. *Kabuki no katachi.* Vol. 2 of *Gunji Masakatsu santei shū.* Hakusuisha, 1990.

______. *Kabuki ronsō*. Kyoto: Shinbungaku Shuppan, 1979.

______. *Kabuki yōshiki to denju*. Gakugei Shorin, 1969.

______ et al., eds. *Meisaku kabuki zenshū*, vol. 7. Sogen Shinsha, 1969.

Hare, Thomas B. *Zeami's Style: The Noh Plays of Zeami Motokiyo*. Stanford: Stanford University Press, 1986.

Hattori Yukio. "Danjūrō no aragato to shomin shinkō." In *Ichikawa Danjūrō*, edited by Kanamori Kazuko. Shōchiku, 1984, 50–55.

______. *Edo kabuki ron*. Hōsei Daigaku Shuppankyōku, 1980.

______. *Ichikawa Danjūrō*. Vol. 20 of *Nihon o tsukutta hitobito*. Heibonsha, 1978.

______. *Kabuki seiritsu no kenkyū*. Kazama Shobō, 1968.

______, ed. *Kotobuki kongen Soga*. Vol. 46 of *Kokuritsu gekijō jōen shiryō shū*. Kokuritsu Gekijō Geinō Chōsa Shitsu, 1970.

______, ed. *Ya no ne sannin Kichisa kuruwa no hatsugai*. Vol. 74 of *Kokuritsu gekijō jōen shiryō shū*. Kokuritsu Gekijō Geinō Chōsa Shitsu, 1972.

Hayashiya Tatsusaburō. *Kabuki izen*. Iwanami Shinsho, 1954.

Heilman, Robert. "Tragedy and Melodrama." *The Texas Quarterly*. 3.2 (Summer 1960): 36–49.

Henn, T. R. *The Harvest of Tragedy*. London: Methuen and Co. Ltd., 1956.

Highet, Gilbert. *The Anatomy of Satire*. Princeton: Princeton University Press, 1962.

Hiruma Hisashi. *Edo no kaichō*. Yoshikawa Kōbunkan, 1980.

Hisamatsu Sen'ichi and Nishio Minoru, eds. *Karon shū nōgakuron shū*. Vol. 65 of *Nihon koten bungaku taikei*. Iwanami Shoten, 1961.

Hori Ichirō. *Folk Religion in Japan: Continuity and Change*. Chicago: University of Chicago Press, 1968.

Horida Kasau. *Yakubun Azuma kagami hyōchū*. Meicho Kankōkai, 1979.

Ichikawa Danjūrō I. "Gansō Danjūrō no zangeroku." In *Danjūrō no shibai*, edited by Ihara Seiseien. Waseda Daigaku Shuppanbu, 1934, 109–51.

Ichiko Teiji and Ōshima Tatehiko, eds. *Soga monogatari*. Vol. 88 of *Nihon koten bungaku taikei*. Iwanami Shoten, 1966.

Ihara Saikaku. *Tales of Samurai Honor*. Translated by Caryl Ann Callahan. Tokyo: Monumenta Nipponica, 1981.

Ihara Toshirō. *Kabuki nenpyō*, vol. 1. Iwanami Shoten, 1956.

Ikeda Yasaburō, ed. *Geinō to minzokugaku*. Iwasaki Bijutsusha, 1972.

Ikuro Takeaki. "Yōkyoku *Fushiki Soga* no sakusha ni tsuite." *Hōei Daigaku kō kiyō* 19.9 (1969).

Imao Tetsuya. "Ikkō nikki wo yomu." *Kabuki kenkyū to hihyō* 11 (1993): 21–34.

Inoura Yoshinobu and Kawatake Toshio. *The Traditional Theater of Japan.* New York and Tokyo: Weatherhill and Japan Foundation, 1981.

Kabuki Hyōbanki Kenkyūkai, ed. *Kabuki hyōbanki shūsei.* 11 vols. Iwanami Shoten, 1972–77.

Kadokawa Gen'yoshi. *Katarimono bungei no hassei.* Tōkyō-dō, 1975.

______. "Katarimono to kanrisha." *Kokugo kokubun* 13.12 (1943): 1–19.

Kanamori Kazuko, ed. *Ichikawa Danjūrō.* Shōchiku, 1984.

Kanazawa Yasutaka. "Aragoto ni kiku kami no ashioto." *Kokugakuin zasshi* 57.5 (1956): 73–82.

Kawatake Shigetoshi. *Chikamatsu Monzaemon.* Tokyo: Yoshikawa Hiroshi Bunkan, 1958.

______, ed. *Kabuki meisaku shū.* 6 vols. Kōdansha, 1935.

______. *Kabuki sakusha no kenkyū.* Tōkyōdō, 1940.

______, ed. *Mokuami zenshū.* 27 vols. Shunyōdō, 1925.

Keene, Donald. *The Battles of Coxinga.* London: Taylor's Foreign Press, 1951.

______. *Bunraku: The Art of the Japanese Puppet Theater.* Tokyo and New York: Kodansha International, 1965.

______. *Chūshingura: The Treasury of Loyal Retainers.* New York: Columbia University Press, 1971.

______. *Landscapes and Portraits: Appreciations of Japanese Culture.* Tokyo: Kodansha International, 1971.

______. *Nō: The Classical Theatre of Japan.* Tokyo: Kodansha International, 1966.

______, ed. *Twenty Plays of the Nō Theater.* New York: Columbia University Press, 1970.

______. *World Within Walls.* New York: Holt, Rinehart, and Winston, 1976.

Kitagawa Hiroshi, trans. *The Tale of the Soga Brothers.* 2 vols. Hikone: Shiga University Press, 1981, 1984.

______, and Bruce Tsuchida, trans. *The Tale of the Heike.* Tokyo: Tokyo University Press, 1975.

Kitagawa Tadahiko. "Kan'ami, Miyamasu, Kojirō." *Bungaku* 25.9 (1957).

______. "Yōkyoku sakusha Miyamasu o meguru shiron." *Kokugo kokubun* 26.5 (May 1957): 47–61.

Kitano Beni. "Chikamatsu Soga jōruri: seikaku byōsha o chūshin to shite." *Jissen bungaku* 16 (1962): 31–55.

Kobayashi Shizuo. *Yōkyoku sakusha no kenkyū*. Maruoka Shuppansha, 1942.

Koike Shotarō. *Kōsho Edo kabuki*. Miki Shobō, 1979.

Kokonoe Sayū. "Soga buyō." In *Soga kyōgen buyō shū*, edited by Hattori Yukio. *Kokuritsu gekijō jōen shiryō shū* 50. Kokuritsu Gekijō Geinō Chōsa Shitsu, 1970, 59–64.

Kominz, Laurence. "The Noh as Popular Theater: Miyamasu's Youchi Soga." *Monumenta Nipponica* 33.4 (1978): 441–59.

Kondō Yoshihiro. "Bungaku to josei to shinkō." *Shintō gaku* 5 (1958): 25–43.

Kōsai Tsutomu. "Kosode Soga sakusha to honsetsu." *Kanze* 28 (May 1961): 7–9.

Koyama Hiroshi. "Sogamono no gaikan." *Kanze* 28 (May 1961): 2–4.

______, Satō Kikuo, and Satō Ken'ichi, eds. *Yōkyoku shu*, vol. 1. *Nihon koten bungaku zenshū* 33. Shōgakkan, 1973.

Kuroki Kanzō. "*Ya no ne* Gorō no genkō to keitō." In *Ya no ne sannin Kichisa kuruwa no hatsugai*. Vol. 74 of *Kokuritsu gekijō jōen shiryō shū*. Kokuritsu Gekijō Geinō Chōsa Shitsu, 1972, 30–37.

Leiter, Samuel. *Kabuki Encyclopedia, An English Language Adaptation of Kabuki Jiten*. Westport, CT: Greenwood Press, 1979.

Link, Howard. *The Theatrical Prints of the Torii Masters: A Selection of 17th and 18th Century Ukiyo-e*. Honolulu: Honolulu Academy of Arts, Riccar Museum, 1977.

Machida Hirozō. "Kongen kusazuribiki no hensen." In *Soga kyōgen buyō shū*, edited by Hattori Yukio. *Kokuritsu gekijō jōen shiryō shū* 50. Kokuritsu Gekijō Geinō Chōsa Shitsu, 1970, 68–74.

Maeda Isamu, ed. *Kamigata engei jiten*. Tōkyō-dō, 1966.

Maeda Katsuo, ed. *Ki no Kaion zenshū*. Seibundō, 1977.

Maruya Saiichi. *Chūshingura to wa nani ka*. Kōdansha, 1984.

Masaya Akira. "*Soga monogatari* no minzokuteki kiban." *Kokugakuin zasshi* 69.4 (1968): 41–49.

Matisoff, Susan. *The Legend of Semimaru: Blind Musician of Japan*. New York: Columbia University Press, 1978.

Matsubayashi Yasuaki. "*Soga monogatari* to yōkyoku: *Kosode Soga*, *Fushiki Soga* o chūshin to shite." *Koten isan* 22 (1971): 12–23.

Matsumoto Kamematsu. "Gorō—nagauta kaisetsu." In *Soga kyōgen buyō shū*, edited by Hattori Yukio. *Kokuritsu gekijō jōen shiryō shū* 50. Kokuritsu Gekijō Geinō Chōsa Shitsu, 1970, 115–22.

Matsuzaki Hitoshi. *Chikamatsu shinpojiumu Nihon bungaku*, vol. 7. Gakuseisha, 1976.

McCullough, Helen Craig, trans. *The Taiheiki: A Chronicle of Medieval Japan.* New York: Columbia University Press, 1959.

______. *Yoshitsune: A Fifteenth-Century Japanese Chronicle.* Tokyo and Stanford: University of Tokyo Press and Stanford University Press, 1966.

Mills, Douglas. "Gaikoku ni okeru Nihon koten bungaku kenkyū no kadai: Soga kyōdai no densetsu o megutte." *Tōhōgaku* 12 (1975): 1–16.

______. "Kataki-uchi: The Practice of Blood Revenge in Pre-modern Japan." *Modern Asian Studies* 10.4 (1976): 525–42.

______. "Soga Monogatari, Shintōshū, and the Taketori Legend." *Monumenta Nipponica* 30.1 (1975): 37–68.

Miner, Earl. *An Introduction to Japanese Court Poetry.* Palo Alto: Stanford University Press, 1968.

______. *Japanese Linked Poetry: An Account with Translations of Renga and Haikai Sequences.* Princeton: Princeton University Press, 1976.

Misumi Haruo. *Sasurai bito no geinōshi.* NHK Books, 1975.

______. "Soga no buyō oyobi aragoto." In *Soga kyōgen buyō shū,* edited by Hattori Yukio. *Kokuritsu gekijō jōen shiryō shū* 50. Kokuritsu Gekijō Geinō Chōsa Shitsu, 1970, 15–34.

Miyamasu (attributed). "Hitsukiri Soga" and "Fumisaki Soga." In *Bangai yōkyoku shū*, vol. 2, edited by Tanaka Makoto. Koten Bunko, 1950.

Miyao Shigeo, ed. *Nihon sairei gyōji jiten.* Shudōsha, 1968.

Moore, Jean. "A Study of the 13th Century Tale Collection 'Senjusho.'" Ph.D. diss., Columbia University, 1982.

Mori Shū. *Chikamatsu Monzaemon.* Vol. 4 of *Koten to sono jidai.* San'ichi Shobō, 1959.

Moriya Takeshi. *Kabuki no jidai.* Kikan Ronsō, 1976.

Morley, Carolyn Anne. *Transformation, Miracles, and Mischief: The Mountain Priest Plays of Kyōgen.* Ithaca, NY: Cornell East Asia Series, 1993.

Morris, Ivan. *The Nobility of Failure.* London: Secker and Warburg, 1975.

Muller, Herbert. *The Spirit of Tragedy.* New York: Knopf, 1956.

Nakajima Kaoru. "Hakoneyama no shinkō to bungei." *Kokugo to kokubungaku* 24.12 (1947): 32–42.

Nakamura Yasuo. *Noh: The Classical Theater of Japan.* New York: Walker/Weatherhill, 1967.

______. *Nō to nōmen no sekai.* Tankōshinsha, 1963.

Nishiyama Matsunosuke. *Ichikawa Danjūrō.* Yoshikawa Kobunkan, 1960.

Noda Yukio. "*Soga monogatari* to Chikamatsu." *Koten kenkyū* 6.10 (1941): 36–40.

Okami Masao and Kadokawa Gen'yoshi. *Taiheiki, Soga monogatari, Gikeiki.* Kadokawa Shoten, 1960.

O'Neill, P. G. *Early Nō Drama: Its Background, Character, and Development, 1300–1450.* London: Lund Humphries, 1958.

______. *A Guide to Nō.* Kyoto: Hinoki Shoten, 1954.

Ōshima Tatehiko. "*Soga monogatari* ni okeru koji." *Bungaku ronsō* 35.3 (1967): 62–71.

______. "*Soga monogatari* no keisei." *Kokugo to kokubungaku* 37.4 (1960): 102–19.

______. "*Soga monogatari* no sekai." *Rekishi kyōiku* 15.8 (1967): 30–35.

Ōtō Tokihiko. "Tora ga ame." *Minzokugaku kenkyū* 7.2 (1951).

Pigeot, Jacqueline. *Michiyuki bun poétique de l'itineraire dans la litterature du Japon ancien.* Paris: Maisonneuve et Larose, 1982.

Raz, Jacob. "The Actor and His Audience, Zeami's Views on His Audience." *Monumenta Nipponica* 31.3 (1976): 251–74.

______. *Actors and Audience.* Leiden: E. J. Brill, 1983.

Ristine, Frank H. *English Tragicomedy: Its Origins and History.* New York: Columbia University Press, 1910.

Ruch, Barbara. "Medieval Jongleurs and the Making of a National Literature." In *Japan in the Muromachi Age,* edited by John W. Hall and Takeshi Toyoda. Berkeley: University of California Press, 1977, 279–310.

Salz, Jonah. "Intercultural Pioneers: Otojirō Kawakami and Sada Yakko." *The Journal of Intercultural Studies* (Kansai University of Foreign Studies Publication) 20 (1993): 25–74.

Sansom, Sir George. *A History of Japan to 1334.* Palo Alto: Stanford University Press, 1958.

Sasano Ken, ed. *Kōwaka bukyoku shū.* 2 vols. (with texts and commentary). Rinsen Shoten, 1974.

Shigetomo Ki, ed. *Chikamatsu jōruri shū* 1. Vol. 49 of *Nihon koten bungaku taikei.* Iwanami Shoten, 1958.

Shimada Itsuko. "Chikamatsu Soga jōruri no kenkyū." *Nihon bungaku* 14 (1965).

Shimazu Hisamoto. "Kōwaka no Sogamono." *Kokugo to kokubungaku* 10.4 (1943): 459–70.

Shinoda Jun'ichi. "Kiri jōruri *Sonezaki shinjū* no seiritsu ni tsuite." *Ōsaka kokubungaku kenkyūshitsu* 39 (1981): 1–9.

______ and Saitō Seijirō. *Noroma soroma kyōgen shūsei.* Daigakudō Shoten, 1974.

Shively, Donald. "Tokugawa Plays on Forbidden Topics." In *Chūshingura: Studies in Kabuki and the Puppet Theater*, edited by James Brandon. Honolulu: University of Hawaii Press, 1982, 24–53.

Shuzui Kenji, and Okubo Tadakuni, eds. *Chikamatsu jōruri shū*, vol. 2. *Nihon koten bungaku taikei* 50. Iwanami Shoten, 1959.

Stramigioli, Giuliana, trans. "Preliminary Notes on Masakado-ki and the Taira no Masakado Story." *Monumenta Nipponica* 28.4 (1973): 261–94.

Suwa Haruo. *Genroku kabuki no kenkyū.* Kazama Shoin, 1967.

______. "Goryō shinkō to aragoto gei." *Bungaku* 47.8 (1979): 1–16.

______. "'Kaneko Ikkō nikki' ni miru Chikamatsu to Kaneko Kichizaemon no kankei." *Kabuki kenkyū to hihyō* 11 (1993): 35–44.

Suzuki Tōru. "*Soga monogatari* to futari bikuni." *Gobun* 21 (1958): 25–34.

Takahashi Hiroshi. "Uji Kaganojō." In *Engekishi kenkyū.* Daiichi Shobō, 1932, 147–72.

Takano Masami. "Chikamatsu Sogamono kō." *Kokugo to kokubungaku* 10.4 (1943): 471–98.

______. *Chikamatsu to sono dentō geinō.* Kōdansha, 1965.

Takano Tatsuyuki and Kuroki Kanzō, eds. *Genroku kabuki kessaku shū.* Waseda Daigaku Shuppanbu, 1925.

Tanaka Makoto, ed. *Bangai yōkyoku shū.* 2 vols. Koten Bunko, 1950.

______, ed. *Mikan yōkyoku shū.* 31 vols. (with texts and textual information). Koten Bunko, 1963–80.

Thornbury, Barbara. *Sukeroku's Double Identity: The Dramatic Structure of Edo Kabuki.* Michigan Papers in Japanese Studies, No. 6. Ann Arbor: Center for Japanese Studies, The University of Michigan, 1982.

Toita Yasuji. *Kabuki jūhachiban.* Chūō Kōronsha, 1969.

______, ed. *Kabuki meisaku sen.* 15 vols. Kōgensha, 1952–57.

______. *Kabuki: The Popular Theater,* translated by Don Kenny. New York: Weatherhill/Tankōsha, 1970.

Tokyo Daigaku Engeki Shi Kenkyū Gakkai, ed. *Engekishi kenkyū genroku geki hen.* Kogeisha, 1936.

Torigoe Bunzō. "Edo Jōruri." In *18th Century Japan: Culture and Society*, edited by C. Andrew Gerstle. Sydney: Allen & Unwin, 1990, 51–60.

______. *Genroku kabuki kō*. Yagi Shoten, 1991.

Torii Fumiko, ed. *Tosa jōruri shōhon shū*. 3 vols. (with texts and commentary). Kadokawa Shoten, 1975.

Tsukazaki Susumu. "Kyōdō bungei to shite no *Gikeiki*, *Soga monogatari*." *Kokubungaku* 11.2 (1966): 66–70.

______. *Monogatari no tanjō*. Vol. 42 of *Minzoku mingei sōsho*. Iwasaki Bijutsusha, 1969.

Tsunoda Ichirō. *Ningyōgeki no seiritsu ni kansuru kenkyū*. Osaka: Asahiya, 1963.

Umehara Takeshi. *Koten no hakken*. Kōdansha, 1973.

Utsumi Shigetarō. *Ningyō jōruri to bunraku*. Hakusuisha, 1958.

Wakatsuki Yasuji. *Ko-jōruri shin kenkyū (Keichō kanbun hen)*. Shingetsusha, 1958.

Waseda Daigaku Engeki Hakubutsukan, ed. *Engeki hyakka jiten*. 6 vols. Heibonsha, 1960.

Watsuji Tetsurō. "Yōkyoku ni Arawareta Rinri Shisō—Japanese Ethical Thought in the Noh Plays of the Medieval Period" (translated by David Dilworth). *Monumenta Nipponica* 24 (1969): 467–98.

Yamane Tameo. "*Uchiwa Soga* to *Hyakunichi Soga* shiron." *Geinōshi kenkyū* 78 (1982): 1–17.

Yokomichi Mario and Omote Akira, eds. *Yōkyoku shū*. 2 vols. *Nihon koten bungaku taikei* 40, 41. Iwanami Shoten, 1960, 1963.

Yokoyama Shigeru. *Kaganojō danmono shū*. Koten Bunko, 1958.

______, ed. *Ko-jōruri shōhon shū*. 6 vols. (with texts and commentary). Kadokawa Shoten, 1964.

Yokoyama Tadashi. "Chikamatsu no Soga jōruri." *Kokugo to kokubungaku* 25.6 (1956): 14–27.

______. *Jōruri ayatsuri shibai no kenkyū*. Kazama Shoten, 1964.

______. "Minzokugaku yori mita aragoto no bijutsu." In *Geinō to minzokugaku*, edited by Ikeda Yasaburō. Iwasaki Bijutsusha, 1972.

Yūda Yoshio. "*Hyakunichi Soga* o meguru mondai." *Yamanobe no michi* 7 (1961): 1–11.

______, and Torigoe Bunzō, eds. *Kamigata kyōgen bon*. 6 vols. Koten Bunko, 1977.

Zeami Motokiyo. *Kadensho*. Translated by Sakurai Chūichi et al. Kyoto: Sumiya-Shinobe Publishing Institute, 1968.

______. *On the Art of the Nō Drama: The Major Treatises of Zeami*. Translated by J. Thomas Rimer and Masakazu Yamazaki. Princeton: Princeton University Press, 1984.

Index